Laibon

Laibon

An Anthropologist's Journey
with Samburu Diviners in Kenya

Elliot Fratkin

A division of
ROWMAN & LITTLEFIELD PUBLISHERS, INC.
Lanham • New York • Toronto • Plymouth, UK

Published by AltaMira Press
A division of Rowman & Littlefield Publishers, Inc.
A wholly owned subsidary of The Rowman & Littlefield Publishing Group, Inc.
4501 Forbes Boulevard, Suite 200, Lanham, Maryland 20706
http://www.altamirapress.com

Estover Road, Plymouth PL6 7PY, United Kingdom

Excerpt from "California" by Joni Mitchell in chapter 4 is used by permission of
Alfred Publishing.

British Library Cataloguing in Publication Information Available

Library of Congress Cataloging-in-Publication Data

Fratkin, Elliot
  Laibon : an anthropologist's journey with Samburu diviners in Kenya / Elliot M.
Fratkin.
    p. cm.
  Includes index.
  ISBN 978-0-7591-2067-9 (cloth : alk. paper) — ISBN 978-0-7591-2068-6 (pbk. : alk.
paper) — ISBN 978-0-7591-2069-3 (electronic)
  1. Fratkin, Elliot 2. Anthropologists—Kenya—Biography. 3. Samburu (African
people)—Social life and customs. 4. Ariaal (African people)—Social life and customs.
5. Ethnology—Kenya. I. Title.
  GN21.F37A3 2011
  301.092—dc23   2011022332

∞™ The paper used in this publication meets the minimum requirements of
American National Standard for Information Sciences—Permanence of Paper
for Printed Library Materials, ANSI/NISO Z39.48-1992.

Printed in the United States of America

For Lekati and Kanikis

Contents

Acknowledgments

The descriptions in this book are based on my experiences as an anthropologist conducting field research in Kenya, mainly in the 1970s but also during follow-up visits in the 1980s, 1990s, and 2000s. I am very grateful to the many people in Kenya without whose assistance I could never have conducted my anthropological research, particularly Lugi Lengesen, Kanikis Leaduma, Kordidi Leaduma, Daniel Lemoille, Larion and AnneMarie Alyaro, and two dear friends who are no longer with us, Lekati Leaduma and Kawab Bulyar.

I wish to thank those friends and colleagues who generously read and commented on various drafts of this book—Kris Holloway Bidwell, Cecelia Cancellaro, Ralph Faulkingham, Dorothy Hodgson, Edward Jacob, Donald Joralemon, Anatoly Khazanov, Corinne Kratz, Ella Kusnetz, Arky Markham, Jeremy Miller, Günther Schlee, Susan Sherman, Neal Sobania, Richard Waller, and at AltaMira, my editor Marissa Parks, production editor Emily Natsios, copyeditor Jeremy Rehwaldt, and the anonymous reviewers who made helpful suggestions.

To my family I extend my deepest appreciation: to Marty Nathan, my life partner and collaborator, who read all the various drafts and threatened to kill me if I mixed my tenses in any more sentences, and to our children, Leah, Mulugetta, and Masaye, who have provided me with the belonging for which I have searched so long. I also thank my natal family who followed my exploits with both joy and worry—my late parents Ralph and Millie Fratkin, my sisters, Susan Sherman and Arlene Horowitz, and my l-maoi (twin), Jake Fratkin, who intuited most of this book anyway.

Preface

Foolishness first, then wisdom.

This is a story about a cross-cultural friendship I have with a nomadic community in northern Kenya, and of my relationship with the *laibon* "medicine man" I will call Lonyoki, who adopted me as his son and whose family I have studied as an anthropologist for more than thirty-five years. It is also the story of my personal journey into adulthood, and my love for a foreign culture whose members accepted me and allowed me to join them as they lived and survived in this austere but beautiful part of the world. Much of this story is based on my early fieldwork experiences as a young anthropology graduate student living with an Ariaal (mixed Samburu/Rendille) pastoralist community called Lukumai in the 1970s and my return visits over the next three decades. In the early 1970s, the Ariaal were living a mainly nomadic existence herding their cattle, camels, goats, and sheep in a desert environment. At that time, as today, our community was surrounded by traditional enemies—Boran, Turkana, and Somalis. But many former pastoralists have now settled in towns and farms, having lost their livestock following periods of long drought and political instability. The Lukumai community, in which I lived, has managed to keep their livestock and maintain their way of life.

This book is both a memoir of my own experiences as an anthropologist and an ethnography, an anthropological description, of *laibons*, who are a special family of diviners, prophets, medicine men, and sorcerers among Samburu and Maasai people of East Africa. There are several laibons in this story—Lonyoki, a man in his forties when I first met him; his father Lon-gojine with whom he had a troubled relationship; Lonyoki's older cousin, Lokili, who was a notorious sorcerer; Lobata, a rival laibon and constant threat; and finally Lembalen, Lonyoki's son, who today continues to practice divination, healing, and prophesy among Samburu people. This story also concerns my friends in the community of Lukumai, particularly Dominic and his wives, Naiseku and Rendille, and my age-mates Lalem and Kidenye, who were my warrior friends when I first lived in their *nkang* (nomadic village). All these names are pseudonyms, as are several of the location and village names, as I wish to protect the identities of these people as much as possible. While all the characters in this story told me they had no objections to my using their real names, I fear negative consequences if their identities were known, either from authorities who might disapprove or wandering travelers who might approve too much. I have tried to adhere to the long-established ethic in anthropology to "do no harm."

My first fieldwork experience lasted eighteen months and was a life-altering experience. This book is partly written by the young man I no longer am, when I was searching for adventure, knowledge, and a sense of meaning for my life. Thirty-five years later, I realize this search has been about belonging and having a family of my own.

"Where Are Your Dominic Stories?"

Nearly all of my academic writing has been for a specialized readership, mainly anthropologists working in Africa or studying pastoral nomads throughout the world. I have also written a short ethnography *Ariaal Pastoralists of Kenya*, that has been popular in anthropology classrooms. Students particularly liked the short section in the introduction of that book where I describe my fieldwork experiences. For some time, I have wanted to expand this into a full-length book to share my personal experiences and what I have learned with both anthropology students and a wider audience.

Many years ago while attending an annual meeting of the American Anthropological Association in my hometown of Philadelphia, I delivered an academic paper on my research. These meetings are huge conferences running over four days, with 100 to 150 panels a day and four to eight presenters per panel. Here professors and nervous graduate students have fifteen minutes to deliver (i.e., read) papers summarizing their research. It was and remains a daunting experience for me and countless others. But I told my mother that I was in town to give a paper, and she enthusiastically attended, accompanied by my Uncle Sam, a teacher who was close to eighty years old. Not surprisingly, they sat in the front row, leaning forward in eager anticipation. But their bright gazes quickly dulled as I droned on with graphs and tables about my research on labor, economy, and pastoral production in Kenya. I wasn't quite sure they were able to follow my treatise to the end. I wasn't sure *I* was able to keep up until the end. My main conclusion was that adult women in this nomadic community worked nearly twice as arduously as adult men but had only one-half the rest or leisure time. My wife, Marty, had said to me earlier, "You needed a research grant from National Geographic Society to learn that women work harder than men? Criminy, I could have told you that!" After the meeting, my disappointed mother asked, "Why didn't you just tell them your Dominic stories?"

"Dominic stories" were the personal accounts of my fieldwork that I had related to my family in letters and stories. They were about life in the Lukumai community and the people who lived there and particularly my relationship with the laibon Lonyoki and our mutual friend Dominic. My mother wanted me to communicate my empathy for and understanding of people living in a culture very different from our own. She understood what academic writing seldom reflects but most anthropologists know, that these are real people we study and live with, with real triumphs, sorrows, expectations, and experiences.

I decided to write this book now because I am finally able to do it. My career has reached a satisfying plateau following thirty years of teaching, research, and writing about anthropology. I am a professor at Smith College, a wonderful institution (and one of America's few women's colleges) whose students constantly inspire me. My three children are grown (mostly), and my partnership with Marty has passed our twenty-fifth year. I am now able to turn to this personal account of my fieldwork.

Different Voices

Instead of writing here *about* the people with whom I lived, I allow people to speak in their own voices. During the time of my fieldwork, I wrote in my field journal almost every evening using notes I had jotted down throughout the day in small spiral notebooks. People in Lukumai went to sleep fairly early (the sun sets around 6 p.m. and there was no electricity for light), so I had plenty of time to record what was said during the day and how it was said. One technique I used that is not usually mentioned in books on anthropological methodology was inspired by the book *In Cold Blood*, which Truman Capote based on extensive interviews with two killers in their prison cells over a considerable period of time. Capote never wrote notes during his interviews, as he thought these would inhibit the men, Perry Smith and Dick Hickock, from speaking freely. Each evening, back in his hotel room, he would type the dialogue as concisely and accurately as his memory would allow. This process was essentially the one I followed, where I tried to repeat word-for-word the conversations of the day. I also begin each chapter with a Samburu proverb; these proverbs are used often in everyday speech and beautifully summarize complex situations. I had a lot of fun writing this way, and I think my mother would have approved.

A Note on Language

The Ariaal are a bridge society between Samburu and Rendille, two very different ethnic groups who have formed an intermarrying alliance over the past few centuries. The Samburu language is a dialect of ol-Maa spoken by Maasai people (an Eastern Nilotic language of the Sudanic subfamily, Chari-Nile family, of the Nilo-Saharan language stock [Greenberg 1955]). Rendille is a Cushitic language of the Afro-Asiatic family, related to Somali and Oromo in the Horn of Africa. Most Ariaal men prefer to speak Samburu, which is the language I used in my fieldwork. Spelling and translations of Samburu words are based on Mol's *Maa: A Dictionary of the Maasai Language* (1978) and the more recent *Maa (Maasai) Dictionary* by Doris L. Payne and Leonard Ole-Kotikash (2008), both of which are excellent sources. Rendille spelling follows Schlee (1989). Samburu masculine prefixes are written as *l-*, as in *l-oiboni, l-oibonok* (diviners), rather than *ol-oiboni, il-oibonok*, as in Maasai. Feminine prefixes are written as *n*, as *nkidong, nkidongi* (laibon's gourd), instead of *en-kidong, in-kidongi*, as in Maasai. A glossary of people and places is included at the end. For a relatively easy approach in pronouncing African words, one should follow the Spanish system of vowel sounds ("ah" for A, "ay" for E, "iii" for I, "oh" for O, and "ew" for U). Samburu is a glottal language, with certain sounds made explosively near the throat, like *nkang* ("n-ka-ang") for village.

CHAPTER ONE

Meeting the Laibon Lonyoki

You know what to say, but you do not know what you might be told.

The road south from Marsabit Mountain into the desert lowlands in northern Kenya had not changed in the thirty-five years since I first came here—it was still corrugated dirt and macadam, with large potholes caused by heavy trucks traveling to and from down country. The Chinese are in the process of paving the three-hundred-kilometer road from Isiolo to the Ethiopian border as I write this, and I know this will dramatically change the region, for better and for worse, in the near future. But this was still the northern Kenya that I remembered: hot and bright as we traveled through a vast terrain of deserts, hilly outcrops, and dark brown mountains, through an area populated mainly by nomadic pastoralists tending small herds of camels, goats and sheep, and cattle.

Despite reports of armed bandits on the road, I was happy to be here. It had been ten years since my last visit, and I was heading to see my adopted brother, Lembalen. Now a man in his forties with a family of his own, I first met Lembalen when he was a boy of eight years old, living with his mother in Samburu District. I had been sent by his father, Lonyoki, to fetch his wife and son back to his *manyatta* (a nomadic community) in Marsabit; he had not seen either of them since Lembalen was born.

Lonyoki was a *laibon* (a diviner/prophet-healer/sorcerer) living in the Marsabit District lowlands, practicing divination with his *nkidong* gourd of stones and dispensing his *ntasim* (medicines) among nomadic Samburu and

1

Ariaal (mixed Samburu/Rendille) communities. As a young anthropology graduate student, I lived with Lonyoki and his close friend Dominic in the large camel-keeping community of Lukumai. After I successfully delivered his wife and son to him from another district, I was adopted as his other son.

"I don't want to hear anyone say, 'There goes the white Lonyoki,'" the laibon said when he adopted me. "There are no white Lonyokis, there are no black Lonyokis; there are only Lonyokis!"

This book is the story of my anthropological fieldwork living with the nomadic camel-keeping community of Lukumai of northern Kenya and the family of the laibon Lonyoki. I lived with Lonyoki and Dominic in Lukumai for a year and a half during my first fieldwork experience in the 1970s and have returned many times between then and now. My first fieldwork was the most intense, where I followed Lonyoki as he traveled to various villages to practice his divination and ritual medicine, mainly to treat people inflicted by sorcery. I also experienced with the people of Lukumai the arduous routine of raising livestock—moving our settlement and livestock camps to feed and water our camels, cattle, goats, and sheep, with periodic disruption brought about by raids from neighboring groups, attacks on livestock by lions and hyenas, and the ever-present threat of drought. Looking back on those experiences and reading my field notes, many of them handwritten in a dozen lined-paper notebooks, transported me back to this magical time in my life. What impressed me most then, as it still does today, was the recognition of a common humanity with the people I lived with. Through conversation and laughter, meals and travel, Lonyoki, Dominic, and I bonded in a genuine friendship that has survived decades of shared joys, pain, humiliations, and loss.

Samburu are an exotic culture, even to Kenyans who embrace a large number of distinct cultures and traditions. Samburu warriors, like their cousins the Maasai, still keep their hair in long red braids, wear swords on their belts, and carry spears. Women dress in leather skirts and colorful cotton cloth shawls and adorn themselves with elaborate and colorful beadwork strung on wire and worn around their necks, foreheads, and arms. Yet once I joined their community, my sense of their exoticism declined and people became remarkably familiar to me, emoting love and desire, pride and achievement, shame and embarrassment, anger and jealousy. Lukumai village, nomadic as it was, showed a similarity to most communities around the world, both small towns and large urban neighborhoods. People tried to be civil and polite in their interactions with one another and to promote good behavior in their children, but they were not immune to jealousies and rivalries, hurts and resentments both within and between families. And these jealousies sometimes resulted in great harm. The main difference between our two cultures was that whereas we both used gossip or weapons to settle scores, Samburu added sorcery to disable or kill their rivals. And it was the laibon's powers to combat sorcery that became the focus of my research.

A Journey North

In the 1970s, when I was a graduate student in anthropology, I did not intend to study Samburu laibons, but I did want to do field research in East Africa. I particularly wanted to live and study people like the Maasai, seminomadic pastoralists who raised livestock for a living. Moreover, I wanted to go to places that hadn't been written about, to live in the most isolated area I could find. I wasn't trying to be the sole authority on one "tribe," like Malinowski among the Trobriand Islanders of the western Pacific, although he too was an exile living in a small foreign community. My intention was to get as far as possible from the turmoil and dislocations in my own country. At the end of the 1960s the United States was embroiled in the Vietnam War, the civil rights movement, and urban dislocation and youth protests. Just as it looked like the war was winding down, in 1968 we elected Richard Nixon as president. He continued to escalate the war, cracked down on dissidents at home, and imposed "law and order" policies aimed at urban minorities, hippies, and political activists. So my purpose was not to seek academic fame but to find a quiet refuge, "shelter from the storm," and pursue my own personal journey.

As a graduate student preparing for my fieldwork, I wrote a proposal to the government of Kenya to study Turkana pastoralists, an isolated population of cattle-herding nomads who lived in northwest Kenya. My initial research proposal was titled "The Application of a Structural Analysis to Rites of Passage among Turkana People of Kenya." When I arrived in Nairobi, the immigration officer inspected my research permit and asked, "What in the world is there about those people that deserves such a title? They don't even wear clothes! They have nothing up there in that hot place. If you want to research interesting people, come to my home village, where people are smart and know how to work!"

This was not the first time, and certainly not the last, that I heard disparaging remarks about pastoralists, particularly from "down country" people who grew up on farms and in cities. I know of no country in Africa, with the exception of Botswana and Somalia (when they had a government), in which national states did not despise nomadic pastoralists. Most countries with pastoral populations—Kenya, Tanzania, Mali, Nigeria—have sought to make nomads settle and become "civilized."

East Africa in the early 1970s was an exciting place, full of postindependence optimism for the future. I stayed at the Nairobi YMCA, which housed up-and-coming, but not very wealthy, young African men (no women permitted) seeking their fortunes or education. Colonial rule had ended only ten years previously, and while one occasionally saw British settlers visiting their drinking troughs in Nairobi, they had definitely moved to the sidelines of Kenya's political life. Under the British, East Africa had been a united federation in which Kenya, Tanganyika, and Uganda had an integrated currency, post office, and railroad. That was now changing. Uganda followed a tortuous path to military dictatorship under Idi Amin, while Tanzania, formed from the union of Tanganyika and the island of Zanzibar, was attempting an "African Socialism," or *Ujamaa*, under their president, Julius Nyerere, who was intent on merging traditional African ideas of community with modern ideas of development.

Kenya was quite the opposite of Tanzania, since it was the showcase of Western capitalism and investment. Here English was the national language (unlike Tanzania, where it was KiSwahili), which mainly benefited the educated elite. Kenya was led by the charismatic but stern father figure, Jomo Kenyatta. Whereas Tanzanians called their leader *Mwalimu* (teacher), Kenyatta was always called *Mzee*, a respected elder and "big man."

Uganda, once the jewel in the crown of Britain's African colonies, had gone quite a different route. Their leader, Idi Amin, gave himself the title "*His Excellency President for Life, Field Marshal Al Hadji Doctor* Idi Amin Dada." He was a brutal dictator who came to power in a military coup in 1971 and immediately set out to kill and imprison his rivals and ethnic enemies. He killed at least 250,000 Ugandans in his short reign and expelled all 80,000 resident Indians, which quickly ruined Uganda's economy. Amin foolishly invaded Tanzania, which retaliated and struck back, overthrowing the dictator in 1978.

I enjoyed living at the "Y" and establishing relations with my academic host faculty at the Institute of African Studies (IAS), which was part of the University of Nairobi. The IAS at that time was under the directorship of Ogot P'Bitek, a Ugandan exile and poet and the author of the *Song of Lawino*, a classic in African literature. He encouraged cultural research and was pleased to have me on board. Next door to the institute was the National Museum of Kenya, which was directed by Richard Leakey and housed early human fossils from Kenya and Tanzania. It was a stimulating atmosphere, although a bit separate from the radical politics of the university at the time.

The YMCA offered pleasant enough accommodations, but it was time for me to push off and do what I came for—anthropological fieldwork. I headed to Kenya's northwest, taking buses for two days to Lodwar, the capital of Tur-kana District. But I learned quickly that Turkana was not the place I wanted to study. I stood for nearly four hours outside a Turkana *awi* (homestead) waiting to be invited in. I greeted an elder sitting by his gate, but he ignored me. I waited some more and had very little luck, either in town or in the hin-terland. Later J. Terrence (Terry) McCabe, an anthropologist who worked extensively with the Turkana in the 1980s (and later Maasai in Tanzania), told me, "In the four years I lived with Turkana, I was only offered one cup of tea, once! Never goats like the Samburu gave you!"

I returned to Nairobi, intent on finding a better field site. I decided to travel north into Ethiopia where the Omo River enters Lake Turkana, a very isolated region inhabited by tribal people who combined herding and horticulture. I bought an old English motorcycle, a BSA 250 cc, and joined up with two Peace Corps volunteers, Paul and Peach, who had completed two years in eastern Zaire (now the war-torn region of Democratic Republic of Congo) and were journeying north on their motorbikes. They were good traveling companions.

We drove north from Nairobi through the rich farmlands and forests that were home to Kenya's largest ethnic group, the Kikuyu. On narrow and curving roads we drove around Mount Kenya, at 17,057 feet Africa's second-highest mountain (Kilimanjaro is 19,341 feet). We drove past large wheat estates once owned by white settlers and one of the main areas where Kenyans fought against colonial rule in the 1950s during the Mau Mau rebel-lion. After several hours, we reached the northern side of Mount Kenya and began a descent into the vast red-and-yellow desert that extends hundreds of miles north and east to Ethiopia and Somalia. The paved road ended at the desert town of Isiolo, where there was a barrier and police inspected vehicles traveling into what used to be called the "Northern Frontier District," a for-midable and dangerous area to most Kenyans. After Isiolo, the road became unpaved and surfaced with gravel with washboard corrugations from heavy truck use, and that extended three hundred miles to the Ethiopian border.

I felt we had left the country called Kenya and entered a different world. Isiolo was a predominately Muslim town occupied by Somali and Boran people. It was a hot and dusty junction for livestock traders where pastoralist peoples brought their cattle, goats, and sheep to sell, destined for the feed-lots, butcheries, and tanneries of the south.

The police barrier proved to be no problem as the police assumed we were traveling to the Samburu Game Park, a popular tourist destination. But we drove past the turnoff to the game park and headed north into Marsabit District, entering a world of nomadic herders where men carried spears or

rifles and where rustlers and elephant poachers were known to carry automatic weapons. We stopped briefly on the concrete bridge that crossed the
wide Uaso Nyiru River, the only river in the district where water flowed
year-round. Down below, we could see Samburu warriors with their long
braided and red-dyed hair watering their cattle. But we couldn't turn off our
motorbikes as they would be too hot to start again, so we pushed on. The
few towns we passed through were built mainly around churches and schools
established by Catholic and Protestant missionaries and usually consisted of
little more than a few shops and sometimes a police post.

The Kaisut Desert is a flat plain punctuated by huge rocks and hills.
To the west lie the Matthews Range and Ndoto Mountains, which reach
heights of nine thousand feet. To the east a flat desert extends all the way
to Somalia. Hour after hour we proceeded on corrugated or sandy stretches,
sometimes riding close to one another, sometimes separated by a mile or
so. By evening, we reached the small town of Laisamis, which is situated
halfway to Marsabit town. Here in a dusty restaurant we ate goat stew and
drank Fanta soda, then found a place to camp near the church mission
where we quickly fell asleep.

We pushed off early the next morning, and by noon we began climbing up
Marsabit Mountain. Marsabit is not like Mount Kenya or Kilimanjaro, with
their granite tops and snow-capped peaks. It is gently sloped and was covered
in a green forest on its eastern, wet side, and a dry savanna grassland on the
western side. At the top of the mountain was a large crater lake with an old
tourist lodge built to view some of Kenya's largest elephants. On the outskirts
of the reserve lay Marsabit town, the administrative capital of the district,
with a population (in 1974) of five thousand people. Today the mountain is
home to thirty thousand Rendille, Samburu, and Boran people, with government and NGO offices, a government hospital, and a secondary school.

Pulling onto the main street, we went to a restaurant and bar and again
ate goat stew and chapati bread, now with sweet and spicy tea. I was getting
to like this food. We were approached by a young teenage boy wearing the
khaki uniform of a primary school student. In very polite and well-spoken
English, he asked us if we needed a guide to see the elephants in the Marsabit
Forest Reserve. The boy was friendly, but he had a hungry look that com-
municated there were very few tourists up here. We were all tired from our
two-day ride from Isiolo and I had no desire to hike through a forest right
then. Paul and Peach obviously felt the same, for they excused themselves to
find a hotel and left me with the boy in the bar.

I asked the boy his name, which he gave as Peter (a pseudonym), and I
bought him a soda, feeling he deserved some reward for his effort.

"Well," Peter said in his clipped schoolboy accent, "if you're too tired to see the elephants today, would you like to see my school?"

He was really scraping the bottom of the barrel for tourist attractions in the area, but the school visit prompted the same response as the elephants had.

"No thanks," I replied, "I really don't want to do anything right now; I just want to sit and rest."

I was thinking about our trip to Ethiopia, its border still more than one hundred miles to the north on this miserable road. As if reading my mind, Peter asked me if we were heading to Ethiopia. I nodded yes, and he started shaking his head vigorously from side to side.

"Oh no, that is a very bad place right now. My father works for the government at the water pump. He told me that there is trouble up there now, and the border to Ethiopia is closed. I hear that their emperor Haile Selassie is fighting against his own army in a . . . how do you call it? A cooty something."

"A coup d'etat?" I asked.

"Yes, it is very dangerous; you and your friends should not go there."

Great, my luck in finding fieldwork locations was really headed downstream.

Suddenly Peter brightened up and asked, "How about some native dances? Would you like to see traditional African warriors dance?"

I perked up at this, being a sucker for any anthropological experience. Whether it's a Cherokee tourist shop in North Carolina or an exhibit of Balinese masks at the Museum of Natural History, I can't refuse. Non-Western cultures have always fascinated me.

"Traditional dances, huh? What kind of people are you talking about?" I asked back.

"My kind of people," the boy smiled brightly. "Samburu people, you know, like Maasai peoples. My father's home is at Lorubai. We keep cattle. It is only about fifteen miles from here. Our dances are beautiful, not like those of the Boran or other groups up here. Come, I will show you. I will take you to the manyatta (village) of my father."

I was tired, but not that tired. I was bored walking around the town, so I put Peter on the back of my motorcycle and we drove back down the mountain. This was probably the first time Peter sat on a motorcycle. He wrapped his arms tightly around my waist as we raced down the mountain road; he laughed hysterically as I downshifted to take the curves in the road. Periodically, I could see the desert in the distance below us, vast and white with heat waves distorting the view.

Suddenly, we rounded a curve onto a concrete bridge over a deep gully. But on the far side of the bridge was an enormous bull elephant standing in the middle of the road. He flapped his ears as we approached and took one step back. He trumpeted a cry and looked like he was going to charge right into us.

"Quickly, don't stop!" yelled Peter into my ear. "Drive past him fast before he has time to charge us."

I didn't want to get stuck on that narrow bridge with this monster, so I did as the boy instructed, downshifting to third gear and revving the accelerator. We swerved to the right of the elephant, fishtailing around him as I balanced the bike with my left foot, and we made off like demons down the mountain.

Peter's village was called Lorubai by the Samburu. It had a few shops on one side of the road and a half dozen manyattas on the other side. "Manyatta" in Maasai literally means a "warrior's village," but the name has entered general usage in Kenya to mean nomadic communities or settlements. Samburu manyattas are circular in shape, with livestock pens inside surrounded by a ring of houses. The houses here were of permanent design, made with mud and dung pasted on domed roofs resting on strong timber frames. Each had a hearth inside, and one could see smoke wafting through the cracks in the sides of the house.

This community included a mixture of Samburu and Rendille people. A bit of anthropology: Rendille, who are distantly related to Somalis, are camel pastoralists who for the most part live in the lowland deserts of Marsabit District; Samburu are cattle-keeping people closely related to the Maasai, and who live in the highlands or closer to permanent water sources in Samburu District and Marsabit District. Both Maasai and Samburu are descended from migrating pastoralists who arrived in Kenya in the last five hundred years from southern Sudan. The Rendille and Somali have been here longer, and probably originated in southern Ethiopia. Sometime in the past few centuries, Samburu and Rendille formed an alliance, intermarried, and fought against common enemies. The Ariaal as a group were formed by that alliance, made up of Rendille men who joined to take up cattle husbandry and Samburu who raised camels. The Samburu (and the Maasai) borrowed from Rendille the customs of male and female circumcision, something not practiced by other Nilotic pastoralists of southern Sudan.

When we arrived at Peter's village, few people paid attention to me. Most were gathered in the western side of the settlement watching an intense ceremony of the l-murran (warriors). There were perhaps thirty warriors dancing and singing in a tight circle, twirling their long spears in the air and flipping their hair to the side as they jump-stepped forward. Moving around the warriors were older men with shaven heads wrapped in gray blankets thrown over their shoulders. These were the village elders supervising the dance, admonishing and directing the warriors with their cattle sticks. Among the elders I saw a short man moving among the warriors, flicking milk from a bowl onto the heads of the warriors. Unlike the other men who were dressed in red or white, this man was wearing a bright green cloth, and he had an intense and concentrated expression on his face.

I cautiously moved closer to watch the dancing, standing near the women and children who stood at a distance from the warriors, but clapping and watching the dance with great attention. As the warriors danced, a group of teenage girls stood to their side, dancing and singing in unison. Their bodies glistened with red ochre and oil spread on their neck beads and bared breasts; their heads were shaved close and were blackened with charcoal and oil.

"What's going on?" I asked Peter, my only link at that moment with these people.

"Oh, it's the warriors dancing," he replied in a nonchalant tone. "Come and meet my family."

But I could see this was no ordinary dance. These people were involved in something large and important, and I wanted to know what it was. It turned out I was correct; as I learned later, I had been observing a serious ceremony of the warriors throughout Samburu, an age-grade ritual called an *l-mugit* where each warrior sacrificed an ox, something done on four ritual occasions during their period of warriorhood.

Some more anthropology: neither Rendille nor Samburu had chiefs or a hierarchy of political authority; communities were run by married male elders, who were organized by both kinship ties and their members in par- ticular age-sets. Age-sets were formed every fourteen years and consisted of young men who were initiated with circumcision and served as warriors until a new set was initiated. Each age-set had a specific name, like *l-Kishili* or *l-Kimaniki*, similar to one's year of graduation from high school or college in America. In Samburu and Rendille, men passed through successive age "grades" as warriors, junior elders, and senior elders. The warriors are initi- ated in groups of young men ranging in ages from the early teenage years to early twenties. They are circumcised in a collective ritual during which they kill their first ox, one of five ox slaughters or *mugit* held during their warriorhood.

The warriors looked like the ones we saw on the bridge coming up from Isiolo. They were particularly striking in appearance, with long red-dyed braids, beaded necklaces and bracelets, and imposing spears and weapons. After completing their twelve- to fourteen-year warriorhood period, these men married as a new age-set was initiated. They then became elders who looked much less glamorous, with shaved heads and earlobes stretched long by brass earrings. Nevertheless, the elders held political power in the society; they made the major decisions including where and when to move for grazing or warfare. Village elders were often men of the same lineage or clan who had lived together most of their lives.

Warriors (in Samburu called *l-murran*, or singular *l-murrani*, meaning "the cut ones") formed their own semi-independent society, eating and living apart from the main settlements of adults and children. Their main jobs were herding cattle or camels to distant mobile camps and protecting the villages from attack by enemy marauders. The age-set system had allowed these groups to create mobile armies in the past, which the Maasai used with great effectiveness in the nineteenth century, mainly to fight each other for grazing land and livestock. Samburu and Rendille warriors continue to fight with their pastoral enemies, Turkana and Boran, but automatic weapons have begun to replace spears and clubs.

Women were not organized into age-sets, but they did pass through defined statuses of girl, adolescent, and married woman, reaching full status when they had children. Where villages were typically composed of men related to each other through the male line (the Samburu name for village, *nkang*, means "ours" or "family"), women moved to their husband's *nkang* from their own villages and formed their own friendships with other women outside of their family. In many cases women also had to adjust to the presence of other co-wives, since the society was polygamous; this situation usually did not cause tension unless the husband unduly favored one wife over another. Women wore leather skirts with intricate beadwork and large strands of colored beads on their necks; they also wore brass hoops on their upper arms and ankles. Warriors wore beaded leather bracelets and armbands made by their girlfriends; as married elders, they wore only a single strand of neck beads and an old cloth or blanket thrown across one shoulder.

As I watched the warriors dance, I asked Peter, "Who is that man, the one dressed in green sprinkling milk on the warriors? What is he doing?" I persisted, trying to figure this all out.

"Oh, he is Lonyoki, the *laibon*, a medicine man. Come on, let's leave here and go to my house."

I went with the boy, somewhat reluctantly, as I wanted to see the entire ceremony. I was fascinated by this direct exposure to an African ritual, and I knew immediately that I wanted to stay here a few days if I could arrange it.

As if reading my thoughts, the boy said, "You want to see the dancing, no? Don't worry; there will be more dancing today and tonight, and more tomorrow morning. You will see it all."

Peter's father was much older than I expected a man with such a young son to be, perhaps in his late fifties or early sixties. He was a tall and dignified man dressed in Western khakis and a black beret, the ubiquitous uniform of a government employee. As the caretaker of the government water pump, he had an important position and a steady income. The position also allowed him to watch over his own cattle, as the pump was not far from the settlement. We entered his house, where I presented some small gifts that Peter had suggested I buy in town, including small bags of sugar, tea, and tobacco, whose hard coarse chunks were chewed by the men and ground into snuff by the women.

Peter's mother greeted us warmly; Peter was obviously a favorite child. As she made the tea, the father began speaking to me in KiSwahili, but seeing that I didn't understand, he lapsed back into Samburu, which his son translated.

"*Habari gani?*" he asked, the traditional KiSwahili greeting meaning "What is the news?" In Samburu, the greeting is *serian ake*, "How is the peace?"

"It is fine. I've come from Nairobi, via Isiolo and the lowlands."

"And how is the weather there? Is there any rain?"

"No, no rain, but it is cloudy." Later I found out that weather was usually the second question Samburu ask a visitor. The first question usually was, "What family are you from?" (*Le'nkang ira iye?*), meaning what is your origin, and more specifically to another Samburu, "What is your relationship to me? Are we cousins, in-laws, friends—in other words, how should I behave toward you?"

When I told him I was an American, the man began a long description of his service as a soldier in World War Two. He lifted his shirt and showed me a long scar across his abdomen.

"I got this in Burma, killing Japanese for the British. Many Samburu warriors joined the British army, and many fought the Japanese. We also helped the government put down the Mau Mau."

Peter's father was pleasant, and he told me I was welcome to stay as long as I liked. I told them I would like to spend the night here, and they offered me a small house next door, recently occupied by their daughter who had married and moved away. I accepted, and after an evening meal of canned spaghetti that I prepared for myself, which my hosts graciously declined (with looks of horror on their faces), I went to sleep.

The house was near the cattle enclosure where the animals had settled in for the night. It was low and dome shaped, and it had woven sisal mats on its roof and leather skins tied to the sides of the wooden frame. Inside a small fire burned in an earthen hearth near the door, while the floor in the rear was covered with cattle skins to sleep on. The structure was quite old; the ceiling was black and shiny from the cooking smoke, which emanated from all the residences in the village. I was enthralled by the experience of being in a Samburu manyatta; I felt I was transported to another century, to the American West inside a Cheyenne lodge before the whites came. This was a dream come true and I wondered if I could stay here with these people. Why not, I thought, it's as good a place for fieldwork as any. They're certainly a lot nicer than the Turkana, who wouldn't give me the time of day. The manyatta was large, there were many cattle and goats, the people were welcoming; it was shady and cool, the . . .

Suddenly I jumped up; something had pinched me on my leg, something sharp and small. There was another, and another. Jesus, I was getting bitten by something! They were fleas, and they were all over me! They were in my hair, on my chest. Oh god, they were in my crotch! I was covered with them; they must have been on the calfskin mat. I pulled a sheet over my head and fell into a fitful sleep, my dreams of joining this primitive romance slipping into nightmares about snakes, scorpions, lions, and hyenas.

The Laibon Extends an Invitation

The next morning I was awakened by what I later called the "Samburu alarm clock"—flies buzzing around my head and landing on my face. This, on top of the fleas, gave me an inkling why few anthropologists came to study in these places. I got up quickly and walked outside. It was very misty; I could hardly see the next house. But I could hear metal cowbells ringing and the sound of women singing to their cattle as they milked them. As the mist cleared, I could see cattle in pens throughout the village and women and girls carrying their calabash gourds filled with milk back to their houses. It was a lovely sight.

Peter came out of his house and invited me in for tea. His mother was sitting by the cooking hearth, pouring hot tea from one cup to another to cool it down, and then she served it to me. It was delicious, made with lots of sugar and warm smoke-flavored milk. (The women cleaned their milk gourds out each evening with smoky sticks from the fireplace, giving it a distinctive taste.) I had to keep my cup covered with my hat when I wasn't drinking to keep out the houseflies. As we drank I could hear the warriors singing, and I knew the ceremony was continuing.

After breakfast, we went over to the dance area and saw the warriors move into an enclosed area called the *na'abu*, the manyatta's ritual center. The enclosure was surrounded by a thorn bush fence; inside was a small fire, which Peter told me was the site of evening prayers and had to be lit continuously for as long as the settlement stayed in that place. A warrior was blowing the horn of a kudu, a large antelope whose spiral-shaped horns were four feet long. This was one of the few Samburu musical instruments, and it was used both in rituals and to warn of enemy attacks. The laibon, dressed in his green cloth, was marking the foreheads of the warriors with a yellow powder as they entered the men's enclosure. The elders greeted the warriors by lifting their cattle sticks in blessing. The warriors sat in the circle, and the elders spoke, telling them something the boy couldn't or wouldn't translate.

Soon, the warriors rose and left the inner enclosure and dance-skipped to the outside of the settlement, where adolescent girls waited in a group to dance with them. Like the warriors, the girls had made themselves up, darkening their shaved heads and eyebrows with charcoal and grease, marking thin orange lines on their faces and red ochre and fat on their neck beads and exposed chests. The men lined up shoulder to shoulder, five across and fifteen deep, and twirled their spears in unison as they jumped forward into the semicircle of girls. The dance was incredibly erotic, and I wished I were part of it.

Later in the day, when everyone was resting in their houses, I asked Peter to introduce me to the medicine man.

"The laibon? What do you want to meet him for?" he replied with alarm.

"He seems like an interesting person; I want to meet him."

"You just stay away from him," Peter said emphatically. "He is a dangerous man."

"Well he can't be *that* bad," I said. "Let me meet him and introduce myself."

"You don't understand," the boy said. "He makes dangerous medicines. He's a sorcerer; do you know what that means? He kills people. His cousin Lokili is even worse. I heard he cursed a woman in Marsabit who became very sick and died just a short time ago. Look, you want to meet nice Samburu, don't you? You stay with my father and my family. We will help you with whatever you need to do. But don't go meet that man, he's no good."

"Come on, let's go. It won't kill you," I said, immediately regretting my choice of words. Off we went to the house where the laibon was staying, the boy announcing us in KiSwahili: "*Hodi,*" may we come in?

Lonyoki was sitting on a stool inside the house near a young woman who was sitting on the floor tending the fire. The laibon looked much less formidable than at his performance in the ritual. He had a handsome and kind face with an engaging smile, accompanied by arched eyebrows inviting agreement. It was hard to tell how old he was—he had a smooth face but faint lines around his eyes and mouth. I thought him to be in his forties. Smiling, he gently took Peter by the arm and had him sit by his side, motioning for me to sit as well. Peter told me the woman was named Correa, and she was the wife of Peter's father's brother. She remained silent during our conversation.

With Peter as translator, I began a conversation with Lonyoki, speaking in a very respectful tone.

"Please, I bring you this small gift of tea, sugar, and tobacco. My name is Elliot, I come from America. I very much wanted to meet you."

I expected the normal formalities to follow as in the boy's house, where the visitor brings tea and the host and visitor drink the tea and make small talk for half an hour. But the laibon tied the small tea, sugar packets, and hard tobacco in his green cloth and asked me in an even tone, "Why have you come here?"

"I heard there was dancing here. I wanted to see it."

"But why have you come here, from America to Africa?"

It was a fair question. I replied, "I've come to learn about the Samburu people. I want to learn your language and your customs so I can write a book about it, so people in my country can learn about the Samburu and your ways."

Most of what I said was true, although I had left out the part about wanting to study laibon medicine men, whom I had heard were a reclusive and unsociable lot.

There was silence for a while. Finally, Lonyoki asked me directly, "Would you like to write a book about the laibon?"

I stumbled for a minute. I couldn't believe he was asking me this. If I said yes I might be run out of that village for my arrogance. Those warriors had sharp spears and seemed awfully loyal to the laibon. But if I said no I would lose a wonderful opportunity forever and be just a run-of-the-mill ethnographer.

I gulped and said, "Yes, I would like to write such a book. I want to learn about the laibon, about what you do. People need to learn about your customs and practices, before all this knowledge is gone. If you allow it, I can watch you and talk to you, and write this book."

My body was tense and my hands sweaty. I looked down at my shoes in the dusty floor, wondering what he would say.

"This is good," he said. "You are right; soon this knowledge will be gone. There are only a few of us laibons left. I think it is important for our children to go to schools, to become doctors or learn medicine for the animals. But it is also important that they know the old ways too. I want you to write a book about me, Lonyoki. I want you to come with me and learn the ways of the laibon."

I couldn't believe my luck, and I would start right away. I took out my small notebook and pen and asked, "Tell me, what was this ceremony about?" I was tempted to say, "I'm new to the ways of the Samburu, someone who knows nothing about your people," but that sounded insincere and was unnecessary, so I stayed quiet. He seemed very direct, so I had better be too.

"This was a 'Mugit of the Bull' [Mugit lolai'ngoni]. It is the final mugit [ritual ox slaughter] before a new age-set is initiated. Now these warriors can find wives and marry."

"What was that yellow powder you put on their heads this morning?"

"That was my ntasim, my medicine. There is nothing stronger then the ntasim of the laibon. Now nothing will harm the warriors of Lorubai settlement."

"What exactly is a laibon?" I asked.

Lonyoki looked serious and said, "l-oibonok can see the future and prevent bad things from happening. The word a-ibon in Samburu means 'to predict,' and we do this with our nkidong [divination gourd] and by dreaming. We also know how to make medicines [ntasim] which can protect you from harm." He held up his necklace, which consisted of a half dozen dik-dik horns and a large crocodile tooth attached to a string of blue glass beads. "There is ntasim inside these horns. They protect me, and can harm people if I wish. I could stop your car by pointing this at you, even if you are far away. But I never use my ntasim to hurt people. Only to help people."

"How does one become a laibon," I asked, although I knew the answer from my reading about Maasai laibons.

"We all come from a single family in Maasai, the family of Supeet who was our ancestor. My grandfather came from Laikipiak Maasai long ago, and joined the Samburu living on Marsabit Mountain. You have to be born to a laibon family, but not everyone has the power to predict. My father knew I was a laibon before I was born, because when my mother was pregnant, she had dreams that came true. After I was born, her dreams were like everyone else's," he laughed.

This was fantastic! Here I was with my own private medicine man who was willing to talk to me. Laibons had the reputation of being severe and not very cooperative people, and I knew few Europeans (that is, whites) who were able to meet and interview them directly.

I had never given much credence to the supernatural world; I always suspected it existed only in the minds of people and not outside it. Still, religious beliefs were central to many cultures, and beliefs in laibons were obviously important to Samburu. My thoughts were interrupted as Lonyoki asked a few questions of his own. Speaking through Peter, he asked,

"Tell me, do you know the stories of *Jesu*, from the Bible?"

"Well, not very much, but I know a little," I replied. I was raised in a Jewish household and was pretty ignorant of Christian beliefs. My main source of information was watching Jeffrey Hunter play Jesus in the movie *King of Kings*.

Lonyoki asked, "Is it true when it says that *Jesu* was the son of God, and that he himself was God?"

"That's what Christian people who believe in Jesus think," I replied. "But I don't think it is true. I don't believe it myself."

"I don't believe it either. I think *Jesu* was a great laibon, but not God. Do you know that story where they say *Jesu* turned one fish into many, and one piece of bread into many?"

"Yes, I heard that story," I said. "I don't know if it's true, but that's what the story says. People were hungry and Jesus took two small fish and five small loaves of bread. He laid them down and then there were many."

The laibon laughed softly and with a twinkle in his eyes said, "That *Jesu* must have been quite a laibon. That's a really nice trick!"

"Where did you learn these stories from the Bible?" I asked.

Lonyoki turned and said something to the woman Correa, who reached and handed a small blue bag to him. From the bag he drew out a small dog-eared book and handed it to me. It was a Maasai Bible, published by the African Inland Mission in 1948. Lonyoki also passed me a book in KiSwahili published by UNESCO and subtitled in English "Papers Presented to the World Congress of Ministers of Education on the Eradication of Illiteracy," published in 1965. Finally there was a small hardbound ledger, where written in a childish scrawl was his name, "LONYOKI." Inside there were two small machine photographs of Lonyoki, and written on the first page of the book in the same childish handwriting was the word "Lembalen," with the birth date 1965. I assumed, correctly, this was his son.

"Where did you get these?" I asked politely.

"From a man named Janeck, a white farmer in Rumuruti. When I was a warrior I worked for him on his farm. He taught me to read and write in KiSwahili, and to do accounts in his book."

"When did you know you were a laibon?" I asked.

"I knew when I was very young, because I would have dreams and they would come true. Warriors would come to me and ask me to prophesy and make *ntasim*. But I did not start using my gourd, the *nkidong*, until my son Lembalen was born. This is my gourd," he said, motioning again for the woman to pass him the large round container. The gourd was the size and shape of a football, with a shiny yellow patina and a black ostrich feather on its leather lid, which sealed its neck and opening. Lonyoki held the gourd fondly, wiping it with a small blue cloth. He laid the cloth on the mat in front of him, spit into the mouth of the gourd twice, and then shook out some objects from the container. They were mostly polished stones—brown, red, white—but also seeds, crystals, leather ties, red glass beads, and store-bought marbles. There must have been several hundred objects in the gourd.

"After my father got older, and a little crazy, the Lorukushu [Lonyoki's clan] elders asked, 'Who can be our laibon?' now that my father was no longer able. But I refused, as my father was still alive. On the fifth time, my father came to me and said, 'You must be the laibon now,' and he gave me the nkidong gourd, the blue sheet, and some sugar. He blessed me and the nkidong, and the elders blessed me in the house."

Lonyoki unwrapped from his green cloth the tea and sugar I had presented earlier and passed them to Correa, telling her to make us some tea. I had forgotten she was here; I was so wrapped up in Lonyoki's monologue. But as I was to witness in many discussions among men in Samburu and Rendille, women often stayed quiet and in the background. It was only after guests had gone that the wife would speak her mind, and often quite forcefully. But this wasn't Lonyoki's wife, and I wasn't quite sure how to address her. She was very beautiful; I learned later from Peter that she was Lonyoki's mistress when he visited Lorubai.

Lonyoki looked squarely at me and asked, "Shall I throw the nkidong for you?"

I nodded enthusiastically, and Lonyoki spread out the blue cloth between us. Peter sat to our side, also very excited, and told me he had never seen this before.

Lonyoki held the gourd close to his mouth, spitting air as a blessing into it. He passed the gourd to me and had me do the same. I blew into the gourd's open mouth a few times, and then handed it back.

Lonyoki began his divination session, "This nkidong knows my truths and my lies. Speak the truth now to us here at Lorukushu."

He shook the gourd and poured a few objects into his hand, letting them go and watching them spread onto the cloth. Four objects appeared.

"Is there peace? Tell us good news about this young man who visits us."

He shook the gourd again and threw three handfuls, totaling sixteen pieces. A large lion's tooth was among the stones thrown.

"What is this about? Where is there a lion? Will he bother the peace of Lorukushu?"

He threw again, and a large group of stones fell onto the blue cloth. He collected the others and put them into three piles to the side.

"Is that *ntasim* medicine for the Turkana? What is it you say that is not good?"

He threw again. "No, everything is fine here, I can see it. We will drink plenty of milk at Lorubai. How is the peace of this young man?"

He threw ten pieces, including a leather knot. He threw again.

"Is it us who will be surprised?" Lonyoki asked out loud to himself. Then he said, "We will be giving *ntasim* to protect all of us, but I don't know when." Lonyoki turned to me.

"Have you been to Turkana country recently?" he asked. "This shell shows me something comes from Lake Turkana."

I was surprised, because I didn't think that I had mentioned my trip to Turkana to Peter, and I certainly hadn't said anything to Lonyoki. I replied, "Yes, I have been there recently."

Lonyoki threw again.

"Yes, you are standing at a Turkana homestead. But you are standing alone; there is no one else there. But there is someone in that *nkang* you cannot see, someone looking 'the wrong way,' but I know about this person. The Turkana envy our cattle; they may come here or to our friends the Rendille. I cannot see if they come to us, or we go to them. Is it true?"

He threw again. Several stones and objects fell onto the blue cloth.

"Ah, you are cheating me now. You are lying to me. Tell me truths."

Again Lonyoki threw and counted the pieces.

"What do these two tell me? Speak to me truths."

Again out came the shell from Lake Turkana. He threw again.

"This is good. I see a meeting, I see peace."

He threw again. "We are shifting. Not Lorubai, but a few of her people. And I see this young *mzungu* [white person] coming with us. Is there a meeting?"

He threw again. Then Lonyoki smiled at me. He said, "We have peace."

Lonyoki then collected all the stones. He placed some in my hand and showed me how to touch my head, shoulder, and knee with them. Lonyoki did the same, then collected all the stones and poured them back into the gourd, closing it firmly with its leather lid.

The tea was ready and Correa served us each a cup. It was sweet brewed tea made with hot milk and plenty of sugar. I could see Correa better now; she was stunningly beautiful, a woman in her mid-twenties with a narrow face and slender features. I thanked her and she smiled, which seemed to light up the darkened hut. I turned shyly from her and asked Peter to ask the laibon what the stones said.

Lonyoki responded, "Everything is fine. You will return to Nairobi and have a meeting with government people, then you will return here. We will leave this place together. I also see that you will do a very great thing for me. But I cannot discuss that anymore at this time."

Then with that mischievous grin of his, Lonyoki asked, "Well, what do you think of the *nkidong*?"

"Can you see things without using the *nkidong* stones?" I asked, trying to pin down exactly what this guy was supposed to be.

"Yes, I can dream. Especially when I have beer or honey-wine and feel sleepy, I can dream while I am still awake. When I dream, I see many things that you cannot see, things that will happen or have already happened but we don't know it."

"What do the stones tell you? I mean, how do you read them? I saw there was a lion's tooth, and you mentioned a lion, and so on. Is that how you can tell?" I asked.

"Well, some stones tell me things directly—a red ball, for instance, it means danger, that there is sorcery about. The shell from Lake Turkana tells me something about that place, like the fact you have been there recently. That is true, isn't it, that you were there?" he asked with a grin and raising his eyebrows, fishing for compliments.

"Yes, that is true. I was there and I did stand for a long time outside a hut. But does that mean anyone can look at the stones and read them?"

"No," he continued, "people who are not laibons can only see a few things. But only the laibon can read all the stones and tell you what they mean. When I throw the stones, it is like looking in a mirror. I can see life in there, I can see things happening. And I can tell you that nothing bad will happen to you in this place. Only good will happen to you. You have nothing to fear here."

Peter and I emerged from the house. Wow, I thought, this was something; the laibon was offering me a unique opportunity, and I decided then and there that I would stay and focus my research on laibons and their relation to Samburu society. I set up my small blue tent near Correa's house, no longer wanting to sleep in the flea-infested house. I settled into living with Lorukushu clan for the next period of time. My motorcycle companions Paul and Peach came by one afternoon to see how I was doing and whether I would join them as they continued their journey north. They did not seem surprised that I had chosen to stay here, and they went on their way.

Alone in my tent at night, I wrote up notes about Lonyoki and about laibons. I knew from reading ethnographies on the Maasai that laibons were prophets and healers who could divine the future and give "medicines" that could defeat one's enemies. The ability to prophesy was inherited, and all laibons are said to have come from one family, the lonkidong'i lineage of Laiser clan among the Maasai.

Some laibons rose to positions of great political power, particularly in the nineteenth century when various Maasai groups fought each other for grazing land and water sites in central and southern Kenya. The most famous laibon was Mbatian, who is remembered for orchestrating the defeat of the Laikipiak Maasai in a great battle by a combined force of Purko and Kisongo Maasai in the 1870s. Although he died before the Europeans colonized East Africa in 1895, Mbatian is remembered for predicting the coming of the whites and their building of an "iron snake" (the railroad) that would divide the Maasai in half. Mbatian's sons Senteu and Olonana fought a civil war, and, in keeping peace with the British, Olonana negotiated the removal of Maasai from Laikipia District to make way for white settlers. Once the "Lords of East Africa," the Maasai were now a small population in Kenya without much power or economic development. While the Maasai in southern Kenya and Tanzania saw their grazing lands diminished by the expansion of tourist game parks (Amboseli and Masai Mara in Kenya, the Serengeti and Ngorongoro in Tanzania), the influx of farmers onto Maasai lands, and the growth of Nairobi, the Samburu were left relatively alone. Most of the arid north of Kenya was occupied by nomadic pastoralists with little appeal to farmers and "down country" needs.

The next morning, I rose and walked over to the house where Lonyoki was staying. Calling Peter to translate, I interviewed the laibon further about his family's origins.

"Are you related to the Maasai laibon Mbatian, the one who defeated the Laikipiak?" I asked Lonyoki.

"We all share Supeet as our ancestor," Lonyoki replied. "Our war cry is 'I am from Supeet!' Supeet was the father of Mbatian, so we are somehow related. The nkidong divination gourd is only found in three peoples—Maasai, Laikipiak, and Meru—but we are all descended from that one family. No one else can get the nkidong.

"The Lonyoki family came from the Laikipiak Maasai during the time when l-Kipeku age-set were warriors [approximately 1837–1851]. It was during this time that our family grandfather, Kocheke, was adopted by the Lorukushu clan of Samburu. His real name was Charrar, but everyone here called him Kocheke ["the stomach," possibly because he was rotund, which was a sign of wealth]. He left Laikipiak and joined the Samburu, living up here near Marsabit Mountain and sometimes over in Maralal. People moved around a lot in those days."

Sour Milk and a Christian Dinner

I wanted to stay here at Lorubai as long as possible before I had to return to Nairobi to straighten out my research permission with the government. With such a short time frame, I needed to be clear about what I could actually accomplish. That was not difficult to figure out because I realized that I knew absolutely nothing about these people or the area. I took out my small spiral notebook in which I had begun to keep notes, including a description of my conversations with Lonyoki.

I wrote at the top of a new page: "June 19, Marsabit Mountain. Explore social and physical environment: Cattle, water pump, manyatta, government officials, missionaries."

Declaring my intentions in writing has always been very satisfying. Just writing specific goals down makes me feel like I've already accomplished them. I closed the notebook and stepped out of my tent, ready to choose one of my many tasks—meeting people here at the Samburu settlement, going out with the animals, or talking to various government and other officials with whom these people interacted.

Peter and his father had gone off for the day to the water pump. I had cheerily told him I didn't need him, that I would just hang around the village by myself. Now that he was gone, I was terrified. There were dozens of houses, vast networks of livestock enclosures, and worse, scores of strange people around—warriors with their spears and long braided hair, women with shaved heads and naked chests, and dozens of little children running around. What had looked charming and distant before now became real and very unfamiliar. I was trying to look unobtrusive despite my long curly hair and unusual garb: a yellow T-shirt, army pants, and hiking boots. People were glancing at me and seemed as scared as I was to make contact. I asked myself, "What do I say to these people? What if somebody comes up to me? Everybody must be looking at me. Oh my god, that man with the limp, he's coming directly to me!" He was a broad-shouldered man with close-cropped hair and long earlobes pulled down by brass earrings. He was leaning on a stick, and I could see he had a shriveled leg, probably from polio. But he was strong and agile, and there was no way I could turn around and pretend I didn't see him.

"*Jambo, Bwana,*" he greeted me. I shuddered, but nodded meekly back. He spoke rapidly to me in KiSwahili, which I did not understand. He gestured, moving his closed hand across his cheek while saying "*Reza, Reza!*" but I didn't understand. He was getting mad that I didn't understand, and he grabbed my hand and moved it across his face, then my face. "*Reza, Reza,*" he repeated.

"Oh, razor, you want to borrow a razor," I said.

"*Ndiyo,*" yes, he smiled but with a look that questioned my sanity. OK, a razor I could do. I went into my tent, hunted around and brought out my safety razor, wondering what setting he preferred. He took the razor but immediately started fiddling with it so he could take the double-sided blade out of its handle.

"No, no," I interrupted. "Like this," and I took the handle and showed him how I shaved my face. But then he interrupted me, grabbed the razor from my hand, and shook his head with an expression of disgust, as if I thought he had never shaved before, and he continued to remove the blade. He turned to view himself in the mirror on my motorcycle, and with the bare blade held between his thumb and forefinger, started shaving his dry face. I couldn't believe this. Don't you even want soap and water, I wondered? But he shooed me away; he wanted some privacy.

I returned to my tent, a little piqued at this rude interaction. But in a few minutes the man returned and gave me back my razor blade. Surprisingly clean shaven and smiling now, he introduced himself as Lenkera and offered his hand, which was huge and crushed mine in a strong grip. While this man had obviously suffered polio, all of his body except for his leg was muscular and thick like a wrestler. He refused to let go of my hand and began dragging me to his house at a fast gait. "*Oh, Oh-weh-nay,*" he repeated, which I assumed meant "come with me," pulling me inside the round hut.

His house was smoky and crowded, with several small children sitting on the skin mat; they had runny noses and mucus in their eyes. His smiling wife was sitting near the cooking hearth, nursing a young infant as her two other children played next to her. Flies, which the mother occasionally shooed away, buzzed around the baby's eyes. As Lenkera sat down on his elder's stool, one of his children jumped on his lap and the father playfully bounced him on his good knee. He then set the boy down and asked his wife to pass him a large round gourd of milk, which was nestled against the wall with the other containers. He took off the large leather lid from the gourd; he poured some milk into it and handed it to me to drink. But this wasn't the fresh warm milk I had been drinking at Peter's. This was that thick, heavy, lumpy sour milk that the elders drink, *kule na oto*, the "milk that slept." It was disgusting. It smelled like milk that had gone really bad.

I took a small sip and then tried to return the container to the elder. His eyes narrowed and he defiantly pushed the leather cup back to me.

"Drink this!" he ordered.

I sipped from the cup feebly, swallowing the thick curds and chewing those that wouldn't go down. The milk was very warm and very sour. I finished the drink and gave it back, thanking him profusely as I tried to keep my stomach still. Good, he smiled, and then poured another cup for me. Please no, I begged, but again he demanded that I drink it, in a tone that brooked no opposition. Was he trying to kill me? I sipped the second offering and immediately felt hot, sweaty, and dizzy. I could hear the flies buzzing around me and could see vaguely in the background the elder filling the cup again. His face was blurred as he handed it to me, but I could feel him lifting my hand so I would drink it. I knew that I was being treated to outstanding Samburu hospitality, but he was killing me with his kindness. As I drank this last cup, I felt the room spin as my head lolled backward and I fell back flat on my back. The elder's concerned and clean-shaven face was the last thing I saw before passing out. I wasn't out long but did feel sick to my stomach. My host Lenkera was laughing heartily, as if he always suspected that the wazungu weren't very tough. I got up, thanked them all in a loopy way, and headed back to my tent.

It was late afternoon when I heard the sound of a car engine driving into the manyatta. It stopped close to my tent, and I could hear the car door open and slam shut. I heard KiSwahili with an unmistakable American accent; a man was greeting people with "Jambo, Jambo, Bwana," sounding like "Howdy, howdy, partners."

I stepped out of the tent to have a look, and sure enough there was an American man in a cowboy hat standing next to a Jeep pickup truck. Peter's father was getting out of the truck, and the American was talking to some elders gathered around him. The man was my age, about twenty-five years old, clean-shaven but with long sideburns and wearing blue Levi's jeans, a plaid shirt, and work boots. I approached his car and he greeted me with the same wide smile he had for the others.

"Hey, how-do-ya-do?" he said, offering a firm shake. His hand was like a rough piece of wood. "My name is Steve, and I'm a water engineer with the African Inland Mission (AIM). I heard from Peter's father that you were staying here for a while, and I wanted to meet you and see if you needed anything. Why don't you join us for dinner at our house, it's just down the road at Logologo? I'll give you a ride in the jeep, and get you back after dinner."

Sounded good to me, especially if it wasn't "milk that slept" they were serving for an appetizer. In his open truck, Steve had made room for eight

Samburu, mostly women and children, who needed a ride down the mountain. He was very jovial, patting women on the shoulders, helping lift their babies up, telling them to "Watch your step, Mama" or "Careful, there we go." He obviously enjoyed being here.

As we drove down the road, he talked continuously in a rapid fashion, telling me about the water situation.

"Yeah, Marsabit Mountain is rich in untapped water, which is pretty unusual for volcanic rock since it is so porous. It's amazing because even though we're in the middle of a desert, there are places both on the mountain and in the lowlands where water gets trapped." Driving down the mountain, Steve raised his voice over the engine noise.

"Logologo was built by Earl Anderson. He first came out here in the 1960s with the African Inland Mission and mechanized the boreholes that the Samburu used. We also put in a pump at Naiborr way out in the desert where the Rendille water their camels, but now the Catholics have gone out there and built a whole manyatta where they give away famine foods. I tell you, it's not charity these people need, but the opportunity to make a decent living in this barren land."

We passed a dirt road leading off into the mountain to the left, with a wooden sign that said "Nasikakwe Agricultural Scheme, National Christian Council of Kenya."

"We helped start that project. There, impoverished Rendille and Samburu who don't own any animals can grow maize on rain-fed plots. It's been going three years now."

I cringed at the idea that so many of these mission projects were undercutting the pastoralist basis of the Samburu economy based on raising livestock for food and cash. Why didn't the missionaries offer assistance that was aimed at improving livestock, which seem to do well up here?

"How many years has that project had a crop?" I asked.

"Well, only once," he admitted, "but that's because the rain has been very bad recently. But there's another agricultural scheme we started in Songa, on the other side of the mountain. That side is green and forested with deep pools and springs. We set up an irrigation system, using those thin plastic pipes that drip water into the plots. The Israelis invented this pipe; it's really a flat hose with lots of small holes for the water to drip through. Those Israelis, well they certainly know how to turn a desert green, don't they?"

I asked Steve if he thought anything besides raising animals would work in this area.

"Well, the desert is moving south, you know," Steve responded. "Most Samburu and Rendille now like eating *posho* [maize meal]. Many older people and young families want to settle down. Only the warriors like to run around in the bush, drinking their milk and blood. But when they grow up and start handling the responsibilities of married men, then they want to settle down, too. That's why we're doing so much work mechanizing the boreholes, to make it possible to live at one place all year round."

"And make it possible so they can become Christians too?" I asked in my politest tone.

"Well, yes, that's true. But we don't just convert anybody like the Catholics. We have Bible teachers who live in the manyattas preaching the Word, but we set up schools and dispensaries too," he said a bit defensively. "We also have our church services every Sunday, and a preschool center, and a Bible study for adults, but you have to want to be there. If you don't accept Jesus willingly and with your heart, then it just isn't real."

We reached Logologo, an unattractive place with a few buildings and even fewer shade trees. The mission compound consisted of a modest cinder-block house, a storeroom, a pump house, an open-air church, and a school. There were a few small Samburu huts nearby, but they looked very poor, without animals and with old burlap bags and cardboard as roofs. We got out of the car and went into the house to wash up.

The missionaries' house was simple but unmistakably American, with a large dining room table set with plastic dishes and aluminum drinking glasses filled, if you can believe it, with ice cubes and cherry punch Kool-Aid. Earl Anderson and his wife were both in their late sixties, I guessed. There was also one of their sons, Howard, and a Canadian nurse named Helen. I shook hands with everyone and sat down at the table.

With hands clasped, Earl led the prayer: "Dear Lord, we thank you for another blessed day in our work, and for bringing everyone safely home this evening. We thank you for welcoming our guest, and for this food you have enabled us to eat. We pray for the medicines we ordered, and speed our son Dilly home with the new water valve. In Jesus's name, Amen."

Dinner was grilled hamburgers and potato salad, with servings of canned corn and green beans. The dinner conversation was of a surprisingly practical nature—how the new diesel engine was now pumping 750 gallons a minute, but what a chore it was last week when the elephants trampled the tap at the water trough, and soon Dilly would bring a new spigot valve when he came back from Nairobi, hopefully later that night.

Over coffee, I asked about the mission's activities delivering health care.

Helen was the nurse in charge of the dispensary, and this was clearly her territory. She was a no-nonsense type of woman, someone you would want to see in charge of a dispensary.

"Well," she explained, "we have an outpatient clinic here, and a large hospital on top of Mount Kulal (below Lake Turkana in Samburu District) where we will fly people who need surgery or serious attention. Let's see, we do childbirth, give out a lot of antibiotic treatments for cuts, and we treat malaria, which gets pretty bad after it rains. A lot of old people get pneumonia and tuberculosis."

"Do you charge money for these services?" I asked.

"Well, yes we do, but it's usually just one shilling a treatment. It's just so people know that we're not a charity, and it teaches the Rendille responsibility. It's very cheap and they can afford it. Except for VD, that is. Those warriors come in with gonorrhea and want a shot of penicillin, just demand it straight out, you know, like we'll just clean them up so they can go out and fool around some more. They have no care in the world about the consequences of their actions, as if we're responsible for cleaning up that mess. But I'll tell ya, we make them pay for that shot, plenty! Twenty-five shillings," she laughs, her face turning red.

("Well, that will surely slow down the spread of disease," I thought to myself.)

"But actually," she continued, "the health of the Samburu and Rendille at Lorubai is pretty good. Samburu and Rendille have a pretty good diet with all their animals; the kids get milk every day. That's quite a difference from over at Naiborr, where that priest," she said with a frown, "has been giving out *posho* every day to anyone that asks for it. Now the Rendille there don't even bring their animals to Naiborr anymore. They just wait for handouts from the Catholics."

Apparently the battle of the Reformation was still being waged up here in Marsabit District, with the Protestant ethic as the standard to judge all actions.

Changing the subject a bit, I asked, "Can you tell me something about the differences between the Samburu and the Rendille? I keep getting mixed up. Are the people at Lorubai Samburu, or Rendille, or both?"

"Now there's an interesting question!" Steve responds. "I've been making a study on it, and maybe as an anthropologist you can help us out on this. I'm actually trying to write a translation of the Bible into Rendille, and it is a very hard language, let me tell you.

"The Samburu are Maasai, they speak Maasai, keep cattle like the Maasai, and have age-sets for their 'moran' warriors like the Maasai. But the Rendille, they're different. Their language is like Somali, almost Arabic sounding, and they keep camels and goats and sheep mainly in the desert. But they are not Muslims like the Somalis.

"As far as I can tell, the Rendille and Samburu have been friends for some time, although it's not always that friendly. Sometimes a Samburu man will move to the low country; he'll take a Rendille wife and raise camels. Sometimes a Rendille man will start to raise cattle, and he will become more Samburu like and move up the mountain."

Earl now spoke, and Steve quieted down.

"I'll tell you something," the old man said. "I think the Rendille are one of the lost tribes of Israel."

This was an old chestnut the early German ethnographer Meritz Merker proposed in *Die Masai* (1904). Part of the thinking then was the racist view that Maasai and other African pastoralists (called Nilo-Hamites) were "more white" than other Africans; a similar explanation was used to describe Tutsi dominance over Hutu farmers in Rwanda and Burundi.

"Why do you think that is?" I politely asked.

"Well," Earl said, "for one thing, they're circumcised. The Hebrews were the ones who originated that. And they have this ritual that's a form of the Jewish Passover. Every spring, around Easter time, the Rendille have this blood sacrifice, where every house kills an animal, and they wipe the blood on their livestock and over their doors. I believe it is so the Angel of Death passes over their houses, as the Hebrews did when Moses cast the ten plagues on the houses of Egypt."

"I think they believe in atonement for sin," said Earl's wife, "because they also mark themselves with blood. They're asking for forgiveness."

This conversation was getting depressing. If there is anything cultural anthropology teaches, it is to respect all cultures and to try to understand them in the context of their own history, beliefs, and customs, not through the values of outsiders imposing their own cultural beliefs. In the 1920s Franz Boas, the "father" of American anthropology, called this approach of respect and understanding "cultural relativism" and called the study of cultures "historical particularism" to emphasize that each culture was the product of its own internal dynamic. Missionaries, while earnestly trying to do good works, had a pronounced history of imposing their own beliefs and values on the societies they were missionizing; indeed, their raison d'être was to convert people to the missionaries' religion.

Everyone was quiet now, thinking, I imagined, about their work and what effect it was having on the area. Their leader Earl then said, almost to himself, "We've only been here eight years so far. It's not enough time to determine our effect yet."

It was time to go. I thanked them all for their genuine hospitality and the interesting conversation. Steve drove me back to Lorubai and I walked through the dark toward my tent. I was depressed about our dinner conversation. Like many Americans and Europeans in Africa, the AIM naturally assumed that the Rendille wanted their help, and they were certain they could improve the Rendille's lives through their gifts of both Western technology and Christian ideology, where clean water and eternal salvation would solve all their ills.

Herding with Warriors

I rose early in the morning and left my tent to urinate. I soon discovered it was fine for anyone, including women, to have a pee near or inside the animal enclosures, but one should take "the long walk" away from the village to defecate. It was foggy and not yet bright. Most people were still asleep. I was startled when I saw two warriors standing near me, leaning casually on their long spears. They were armed with various weapons including a long sword sheathed in leather and the ever-present *rungu*, a wooden club with a large metal piece—a heavy nut or transmission gear on the end. One touched me on the arm and whispered in a conspiratorial tone, "*Oh-weh-nay*" (Come here).

"*Kore Peter?*" (Where's Peter?), they asked.

I walked from my tent to Peter's house and called softly, "Peter, come here please. There are two warriors here who want to speak to me." I was a bit frightened. I didn't know what these two daunting characters wanted.

Peter came out and talked softly with the two *l-murran*. Peter turned to me and said, "These men want to know what age-set you're in. They want to know if you are a married elder or a warrior in the *l-Kishili* age-set like them."

"I'm not married, so I guess I'm in the warrior set like them," I replied.

"They say if you are in the *l-Kishili* age-set, you must sleep and eat with them. They want to know why you are eating milk with elders and women."

"Well, tell them this is where the food is," I joked, hoping they would laugh rather than spear me. Fortunately they laughed.

"Tell them I would prefer to drink milk with them," I said, not quite certain what I was getting myself into.

"They want to know if you can herd cattle."

"Sure, why not?" I asked.

"They ask can you run an hour without stopping?"

"I don't know," I said, although I highly doubted it.

"They ask if you can live on nothing but milk and blood for weeks at a time?"

"As long as it's not that 'milk that slept,'" I said, and the warriors laughed again. We were warming up to each other.

One of the men then touched my arm and said directly to me, as Peter translated, "Get a spear from this boy's father and come with us."

"Tell them that sounds OK to me. What do I call them?" I asked.

"You must call them *murratai*, 'my *murrani* [warrior] brother,'" Peter replied.

As we were talking, I saw the short silhouette of Lonyoki approach us.

"*Sopa!*" he greeted us.

"*Sopa, apaiya*" (Greetings, father), the warriors replied.

"*Serian ake?*" (How is the peace?), Lonyoki asked.

"*Ey, serian*" (There is peace), replied the warriors.

Lonyoki then talked to the two men awhile but held my hand and mentioned my name as he talked. When he was done, Peter translated:

"The old man says that the warriors must take care of you, and see that no harm or danger comes to you. He told the warriors to stop at his house before setting out, and he would give you some medicine to protect you from the buffalo and elephants in the forest."

Lonyoki turned to depart, and said, "*Miki-tajapa nkai*" (May God carry you).

"*Nkai*," we responded, and everyone departed for Lonyoki's house. He was sitting on a short stool, mixing yellow powder and water in an open seashell. He told us to bend over him, and he marked our foreheads with the yellow *ntasim* powder. He also tied a string coated with the same *ntasim* around our right wrists. He did this without ceremony, only telling us the medicines would protect us from dangers in the forest.

"*Ma'apetin!*" (Let's go!), one of the warriors said. They carried nothing but their spears, wearing their red *shukas* (cloths) and sandals made from old tire treads. Unlike them, I was wearing walking boots and baggy military pants and carried my shoulder bag with notebook, pen, camera, and roll of toilet paper. We left the manyatta and headed toward the large woods of the Marsabit Forest Reserve. Jogging at first, I petered out after a mile. The warriors could easily have run five miles but slowed down to wait for me. Soon our path became a winding trail through the mountain woods of tall hardwoods, fig trees, and vines.

After some miles we came to *l-chota*, a series of wells with hundreds of cattle and scores of warriors about. Several warriors stopped to shake my hand, while others glared at me with unfriendly faces, which told me this was not a good time to take pictures. My companions motioned me to one of the wells and soon had me working, passing water buckets up from the well in a three-man chain. I enjoyed the rhythm of the work, adding my voice to their singing "wooah, wooah" to everyone's delight.

When we finished watering the cattle, my companion flicked a finger on the side of his neck and motioned me to follow him and his two friends. The flick at the neck, I soon realized, meant snack time, specifically blood tapped from a living cow. We approached a large gray ox (castrated male), and as one warrior held it by the horns, the other tied a long leather cord tightly about the neck, exposing a large jugular vein pulsating on the side of the neck. With a small bow, he shot a short arrow into the vein and out flowed a steady stream of blood into a small bowl held by another warrior. After a liter or so of blood was collected, the warrior released the leather cord and the bleeding stopped. The ox looked a little woozy, but no worse for wear, and moved away. One of my companions took a swig from the bowl and, smiling in delight, passed it to me. Deciding this would not kill me (I was in strong denial of germ theory at the time), I slowly sipped the frothy blood, surprised at its warmth and salty sweet taste. I had little time to savor the moment, however. Running quickly into the bushes, I had not yet learned that I could expect a bout of diarrhea every time I drank blood.

I stayed with these warriors for one week in their mountain camp, drinking milk and blood, herding and watering cattle during the day, and staying up late at night trying to sing their melancholy songs. Although I was generally incompetent at most tasks they normally performed (milking cattle, killing snakes, or throwing spears and clubs with accuracy), I always tried to join in.

One evening, two warriors I did not know came over to greet us. One of the warriors looked at me with a stern expression. "Tell me," he said, "Where are you from?"

I knew enough Samburu words to follow most of the conversation.

"America," I replied.

"A-mer-ika," he repeated. "So tell me this. Is it true that Americans sent an airplane to the moon?"

"Ey, kedede," I replied, it is true. (I would hear this disbelieving question many times during my stay in Kenya.) He went on, "So is it true that the Americans are going to build a tourist lodge up there?"

All the warriors cracked up laughing, and I laughed too. It was a pretty good joke.

One day, a warrior gave me a red *shuka*, the strong cotton sheets they wear around their waists or toss over their shoulders when it is cold. He told me, "Here, wear this. You are a warrior like us and you should dress like us."

I felt pretty sheepish but took off my army trousers and folded them up in my pack. Another warrior laughed pleasantly and took off a string of beads, which he gave to me to wear across my chest, over one shoulder and under the opposite arm. Another warrior gave me some wrist beads, and another some beads to be worn around the neck, until I was transformed into a warrior, at least in dress. One of my age-mates then applied some thin red lines of ochre to my face, drawing them into the patterns they wore. Looking approvingly at me, he said, "Now you look like a man!" Fortunately, I could not see what I looked like until later photographs revealed how white and out of place I looked.

But in truth, the *shuka* was much more comfortable than my thick trousers, and the beads and spear they lent me gave me a wonderful feeling of empowerment. After a few days, I was no longer conscious of how I looked. I felt a part of this age-set as we herded cattle to grazing fields or water wells. I was happy and felt lucky to be here. Some anthropologists, and more than a few graduate students studying to be anthropologists, have found themselves in fieldwork situations that are unbearable. A professor demands that a student work in the Amazon rain forest to assist in research, and the student finds that he or she can't stand the tropical heat and humidity or, worse, the people to be studied. A couple may begin their fieldwork as a married pair, only to separate when they find the solitude and intensity of close contact unbearable. But my situation was different. I loved it here—I loved the terrain, the desert heat, the smell of burning wood and cow manure and red ochre and roasted goat. And, most of all, I loved the people. Yes, they were alien and exotic to me, but they were also profoundly human and familiar. These Samburu warriors seemed a stoical and serious bunch, but not without humor and wit.

But these feelings became heartbreaking when we returned to the village and I was told by the authorities that I had to leave. Shortly after I came back, I was paid a visit by the local government official, Chief Leruk, who had come to find me at Lorubai. I had been around too long and "people" were asking about me, he said.

"You do not have official permission to stay here in this place. You are a foreigner who is doing research, and you need official permission from the government to conduct research. I could get into trouble if anything happens to you here, or if you do something you should not be doing. You need to get papers from the office of the president in Nairobi, which must be stamped by the district commissioner here in Marsabit. Please go to Nairobi and come back when you have your documents in order."

Lonyoki the laibon joined the conversation. "Yes, Elliot, go get your papers. Then come back and find me. I know we will meet again."

I did have a research permit for Turkana District, which had proved to be a disaster, but those documents were not correct for Marsabit District.

My alternative plan to go to Ethiopia and research isolated groups there was a bust with the coup d'etat against Haile Selassie. I dreaded returning to Nairobi because I knew it would be a long ordeal to obtain a new research clearance. But I had no choice; I had to do this research properly and with government permission. Marsabit was the place where I wanted to live and conduct research, and I wanted to focus on laibons and their influence among Samburu.

That I found this place was totally accidental; I had no research agenda, no knowledge of this group, nothing that remotely resembled formal preparation that graduate students were required to do. What I did have, however, was a deep desire to live with and learn about this community. I knew I had found the place where I wanted to do my research. I packed up my *piki* (motorcycle) and began the arduous two-day drive down to Nairobi, not knowing when I would return.

CHAPTER TWO

Living with Nomads

Home is not far away when you are alive.

It took two months for me to obtain my official permission to conduct research in Marsabit District. Perhaps a bribe would have speeded this up, but I preferred to play by the rules, or at least the rules of my culture. My stay in Nairobi had not been wasted. I had time to write to the Smithsonian Institution for a "Disappearing Worlds" grant, which miraculously awarded me $4,000. This was enough to buy a used Land Rover from two American "world travelers" who had driven across Africa from Morocco to Kenya; after eight months their car and marriage had run out of gas. The Land Rover was a blue short-wheelbase hardtop, with a roof rack and two spare jerry cans attached to the rear. It was the coolest car I had ever owned. Although I was able to go up and down riverbanks, it could not go faster than fifty-five miles per hour, got only thirteen miles to the gallon, and did its best to destroy my kidneys on the corrugated roads.

When I finally returned to Marsabit in June 1975, I learned that Lonyoki had moved to Naiborr in the lowlands where the Rendille lived. At the government offices I presented my documents to the district commissioner, who welcomed me and invited me to stay in touch if I had any problems. Wasting no time, I headed down the mountain with several passengers, including a local schoolteacher who could direct me to the town of Naiborr. I drove south on the main road to Logologo and then turned east on the dirt road to Naiborr.

We arrived at Naiborr in a cloud of dust as the sun was setting. Naiborr was the most desolate place I had ever seen; it lay in a treeless hardpan desert midway between Marsabit Mountain and the Ndoto Mountains. Its only important feature was a permanent water well used by Rendille herders. There were a few shops, but the town was devoid of vegetation and livestock. It was home mostly to impoverished Rendille living around the Catholic mission, which distributed famine relief foods including soy flour, beans, oil, and powdered milk. I made my way to a small Ariaal manyatta behind the church, looking for Lonyoki.

I found the laibon resting in the shade outside a domed Rendille house. These houses were larger and taller than the dung- and mud-covered Samburu houses on Marsabit Mountain. Lonyoki was sitting next to Chief Leruk of Lorubai, the one who had asked me for my papers, and another man whom I did not recognize. I showed Chief Leruk my new Kenyan research identity card, which he looked at with approval. Leruk then said, "Lonyoki dreamt that a white man would come in a car today."

Lonyoki chuckled; he was happy to see me, smiling, winking, and holding my hand.

"I want you to meet my good friend Dominic," he said. I shook hands with Dominic, a slender man with a narrow face and a bald head. He remained quiet but periodically glanced at me during the conversation. There was also a teenage schoolboy named Kenneth who was Lonyoki's nephew-in-law. He was en route to his home in Maralal and would accompany us and serve as my interpreter for a while.

"We have a big favor to ask of you," Lonyoki said. "We want to go to Dominic's manyatta of Lukumai, near Lenguas town in the Ndoto Mountains. We want you to take us there and stay with us."

This sounded good to me. "Ma'ape" (Let's go!), I said, using my new Samburu idiom.

We stayed the night in Naiborr, eating a goat that Dominic acquired from his kinsmen. The next day we loaded up the Land Rover with Dominic, Lonyoki, and two other men including my new interpreter, Kenneth. Dominic strapped a large amount of materials to the roof rack: sisal fibers, which the women use to make roof mats; several large sacks of maize; and boxes of famine relief food including five-gallon metal containers of soy oil that were inscribed, "A Gift of the People of the United States." Each had a picture of a white hand shaking a black hand over a "stars and stripes" emblem.

Once the vehicle was loaded, we drove directly west out of Naiborr on a road leading toward the Ndoto Mountains, with sharp peaks reaching nine thousand feet above sea level (Naiborr is only fifteen hundred feet in altitude). Like a seasoned guide, Dominic pointed out features of the landscape and identified the mountains and hills we passed. To the right was Poi, a sheer rock face more than one thousand feet high. Dominic told me that a man came all the way from Germany ("Cherman") to climb it. Directly ahead of us was a deep cut in the mountains where the town of Lenguas nestled. "There's a river there, and at the top a waterfall," Dominic said, nodding his head vigorously as if anticipating my disbelief. He then pointed to a large hill to our left, about five miles distant, and said, "That is where my *nkang* Lukumai is."

The Ndoto Mountains run in a north-south line along Kenya's Rift Valley, a large trench that was formed by the movement of the African tectonic plates, which began separating fifteen million years ago. This activity dramatically changed the East African landscape, giving rise to the Great Lakes and the mountains of Kenya, Rwanda, and Ethiopia. Creating a rain shadow, the Rift also gave rise to the dry East African savanna environment. No doubt this geologic activity contributed to the evolution of our earliest human ancestors, who came down from the trees and began walking upright on two legs. Just to the north lies Lake Turkana, where Richard Leakey discovered many hominid fossils, including *Paranthropus boisei*, *Homo habilis*, and *Homo erectus*. Further up the Rift Valley in Ethiopia are the Afar lowlands, where the early hominid fossil "Lucy" was found (formally called *Australopithecus afarensis* and dated to 3.2 million years ago).

As we drove, we periodically saw some wildlife, although the animals were few and far between in this desert environment. We saw an oryx, a large gray antelope, resting in the shade of an acacia tree, and a few Grant's gazelles. We even saw a gerenuk, a desert antelope with long legs and a slender neck like a giraffe, standing on two legs to reach the upper branches of a large bush. All of these animals are adapted to the heat of the desert; they also tend to be solitary, since the desert ecosystem cannot support large herds of animals as the grasslands in southern Kenya do.

Just as we reached the Lenguas valley, Dominic told me to turn left onto a small sandy track that cut south, parallel to the Ndoto Mountains. "This road goes to Laisamis," he said, referring to the small town on the main Marsabit road. "Over there is Baiyo Mountain," he added, pointing to an isolated collapsed volcano with a top curved like a Dairy Queen ice cream cone. We drove on a bit until Dominic spotted what he was looking for, a set of camel tracks that went into a very thick layer of bush and acacia trees.

"*Kore nbarabara?*" (Where's the road?), I asked in Samburu.

"*Meti nbarabara*," laughed Dominic, meaning loosely, "There ain't no such road!" Motioning his hand through the air, Dominic said, "Just go straight after you pass this bush." I began to wonder how much experience Dominic had with cars. It was slow going, with Dominic saying, "Go left here, now right, now left." In time, however, we came upon a large herd of camels managed by two men and three boys with long sticks. Dominic motioned for me to stop. He got out of the Land Rover and greeted the men in a friendly way, chatting for a few minutes. He then jumped back in the car and said, "*Ma'apetin*" (Let's go!). We turned to follow the camel tracks, our speed hovering around fifteen miles per hour.

Finally Dominic yelled, "*Towana! Keti nkang*" (Stop! There's the manyatta!). Suddenly we were outside Lukumai settlement. I might have driven right by this place and never seen it. The houses were low and brown colored, and the village was surrounded by thorn bush fences. The manyatta was larger than it first appeared, a cluster of fifty low houses in a circle more than one hundred yards across, inside of which were pens for the camels, cattle, goats, and sheep. The houses were round domes made of sisal mats and leather tied over thin wooden frames. I later discovered that the manyatta was designed deliberately to be defensive, to protect the animals from wild predators—lions, hyenas, even leopards—but also to stay hidden from human enemies like the Turkana or Boran who would try to raid their cattle and camels.

It was around one o'clock, a time when nearly everyone was resting. Slowly people came out to see the vehicle, shy at first because they weren't used to seeing cars or *wazungu* so close to their homes. The young boys came out first and immediately reached for my hand, smiling and jumping up and down. One boy stuck his head into the front seat of the Land Rover and Dominic yelled at him—"*Tshomo iye!*" (Get away you!)—and the kids ran for cover.

The women then began to come out, young and old, all with shaven heads and wearing leather skirts. They were naked from the waist up, although they wore strands of colorful beads around their necks and flat spiral brass earrings. Some women wore the palm fiber *mparua* necklaces over their neck beads; they were smiling and laughing, shaking Dominic's hand; all were beautiful in their red and brown colors. Some of the women approached and greeted me with hands outstretched to shake mine. They were shyer when they greeted Lonyoki, who they recognized as a laibon from his green cloth and large necklace of *ntasim* amulets. Finally, the elders came out from under the shade tree where they had been resting. They were lean like Dominic and wore old white cloths around their waists, and each carried a long slender camel stick.

"*Sopa, Dominic*," they greeted, "*Sopa, sopa!*" and I shook hands with all the elders. After greeting everyone, Dominic took me by the hand and pulled me into the house of his first wife, Naiseku. It had a narrow entrance made of two cow hides turning inward from opposing vertical posts; the house was a large dome with sisal fiber mats on the roof and leather skins on the wall over a strong wooden frame. I entered into a spacious area with a cooking hearth on one side and a resting/sleeping area of leather skins in the rear. Naiseku smiled and motioned to me to sit down. She was a small woman with a pretty face, dark skinned, and (as I was to learn later) a Samburu, unlike most of the women here who were Ariaal or Rendille. She had beautiful beadwork on her necklace and skirt and brass coils on her upper arms. She looked at me directly without shyness; she wasn't flirtatious, she just wasn't afraid of me.

Dominic gave Naiseku a packaged bag of black tea and some sugar he had bought in the shops, and she started to make tea. She directed her eight-year-old daughter, Naisaba, to fetch some water from the large woven container by the entrance while she built the fire with a leather fan. Soon the aluminum pot was boiling and she poured the tea, sugar, and fresh milk from a wooden container into the pot. Dominic called for Lonyoki and Kenneth to join us, and we were soon drinking the delicious brew. I never understood why scalding hot tea, sticky sweet with milk and sugar, was so refreshing in the desert, but it was. I preferred it to the warm sodas or beer that were available in the shops.

Dominic told Naiseku to bring down a small wooden container from the wall of the house. He took off the tight leather lid and offered Lonyoki and I cooked cubes of fat; they were crunchy and delicious. Resting now after our long car ride, I propped myself against the curved wall of the house, absorbing the smells of the fire and looking around. Everything in this house was perfectly neat. Near the cooking fire, on the left, or "woman's side" of the house, were a half dozen calabash gourds with beaded leather lids used to contain milk, one gourd for each member of the household. On the "man's side" on the right were a variety of bags and containers, all rolled and tied neatly to the curved wooden frame supporting the roof. I noticed that Dominic's weapons were also tied there: a long spear, a bow and wooden quiver of arrows, and, toward the entrance, his wide *panga* blade used for cutting bush and firewood.

Dominic reached up and removed a long sword with a highly polished red leather sheath from the rafter. He offered it to me and said, "Here, this is for you. This was my sword when I was a warrior. Now you are a *murrani* of Lukumai manyatta, so I give it you. Pull the sword slowly when you draw it; the sheath is very tight."

I was speechless. This was a very fine gift and I held the sword appreciatively. I pulled the blade slowly, as instructed. The sheath was made of leather stretched over a wooden frame and was indeed tight. The handle of the sword was thin and long and covered with a single piece of leather with no seam. I later learned this was the tail skin from the ox each initiate ritually slaughters at his circumcision. Lonyoki smiled and asked to see the sword. He looked at it in approval, pointing to the impressed figure of a giraffe and the words "Twiga Brand" on the blade (*twiga* is KiSwahili for giraffe).

Dominic said, "Ey, Twiga knives were made by the Ang-lish. The steel was very good then, not like today. From now on you and I are *sotwa*, now, special friends."

The laibon smiled and said to me, "Now ask him to give you a cow, because that's what *sotwa* do." He laughed and continued, "This man Dominic is so poor he doesn't have a cow to give you. He hardly even has a goat." Lonyoki seemed fond of teasing Dominic, who did not seem to mind. But Dominic could dish it out as well as take it.

"This man Lonyoki is so poor he doesn't even have a donkey. He doesn't have but one wife, and she can't stand to be near him anyway. Isn't that right, Lonyoki?"

"*Tu tum menye*," replied Lonyoki, which translates as "your father will meet (and punish) you" but is used when people want to say "go fuck yourself."

"This man Dominic," Lonyoki continued, "is so in need of woman that if he wasn't back home, he would jump on a log if he thought it would let him!"

Everyone laughed, including Kenneth, Lonyoki's nephew, as he translated for me. Dominic's wife Naiseku, who had remained silent by the fire, giggled and said softly to Lonyoki, "Dominic doesn't need the forest when he is at home in Lukumai."

This type of intimate exchange, especially talking about sex in mixed company, took me by surprise, but I learned that it is not unusual in colloquial Samburu. It was a talent of Lonyoki, I discovered, that he could engage people directly and coarsely one moment, and turn into a stern and austere religious figure the next.

A young boy about six years old entered the house and sat by Dominic's side. He was slender with the narrow features of a Rendille. He gently stroked Dominic's arm and held his hand while Dominic spoke softly to him. Displays of affection are rare in public, but not in one's house, and Dominic stroked the boy's shaved head.

Dominic said, "This is my son, Parengi, from my second wife and that little girl is Naisaba, my daughter with the Mother of Larengan [meaning his wife Naiseku]." (Married women were usually called by the name of their first son.) Naisaba smiled shyly and sat close to her mother by the fireplace. She had the same features of her mother—a round face, dark skin, and beautiful smile. Dominic told Parengi to go sit by me. Parengi looked like a young camel, with long eyelashes and slender limbs. He also had a very sweet disposition. He looked shyly at the floor but came over to me as told. I let him sit next to me and, to my surprise, he took my hand and stroked it.

"My name is Elliot," I said, and he repeated softly but correctly "Elliot." He did this better than his father, who had difficulty pronouncing *l*'s and called me "Efriot" when he occasionally used my name. Dominic developed a variety of nicknames for me in time, including *mpirrian* (which is a special age-mate friend) and Lengirrira, the name of a family of Dorrobo hunter-gatherers, meaning to Samburu a "hick" or "dumb ass."

Dominic told us to come to the house of his second wife, whom he called "Mother of Parengi" (*Moto' Parengi*). When not addressed by the name of their firstborn sons, women are called by terms other than their personal names, such as *yeyo* (mother) or *naikitok* (wife of my husband's age-mate). We got up and left Naiseku's, or rather Mother of Larengan's, house and walked immediately into the next house in the row.

"*Hodi?*" I asked, using the polite KiSwahili form for "May I enter?" Moto' Parengi replied in Samburu, "*Wo*" (come). Dominic called her "Rendille" because those were her people. Whereas Naiseku was dark and short, Rendille was light skinned and tall. To her left sat her daughter, Ntenukwa, who was tall like her mother and about four years older than Parengi. Like everyone else, her hair was shaved close to the scalp, and she wore a light string of beads around her neck. Only warriors let their hair grow long, while everyone else shaved their heads. I believe this style was invented for cleanliness, given the lack of water for bathing.

Rendille was older than Naiseku, or at least appeared older. She wore only a few strands of beads, and I had the sense that she thought the beadwork was frivolous. Rendille was a *sapa'ade*, a special class of Rendille women formed every third generation who were not permitted to marry until their older brothers married. Consequently, these women could be in their thirties by the time they had husbands. Because of their age, *sapa'ade* women did not produce many children, but Ariaal and Samburu admired them as second wives because of their reputation for strength and hard work. Rendille spoke very little Samburu, and Dominic spoke with her in Rendille.

I immediately liked Rendille. Like Naiseku, she wasn't afraid of me and looked me directly in the eye. She didn't smile very much, but this was not because she was angry or depressed. She had a quiet dignity about her; she was intelligent and seemed to possess a sober sense of the world. Rendille had prepared some *ugali*, maize meal cooked into moist cakes, which were covered with a meat stew. It was delicious. I learned later that this stew was a rare treat. People usually did not eat meat except on special occasions, and they certainly did not eat large meals in the middle of the day. Lonyoki and I were special guests, at least at first. Until I had my own house, I would sleep either at Naiseku's or Rendille's house, depending on which was the least crowded. With Lonyoki and myself as guests, Dominic's wives had their hands full cooking for all of us.

After a few days, I felt more comfortable in this village and could walk around without drawing too many stares. I particularly liked the early evenings after the animals returned home and the temperature cooled off from its midday high of ninety degrees. After being milked—cattle, goats, and sheep by women; camels by men or boys (but not warriors, I discovered later)—the animals settled into their pens. Throughout the night one heard various animal sounds: cattle moaned softly, young camels and goats made high pitch *eh-h-h* sounds, while adult camels moved about, "tocking" the hollow wooden bells they wore on their necks. I found the sounds and atmosphere extremely pleasant.

But it was the people I was most interested in. Over the next few weeks, I made the rounds and began a census of the 250 residents of Lukumai settlement. Ariaal and Rendille communities were quite large for nomads, ranging from thirty to fifty houses. Lukumai was a subclan of Lukumai section, Lukumai being one of four large sections (or super-clans) of the White Cattle moiety; the other half of Samburu belonged to Black Cattle clans. The White Cattle sections—Lukumai, Lorukushu (Lonyoki's clan), Longieli, and Loimusi—were located mainly in the lowlands, with Ariaal belonging to the first three clans and one they called l-Turia—the "mixed ones." The Black Cattle clans (Masala, Nyaparai, Pisikishu, and Lng'wesi) lived mainly in the highlands, particularly near Mount Nyiru or on the Leroki Plateau near Maralal, the capital of Samburu District. The Rendille people had a clan system that was similar to but different from that of the Ariaal and Samburu, and their clans were ranked in terms of a ritual seniority. Dominic's wife Rendille came from the Wambili family of Dibshai, one of the most senior lineages.

For the first few weeks, I tried to learn the names and families of everyone in the village. I walked around the inside perimeter, greeting people as they sat outside. I had drawn a map of all the houses and was adding names to each of them. If someone was home, I would sit down and ask the names of his or her children so I could begin a household census. Still, it was a big manyatta with more than fifty houses, and I easily got confused. One evening while strolling along the thoroughfare, I realized I was lost and could not identify Naiseku's house. They all looked the same to me. I went up to a woman, I believe it was Dominic's brother Usana's second wife, Nkitari, and said "Yeyo, kore nk'aji?" (Mother, where is my house?). She laughed hard, and in a child's plaintive voice, repeated, "Yeyo, kore nk'aji?" I felt pretty foolish, realizing I was still a child in terms of my knowledge of this culture and language.

My interpreter, Kenneth, who had remained with me in the nkang (village) for a short while, had returned to Maralal, and I was on my own. I had A Masai Grammar written in 1955 by Tucker and Ole Mpaayei, and although there are many differences in dialect between Maasai and Samburu, it was the best source I had. I made a stack of note cards, each with an idiom or word in English on one side and the Samburu translation on the other. I would go through the cards every night and be tested periodically by Parengi, my six-year-old teacher. "What's this?" he would ask, pointing to his nose. "L-gume," I would reply. "What's this?" pointing to the eyes (en-kong'u), "what's this?" pointing to the ears (l-keeok), until finally I said, "Parengi, I know all the parts of the face [kai-yolo l-gomon poke], I need to learn other words!"

Parengi's father Dominic was not as good a teacher as his son, but he was a great listener and interpreter. "Sopa, apaiya," I would say to his brother Usana, "Serian ake? Serian ntamesi?" (How is it going? How are the camels?). And Usana would respond in rapid and slurred speech, made less comprehensible by the absence of many of his teeth. Although I could pick out a few familiar words like "camel," "water," or a place called "Ker'ngera," I could not possibly understand him. Dominic would then look at me and say, very slowly, "His camels are in Ker'ngera, near the Arsim wells. He doesn't know how long they will stay there, but soon he will take them to l-Barta [plains near Baragoi, in Samburu District]." Dominic spoke "ki-Elliot" (the language of Elliot) and was my best interpreter. It was difficult going, but I was managing more each day.

My anthropological research was also taking shape. My census of the manyatta revealed fifty-two houses with 252 people from eight different lineages (families within subclans). Half of the married men had two wives (a few had three); the average age of married men was around fifty years and that of married women was thirty-five, because men married in their early thirties while women married as teenagers. I could never locate exact birth-dates but could age people by an events calendar I had developed that listed, for example, when an age-set had been initiated, when the big drought had occurred, and so on. The combined herds of the manyatta numbered 642 camels, 836 cattle, and more than 2,000 goats and sheep (called "small stock"). Although most Ariaal used camels as baggage animals, those from Samburu backgrounds, including Naiseku, kept donkeys for transport. Many houses kept dogs, which were not very well treated but could warn of predators like hyenas who came to raid in the night. The dogs were small and short haired, brown or black and white in color, with pointed ears and curved tails; they looked like Basenjis but could bark. Most were covered with fat ticks; I wondered how they would look if they were well fed and cared for.

In contrast, the cattle and camels were very well treated. Warriors would stroke the necks and talk to their favorite cattle, and women would sing to their cows as they milked them. Periodically I saw several adults, both men and women, bathing young camels with an herbal solution made from the bark of an acacia tree that killed ticks. People had a variety of herbal medicines and technologies to care for their livestock; they also bought helminthicides (antiworm medicines) and other treatments that were available at the local shops in Lenguas.

The census was a good way to make myself known to each household, and I facilitated the process by presenting tea and tobacco to each household I visited. I didn't want to pay something every time I spoke to someone, but it was polite to present a gift when I was doing a formal interview. This habit certainly made me popular with both men and women in the village. I began to focus my interviews on individuals who were specialists in particular types of knowledge. Dapash knew all the rules of kinship and social structure; he was like a judge explaining the intricacies of Samburu law. Lolongoi, a middle-aged widow, was a midwife and herbalist who taught me many of the plant medicines used to treat men, women, and children with fevers, aches, and burns. Lepere was an expert on camels and could tell me how often they bred, what diseases threatened them, and where one needed to graze them. More than a few people I interviewed thought that my foolish questions suggested that I was not very bright.

Usana's older wife was tanning a goatskin, stretching it out and pegging it into the ground to dry out. "*Sopa yeyo*," I would say, "What are you doing?" She would reply with a "hmmph" and "What does it look like I am doing?"

As with much of cultural anthropology research, my fieldwork was opportunity driven. If I had scheduled an interview with Dapash on kinship, I might arrive at his house only to discover that he was away for the day. I would then drift to some other activity—I would talk to a woman weaving sisal fiber into a roof mat, or photograph a father and son milking a camel. I asked Usana, "Why are men milking camels and not women, who I see milking the cattle and goats."

Usana responded, "Only elders and uncircumcised boys can milk camels. They don't like the smell of sex and won't give milk to women, girls, or warriors."

"Really?" I asked, finding this hard to believe.

"Absolutely. The camels get very nervous when women or warriors get too close." Having seen and kept clear of jittery camels myself, I took his word for it. I had seen camels kick out at people, and even lift a girl by her head with its sharp teeth. I treated her with antibiotic ointment and hoped for the best.

In time I learned about each of the families in Lukumai. Dominic had three brothers; Choma and Usana were older (they were in the l-Mekuri age-set, while Dominic and the laibon were age-mates in the l-Kimaniki set); Dominic had a younger brother, nKong'ini, who was an unmarried warrior (l-Kishili age-set) and away much of the time. Choma, the firstborn, had inherited his father's camel herds, while Dominic, the thirdborn, had received only a few cattle and small stock. Choma was not very friendly, and people said he knew sorcery and kept their distance from him. Usana, the middle brother, was industrious, good humored, modest, and proud of small accomplishments and property such as the new spear he bought from a blacksmith after considerable saving. All the stockowners I met here were concerned about their herds and the security of their families, which were inextricably intermeshed.

Sometimes I visited other manyattas or distant *fora* (herding camps) where warriors moved with the nonmilking livestock. Often while in the village, I went to the men's shade (a place outside the manyatta under a big acacia tree) and listened to the conversations of the older men, asking questions that occurred to me or that I had prepared.

The older men loved to sit under their shade tree and play *ndotoi*, the wooden board game found throughout Africa (widely known as *mankala*). Usana would play with Dominic, moving the small pebbles from hole to hole around the board, stopping at the place where he could accumulate the most stones of his opponent. Slapping his hand down loudly, Usana would say, "Ah-ha! You owe me three cattle!" and chuckle as he added more chewing tobacco to the huge wad already in his mouth.

I asked Usana what age-set he was in. (I knew the answer but wanted him to start reminiscing.) I was not disappointed. Age-set seniority determined social rank, with the oldest members of the society afforded the most respect, although not always.

Usana said, "I am in the Mekuri age-set. We were the strongest of all the warriors and never afraid to fight."

"*Sapardisho!*" (Liar!), said Dominic without any hostility. "Our age-set, the Kimaniki, were the toughest, as tough as the Merisho, our grandfathers who fought the Boran on Marsabit Mountain. Who was it that defeated the *shifta* [bandits] near Laisamis? Was it not the Kimaniki?"

It sounded like a meeting of the Veterans of Foreign Wars in the United States. Samburu used the names of age-sets to date important historical events, and anthropologists and historians have benefited greatly from this. New age-sets were initiated almost exactly every fourteen years. (Samburu followed the Rendille system of naming each year after a weekday in a seven-day calendar; after two rounds or "weeks" they knew when to initiate the new age-set.) Elders might say, "When the L-Mekuri were warriors," and I knew they meant a period between 1936 and 1948. (See Table 1 for age-set dates.) The age-set chronology was essential when I started to unravel Lonyoki's family history of laibons.

Dominic was the most worldly person in the village. As a young warrior he had been arrested for raiding cattle and spent eight months in the Marsabit Prison in the 1950s. Here he learned to speak KiSwahili (the prefix *ki-* indicates a spoken language), and he developed an admiration for the national liberation leaders, including Jomo Kenyatta who became Kenya's first presi-

Table 1. Samburu Age-sets and Initiation Dates

Age-set	Date of Initiation
Meishopo	c.1781
Kurukua	c.1795
Petaa	c.1809
Kipayang	c.1823
Kipeko	c.1837
Kiteku	c.1851
Tarigirik	c.1865
Merikon	c.1879
Terito	c.1893
Merisho	1912
Kiliako	1921
Mekuri	1936
Kimaniki	1948
Kishili	1962
Kororo	1976
Moli	1990
Nateli	2004

(Fratkin 2004)

dent. After his release Dominic returned to the life of a warrior but stayed out of trouble. When the l-Kimaniki age-set began to marry in the early 1960s, Dominic found a beautiful girl, Naiseku, who came from the Soritari clan in Logologo. It was rare for warriors to marry their girlfriends, as marriages were arranged and girls often married strangers much older than themselves. Dominic and Naiseku thought they were very lucky.

Because he could speak KiSwahili, Dominic became an intermediary between Lukumai village and the Kenyan administration. Dominic had good diplomatic skills—he was a thoughtful orator and a skillful negotiator who could speak privately to individuals and work out compromises between people involved in disputes. Dominic had long harbored a desire to be appointed subchief of the region, a paid position with prestige and authority, but he lacked the education and resources to win the position. Still, Dominic was the de facto chief for Lukumai, the one the elders, who spoke no KiSwahili, relied on to speak with government officials.

Not all stockowners were men. Although Samburu culture dictated that animals could be owned only by men, women had rights to milk them, and widows were responsible for caring for inherited animals for their male children until they were grown. One example was an older woman I called "Paker," meaning mother-in-law, or "receiver of the wedding sheep." I called her this because I always teased her eight-year-old daughter that I would marry her one day, to which she would respond with giggles. Paker was a wealthy widow whose husband had died when she was young, and she was responsible for managing the household herds for her male children. In a formal sense, she did not own these animals but was only holding them in trust until her sons were grown and needed cattle as bride wealth in order to marry. But she engaged in many husbandry decisions (deciding which animals to breed) and managed the sale of her livestock. Paker was a shrewd and responsible stockkeeper who would periodically discuss herding decisions, such as where and when to move the settlement, with other Lukumai elders. This was done privately, not in the formal context of men's discussions in the na'abu ritual center, from which she was excluded. However, as her sons began to marry, Paker's status diminished and she became another of the settlement's "old women" (ntasat), lacking prestige, power, and even basic security.

It was not difficult to see how important domestic livestock were to these people. Camels, cattle, goats, and sheep, even donkeys and dogs, were each essential in their own way. Camels produced milk when all other milk animals had dried up. They could survive without water for ten days, sometimes even two weeks, and still produce ten quarts of milk per day. Cattle yielded much less milk, averaging only one quart or so per day in the wet season, compared to American dairy cows, which produce more than six gallons of milk per day. But cattle were the prestige stock of Samburu and Ariaal, and one could hear a warrior singing a praise song about his favorite ox as he scratched the dewlap skin fold along its neck. Cattle were used for sacrifice in age-set and marriage rituals, and were the medium of marriage payments (bride wealth, sometimes called bride price) from the husband-to-be to his bride's father. For Samburu it was expected that the groom would give eight cattle to the father of the bride. These cattle would then allow the bride's brother to pay bride wealth and marry, so cattle were constantly circulating in the society and creating and maintaining social ties among different families. Once the bride wealth was paid, the children born to the union would be members of the father's clan and not the mother's.

Goats and sheep were traded with shopkeepers when households needed to buy posho (maize meal), tea and sugar, or manufactured goods such as cloth, cooking pots, or flashlights and batteries, so necessary in this world without electric power. Dominic once said, "Goats are our bank!" Ariaal and other nomads in northern Kenya often bought on credit from local shopkeepers, who were usually Somalis or Indians, paying their bill when they had accumulated enough animals. And always, offering and roasting a goat for a guest was an important way to show hospitality.

"We can never give up our cattle," Dominic said. "If you give me two hundred acres of land and a tent full of money, I would not know what to do with it. But give me a bull and a cow, and I will make many cattle, I will be a rich man. My head knows cattle, it does not know shambas [gardens]. Kikuyu know farms, Rendille know camels, but Samburu know cattle."

The Samburu and Rendille were allies and intermarried, but they were not always on the best of terms. The Samburu thought of the Rendille (and Ariaal) as great beggars, people who were always making requests of their relatives and neighbors. Dominic once asked me if I knew how to say "thank you" in Samburu. "Of course," I replied, "it's ache-oling." Then Dominic asked, "Do you know how to say thank you in Rendille?" "No," I replied. Dominic laughed, "That's because Rendille don't have a word for thank you! Samburu say n'go'o [here, have this], while Rendille say n-yau [give to me]."

While I gave gifts to individuals in Lukumai, I received much in return. Old Man Lemeti, who was in his seventies when I first met him, was a crusty old coot who was not given to small talk or friendly conversation. He was surprisingly active, despite his age and arthritis, which caused him to stoop over. He had outlived four wives and took care of himself with no help. One day I passed Old Lemeti while he was bringing firewood to his tiny house. He said to me, "*Ero* [youth], give me your hat, it is too hot out here for me." (This was my broad-brimmed safari hat.) To his surprise, I replied, "Here, Grandfather, you take it." He blinked once, put the hat on his head, and shuffled off. That night, Old Lemeti came to my house with his new hat on his head and a gourd of milk in his hand. He handed me the gourd and said, "*N'go*" (Take this). "I don't ever want to hear it said that you have gone hungry in this *nkang*." And indeed, to this day when I go back to Lukumai, one of Lemeti's sons or grandsons (the old man died years ago) brings me a *ma'alo* (wooden container) of milk. As the Samburu say, "A cow has no owner"; all will be fed in the village.

An Eclipse

About two months had passed since I arrived at Lukumai. I was spending more time with Lonyoki, watching him throw his divination gourd for clients and prepare the *ntasim* medicines to protect them from curses and sorcery. Lonyoki was happy to answer any question I asked and he never hesitated to explain the applications of particular medicines.

"This is red *ntasim*," Lonyoki explained, showing me a small gourd containing ground red powder. "It comes from the *reteti* tree [fig trees that grow close to rivers and are sacred to Samburu and Maasai]. The inside of its bark is red, and is very helpful to women. It is the most powerful medicine to help women conceive babies and give birth. And this is yellow *ntasim*, which is protective to the *nkang* and cattle; I give this to men and warriors. And this," he said, holding up a small gourd, "is black *ntasim*. It is quite powerful and can be used to harm someone or protect against sorcery [*nkurupore*]. I can mix this with yellow *ntasim* to give to men, and with red *ntasim* or honey to give to women and children."

"Do you know how to make sorcery medicines?" I asked.

"Yes," Lonyoki replied, "I know how to make *nkurupore*. But I never use them to harm anyone, or sell to someone to use against someone. Some laibons do this, but not me. Sometimes I have to make *nkurupore* to give to our warriors when we fight enemies in battle."

Lonyoki was himself curious about my culture and customs. He asked if there was sorcery in my country, and I said, "Some people have customs about sorcery and medicines. There are many different peoples in my country; some come from Europe, some from China, some from Africa, and some were people living there before the Europeans came. Some African people in America have 'root medicines' which they believe can harm or protect you."

"Yes," replied Lonyoki, "I have heard there are African people in America. Where you find black people, you will find *ntasim* and *nkurupore*."

Lonyoki was curious about the sky and stars, and wanted to know if it was true that the earth moved around the sun, as the *wazungu* (white people) said, rather than the sun revolving around the earth, as Samburu believed. I explained the solar system by drawing figures on paper, and in the evening we would look at the stars and talk about the universe. The stars were utterly amazing in this desert location, where no city lights could interfere with the view. I could see the Milky Way clearly and imagined us somewhere in its middle, spinning like a disc through space. Like many rural people who live without electricity, Samburu were great stargazers, and they had names and stories for the stars and constellations. What we call Orion the Hunter, Samburu saw as a wedding party, in which the husband, best man, and bride (the three stars of Orion's belt) walked between two lines of elders holding cattle sticks. During the first two weeks following a new moon, as the sky got brighter until the full moon appeared, folks liked to sit outside and socialize in the soft light.

The evening of the full moon (*lapa lonyokie*, or "red moon") was the most festive of nights, given how bright it made the desert. Older men and women sat outside their houses and chatted, children played as if it were daytime, and warriors, if at home, danced with their girlfriends late into the night. One evening Lonyoki and I sat on what were probably the only two beach chairs that existed in Marsabit District, waiting for the full moon to appear. We chatted about the stars and looked through my binoculars at the constellations. The full moon always rises at the same time as the sun sets, which in Kenya along the equator meant around six o'clock in the evening. But tonight something was wrong. We had been sitting outside for about fifteen minutes after dusk and it had grown quite dark, but still there was no moon. Then I saw a faint arc of a circle where the moon should have been. It was an eclipse!

People were murmuring in low voices now. A woman near us said, "*Lapa ko-tua, lap ko-tua!*" (The moon is dead, the moon is dead!) Others began moving about, pointing at the dark sky and saying "*Lapa ko-tua!*" I immediately got up, flashlight and spiral notebook in hand, the anthropologist at work. I approached Usana's oldest wife near her house.

"*Lapa ko-tua!*" I said.

"*Ey*, the moon is dead," she replied.

"What will happen now?" I asked. "Will the children get sick, will the animals die?"

She looked at me in astonishment and said, "Why are you saying such bad things? The moon will come back. Haven't you ever seen a *lapa ko-tua* [eclipse] before?"

Burnt my face! While the eclipse was not frightening to the villagers, it was unusual and called for a ritual response. Women from Rendille families went into their houses to don their *sara* aprons, leather skirts with straps of cowry shells and metal bells that made rhythmic sounds as they danced. The women also wore their beautiful *mparua* necklaces. The mood was festive. Women came out of their houses forming a circle for clapping and singing, led by Usana's first wife, who was surprisingly agile. There was much laughter and merriment, especially when the full moon reappeared a few hours later.

The next morning, the mood was more serious. Outside the manyatta the men had constructed a gateway of two fires made of acacia branches. All of the camels were made to pass through the fire, called *ulukh* in Rendille, which was a way to bless and protect camels from unusual and unpropitious events.

Bright moons were the preferred time for community ceremonies and particularly weddings. Weddings were held during rainy seasons when the animals were home and there was plenty of milk for everyone. Daughters of the *nkang* are married to men from other clan villages, and the ceremony occurs in her village. While weddings were festive occasions, they were an intense time for both the bride and groom. The groom must kill a wedding ox swiftly and efficiently for the village to feast on, and the bride undergoes female circumcision early in the morning as the wedding ox is slaughtered.

Early in my stay in Lukumai, one of Lepere's daughters was married to a young elder from Longieli clan. She was an "older" girl around eighteen years; her marriage was arranged by her father and his brothers and I doubt she had met her husband-to-be before the ceremony. The groom had arrived the evening before the marriage ceremony, camping outside the village with his best man and two age-mates. They stayed awake the whole night to guard the ox, lest someone else, presumably the bride's lover, kill the beast and claim the girl for himself.

The wedding began early the following morning when Lepere's daughter was "circumcised" inside her mother's house. I put the term in quotations because there is much controversy, at least in Western cultures, about this act. Circumcision implies a rite of passage for the girl, similar to that for men, although the procedure is quite different. Samburu, as well as Rendille and Maasai, practice a form of female genital cutting called cliterodectomy, and do not practice the more severe form of infibulation, where the lips of the labia are sewed closed after the clitoris is removed, a procedure found in Egypt and northern Sudan. Many societies that practice female genital cutting do so long before a wedding: Maasai will perform the operation when the girl enters her teen years, while Somalis and Ethiopians will do it when the girl is quite young, even as an infant.

I stood outside Rupeeta's house as her daughter went through the cutting. I heard the young woman say to Lolongoi, the midwife who would perform the operation, "I don't want to go through with this. I don't know this man, I don't like this man, I want to call this off." Not surprising, Lolongoi and her mother said, "*Tigerai* [be still], this will be over soon."

While this procedure was going on, the groom arrived in the *nkang* with his best man, leading the wedding ox, a gift to the bride's father, and tying up a sheep next to the mother's house as a gift to the bride's mother. These were the initial payment of a bride price of eight cattle. Lepere came out to inspect the animal, tsk-tsking and chiding the groom that this was a poor specimen indeed to exchange for his daughter. I was taken aback; I thought the white ox was one of the largest and most beautiful I had seen. But Lepere's criticism, I realized, was intended to assert his authority to the future son-in-law and make sure that future favors would be forthcoming. Marriage, after all, was an alliance between two clans and not between two individuals.

Standing outside the circumcision house, the groom assisted by his best man killed the ox in an efficient but dramatic fashion. Grass was placed in its mouth and a leather skin tied around its muzzle and nostrils to suffocate it. Then the groom thrust his knife into the rear of the ox's skull, causing immediate death. This was considered a particularly gentle way to kill an animal, although I must say they seemed more concerned about the well-being of the ox than they were of the bride inside the house. When the sacrifice was completed, Lukumai's elders placed butter and red ochre on Lepere's head and made blessings to both the father and the groom, praying for the newlyweds to have many children and good fortune.

The ox was butchered outside the circumcision house and distributed in an orderly fashion to all of Lukumai's men and women. The elders moved to various circles outside the *nkang* to roast the meat and eat, while women took their portions inside their houses for cooking and consuming. The groom and his friends abstained from eating and stood stoically as they supervised the distribution of the wedding meat. For Lukumai's residents there was much laughter, as one would expect during a large feast. Amazingly, the new bride came out of her house several hours after her operation. Supported by two girlfriends, she walked over and greeted many of the guests. I was amazed at her fortitude.

As the day proceeded, a variety of singing and dancing occurred, first by the married women singing outside the bride's house and later by the warriors and girls dancing outside the village. As it was getting dark, a delegation of Lukumai's elders entered the circumcision house with the groom and his best man. The elders told the bride to obey her husband and told the husband to look after his new wife and their children to come. They ended this mild harangue with a group blessing, saying, "*Nkai! Nkai!*" (God! God!), telling the couple to have many children, both boys and girls; to have many animals, cattle and camels, goats and sheep; and to know prosperity and peace—and also asking God to bless them always. The day ended with singing late into the night by warriors and girls from the village. In a short time, Lepere's daughter would leave Lukumai and join her husband's village. It was unlikely we would see each other again.

The next day I chatted with Naiseku (Dominic's wife) and Nkitari (Usana's young second wife). We had become chummy and were used to teasing each other and kidding around. We were talking about the wedding, and, as if reading my mind, Naiseku asked me, "Elliot, do they circumcise women in your country?"

I replied, "No, that is not done in my country." I refrained from sharing my opinions about what Americans thought about female genital cutting. I was here to learn how their society worked and not impose my own cultural values.

Naiseku was astonished. She said, "It is very bad that you do not circumcise your women. Babies born to them would not be human, would they? They would be like wild animals!"

Nkitari added, "And how can a girl prepare for the pain of childbirth if she has not been cut?"

I was a bit embarrassed to ask, but very curious to know something.

"Tell me," I asked, "Can women enjoy sex if they have been cut?"

Naiseku smiled and nodded vigorously. "Yes, we enjoy it," Nkitari added with a laugh, "but only if the husband is young!" She was in her twenties, whereas her husband was in his sixties.

Naiseku then grinned at me, arching her eyebrow. "Elliot, if you left a baby with us here, what color would it be?"

We all laughed. I responded, "Well, one ear would be white, the other black; the nose would be white, the chin black . . ."

"*Taisho*," (Stop it), Naiseku responded, wagging her head. "It would be white, all white, wouldn't it?"

"Well, what if it were?" I asked.

"Then the men would kill it," Naiseku said calmly. "That happened once before, when a British soldier left a baby with a Samburu girl."

"Why would they kill it?" I asked.

"Elliot, look around you. When the desert is alive it is green. But when it is dead, it is white. White is the color of death," said Naiseku.

"You're really making me feel very good here," I teased them.

"No, Elliot, you know we all love you. But the men would still kill the baby."

Then Nkitari grinned and said, "Elliot, my husband is away. I'm his second wife, he doesn't care about me at all." She laughed and then made a sad face.

I replied, "Which one is your house?" and laughed.

Naiseku smiled and pointed with her tongue, "She lives over there!"

"Not tonight, the moon is too bright," I said. "But tomorrow it will be darker." I hoped she realized I was kidding. I didn't relish the thought of getting killed as easily as that white baby.

Although I never saw a live birth in Samburu, women explained their custom. A woman gave birth in her house, squatting while holding the center pole, assisted by experienced women or a midwife such as Lolongoi. When the baby was born, the father, who was waiting outside, would pass his sandal to the women on the inside. The midwife cut the umbilical cord on the shoe, which connoted paternity and good luck. The husband (or a living male kinsman) killed a goat in front of the mother's house, and for four days she was given blood to drink. Babies did not have a formal naming ceremony but were given names that ideally had not been used by deceased relatives, as such reminders of lost loved ones make people sad. One needed to be creative in coming up with new names. Dominic was named after an Italian priest, and I know of a girl named "Standard One" (first grade in elementary school). There are at least three children now named Elliot in northern Kenya, all girls.

As in much of the Global South, nearly half the population dies before reaching old age, mainly due to infectious diseases including pneumonia, tuberculosis, and malaria. One or two out of five children die before their fifth birthday, mainly from malaria, measles, or diarrhea and dehydration from gastroenteritis. At a person's death, his lineage members, even *l-murran* warriors, would shave his hair. Samburu and Rendille do not bury their dead but leave them in "the bush" where wild animals remove them. If the body has not been eaten by scavengers during the night, a goat is sacrificed to attract them to finish the job. This practice reflects the belief that a bad spirit will reside in the area if the body is not removed. Many nomadic societies leave their dead in the open.

The Rendille (and, by extension, camel-keeping Ariaal) hold special rituals to bless their camels. *Soriu* is held four times a year during special *soriu* months, when all the camels are gathered and returned to the village, even from great distances. During *soriu*, the settlement's men and boys move as a group from house to house, each household sacrificing a goat or sheep (formerly they sacrificed a camel, I was told). Before killing the animal, one man pours milk on its back and on the roof of the house. All of the assembled men dip their camel sticks into the calabash of milk and rub the ends of the stick across the animal's back, saying "*soriu!*" Then a son or another male holds the legs of the goat while the head of the household slits its throat, catching the blood in a waiting calabash. Each male in the family then dips the end of his camel stick into the blood, which is then used to mark the backs of the animals in their enclosures.

Soriu is a sacrifice, or gift, to the Creator, asking for rain so that the grass will grow to feed the animals that ultimately feed the people in the community. On the day following the sacrifice (and the feasting that accompanies it), the camels are led through an *ulukh* fire gateway outside the manyatta, as in the ritual I had observed following the eclipse.

When the *soriu* month came, Dominic asked me what animal I was going to sacrifice. "You don't even own a goat, so what will you kill?" he teased me.

"I can sacrifice a dog, how about that?" I replied.

Dominic laughed and slapped my back, "A dog! No, Elliot, you will not sacrifice a dog because I will give you a goat to sacrifice."

"Fine, then I will have a goat to sacrifice."

When the *soriu* day came, I walked with the men to each house for the sacrifice. When we came to my house, Dominic brought me the goat, as promised. The men dipped their sticks into the calabash of milk, rubbing these across the back of the goat as they said "*soriu!*" It was now time for me to kill the goat. I had never killed anything before—I did not come from a family of hunters; my father was an accountant in Philadelphia, for Pete's sake. I did not want to screw this up, particularly as I didn't want to torment the animal more than necessary. I wasn't even sure I would be able to do this. I had my buck knife in my hand, and I made sure the men were holding the goat firmly. But before I cut its throat, I leaned over, pulled the goat's ear toward me, and said. "*Ache-oling, ey laiseri-na!*" (Thank you very much, and good-bye now!) Dominic cracked up, as did his brother Usana. "Thank you very much, and good-bye," they repeated. Their laughter relieved my nervousness, and I was able to cut the goat's throat quickly and evenly. We moved on to the next houses, and a few times the elder of the house, with a broad smile, repeated to the goat, "Thank you, and good-bye!"

I tell this story to share the joy and camaraderie people feel at ritual feasts, not dissimilar to our Thanksgiving dinners in America. Perhaps the next anthropologist who does research in northern Kenya will find people thanking their animals before killing them.

In the evening of *soriu*, all the men entered the *na'abu* ritual center. Choma led the prayer, and the elders responded to each plea with "*Nkai*" (God), holding their hands outstretched and snapping their fingers to their palms in rhythm.

> God guard and protect your livestock,
> Nkai!
> God guard and protect the young and the old,
> Nkai!
> God guard and protect boys, and God protect girls,
> Nkai!
> God guard and protect cattle, and God protect camels,
> Nkai!
> God guard and protect those at night and during the day,
> Nkai!
> God guard and protect those in the darkness and in the light of the moon,
> Nkai!
> May God give you fresh milk and sour milk and blood,
> Nkai!
> God accept what is said and what we are saying,
> Nkai!
> God accept what we think and what we are thinking,
> Nkai!
> To all this, God says yes!
> Nkai yai [My God].

Lonyoki's Request

I had been with Lonyoki in Lukumai about four months now. One evening shortly after *soriu*, Lonyoki called for me. I walked over to Dominic's house where he and Dominic were sitting on wooden stools outside the house.

"*Sopa, payieni,*" I formally greeted them, as it was unusual for Lonyoki to summon me. Lonyoki smiled at me and set out a leather cow-skin mat, inviting me to sit down next to them. "*To-wana ene*" (sit here), he said, and I sat down, my back against the round wall of the house. "*Serian–ake? (Ey serian),*" we exchanged greetings.

"Elliot, long ago, when I first met Dominic, I told him a white man would come and take him and me to Lukumai, and we would live together at Lukumai. Is that not true, Dominic?" "*Ey, kedede*" (It is true), said Dominic. "So now we have come to know each other, and to love each other, and to live with each other, is that not true?" "*Ey, kedede,*" I replied.

"So now I have a large favor [*paren kitok*] to ask." *Paren* means more than favor; it means a significant request, such as a gift or loan of an animal. It usually involves a long conversation.

Lonyoki went on, "In the time we have known each other, have I ever asked you for anything?"

"*Metii, apaiya*" (Nothing, father). He indeed had never asked me for anything, not even food or clothes, although I once brought him a large green *shuka* cloth to wear.

"What can I do for you, father?" I asked. I was prepared to do anything he requested, although I had no idea what it would be. I was surprised when he told me.

"It is something I know God wants me to do. I want you to go and bring back my wife and son to this place so we can live together in our area. You know I have a son; his name is Lembalen. He lives with his mother in Barsaloi [a small town in Samburu District]. I left Lembalen and his mother a long time ago, when Lembalen was a baby. Now I have a good home to bring them to, here in Lukumai, and I want them with me."

"Fine," I replied, "we can go whenever you are ready."

"I cannot go with you. The Lorukushu clan elders in Barsaloi would not let me leave if I went there with you. They want me to live there as their laibon, because I am from Lorukushu clan. But I prefer to live with the Lukumai."

"OK," I responded. "I would be happy to do this. I need to drive to Nairobi for supplies, but I can pick her up when I return through Maralal [the district capital of Samburu]. But how do I find her? How will she know I am coming at your request?"

Lonyoki replied, "I will send Dapash [one of the Lukumai elders] to go with you. I will also send my wife and son a message in your radio [tape recorder]. You can play it for them and they will know it is me speaking to them."

That sounded like a good idea, and I began to make preparations to go. I needed to replenish my food stock—spaghetti and noodles, cans of tomato paste and cooking oil, Knorr packaged soup and perishables I would consume quickly, including bread and fruit. That evening, as I was preparing for the journey, Dominic came and joined me.

"Tell me, Dominic," I asked. "Why did Lonyoki leave his wife in Barsaloi so long ago?"

"In truth, he was not getting along with his wife; he thought she was not faithful to him. But I don't think she was unfaithful. You know, Lonyoki was driven away from his own father, Longojine, because he also thought his wife was unfaithful and that Lonyoki was not his son. These laibons can get very jealous. So Lonyoki left and he came to this side [Marsabit District] to practice his nkidong. But the elders in Barsaloi wanted Lonyoki to stay there. They are angry with us for taking Lonyoki away from them."

"How did the laibon come to live here with you in Lukumai village?"

As usual, Dominic provided a clear and straightforward answer.

"The elders sent me to bring Lonyoki to Lukumai. We had been having some problems, and we needed a laibon to help us."

"What kind of problems?" I asked.

"Well, first Lemeti's cattle got sick with anthrax [lokochum]. Then Lembere's wife went madai [crazy], you know how she stays in her house all day talking to herself. These and some other things. After some time, we came to learn that we were cursed by another laibon."

I was shocked. I had no idea these things were going on.

"Which laibon?" I asked.

"We think it is Lobata, the laibon from Soritari clan," Dominic replied. "He is a very bad man, and the Soritari have been mad at Lukumai for a long time. We're richer than they are, much richer. So our elders came together to meet—Usana, Lepere, Lemeti, myself. We decided to bring Lonyoki back here to divine and protect us with his ntasim.

"We have not had problems since Lonyoki moved in with us. Lonyoki is very clever; he knows what is happening around us and within our manyatta. He can see things with his divination, such as when our warriors and cattle might face attacks from Turkana or Boran."

The morning of our departure I checked my engine and tires, and saw that I had four jerry cans of petrol on the roof rack of my Land Rover. Several elders, including Dominic and Lonyoki, were standing by the car as I finished packing, and Lonyoki asked me for my tape recorder to make a message for his wife. He held the microphone, and after some initial hesitation, said "Sopa, Yeyo [Hello mother/wife], I greet you from a long time and far away. . . ." He spoke for only three minutes or so, and then stopped. "Sawa," he said in KiSwahili ("all right, enough"). He handed me a large leopard cowry shell filled with ntasim to take. "Carry this in the car, it will keep you safe."

Several of the elders assembled around the car, as they did whenever we went on a journey. "May God grant you a safe voyage [nkai!], may God see no harm your way [nkai!]," they prayed.

As I got into the car, Naiseku ran out and said, "Elliot, n-go" (Here, take this), and handed me a wooden container with roasted meat and a gourd of milk. I appreciated the gesture and smiled, squeezing her hand through the window, and I slowly drove off. She followed the car with her eyes, with an expression that suggested she was wondering where this journey would take us—not just me, but all of Lukumai *nkang*. Having the laibon live in the village was important, and now he was bringing his wife and child, suggesting that he would stay here for some time.

We set out and made our way toward the small road to Ker'ngera, where we would pick up the main road to Baragoi in Samburu District. Ker'ngera was a dismal hot place, with only a few shops and a primary school; I rarely came this way, as I preferred to do my minimal shopping in Lenguas in the forested foothills of the Ndotos. It was about four hours to Baragoi, and another three to Maralal, then on to Nairobi.

Dapash, the elder riding with me, was a quiet man who responded thoughtfully to my many questions. He knew a great deal about Samburu and Rendille history and social organization, and enjoyed explaining social rules and structure to me, telling me about the Black Cattle clans living around Maralal, including the Masala clan, which was the origin of Lonyoki's wife.

"Won't we be driving close to Turkana?" I asked. I knew that Baragoi town lay on the border between Samburu and Turkana districts, and I was curious about how the two societies got along. "Aren't the Turkana enemies to Samburu?"

"Yes, we are enemies, but Turkana people living around Baragoi aren't bad. It is the Ngoroko Turkana who live north near Sudan who come to raid us. We have many enemies—Turkana, Boran, *shifta*."

Shifta is a general term meaning "bandit," but it also referred to Somalis who tried to separate from Kenya in the 1960s and join Somalia. These days, *shifta* were mainly armed robbers who attacked herding camps or manyattas to steal cattle. They also occasionally stopped cars on the road and robbed them, too. In addition to the *shifta*, Turkana and Boran who were also cattle herders raided Samburu and Rendille for livestock. Boran lived in the northern part of Marsabit District and were related to the Oromo people of southern Ethiopia. Many Boran had moved to Kenya in the early twentieth century to escape conscription into the Ethiopian army by Emperor Menelik; some had moved farther south to Isiolo and converted to Islam. The Turkana lived to the northwest of Samburu on the western side of Lake Turkana, a hard desert terrain bordering Sudan and Uganda. Turkana were highly mobile and difficult for the government to control. They were feared by Samburu as ruthless fighters.

I thought it must be good to have a laibon living in the manyatta who could act as an early warning radar.

We drove in silence for some time, and by two o'clock in the afternoon we made it into Baragoi town. It was larger than Ker'ngera, with several rows of buildings in the middle of a broad plain called l-Barta, which was used for cattle grazing by both Samburu and Turkana. The Baragoi road marks the boundary between Samburu District and Turkana District, and there were a large number of Turkana tribesmen walking in the town, side by side with Samburu warriors. Normally, these two groups were bitter enemies, but while they were in town on business, the police post in Baragoi guaranteed a truce. The two groups were "color coded"; the Samburu warriors wore red cloths and had braided red-dyed hair and the women had red ochre on their neck beads, while the Turkana men wore their hair in a distinctive beehive, caked in clay and painted blue. Both Turkana men and women wore flat metal earrings or metal rings in their ears. Women had six or eight earrings in each ear, and older Turkana men also had "lip plugs" made of wood or metal protruding from under their bottom lip. The Samburu, in contrast, had long, hanging earlobes, stretched with metal pendants or, in the case of the warriors, filled with large round rings of elephant ivory. Both groups could recognize the other's silhouette at night and know whether an approaching person was friend or foe.

When I got out of the car, I made a quick inspection of the vehicle. To my horror, the main metal nut holding the left front wheel to the axle was missing; it must have loosened and fallen off somewhere. I was lucky that the whole front tire hadn't spun off, a disaster I might not have walked away from. Where was I going to find a part like that in a town like this? I saw a possible solution in the form of a mud brick building that looked vaguely like a garage and had a few old Land Rovers in the back.

I walked toward the building and saw a middle-aged Somali man sitting outside. He was wearing a green plaid cloth tied around his waist Somali style, a clean white shirt, and a small embroidered white cap.

"*Jambo, habari gain?*" (Greetings, what's the news?), I said. "Are you the owner of these cars?"

He replied "*Jambo,*" and then in English, "Yes, I am Mahmoud and you are welcome. Do you have a problem with your car?"

"Yes, I lost the front axle nut. Do you have one I can buy?"

"Yes, I can get you one off the older car."

"Great," I say. "How much is it?"

"It will cost you two hundred shillings" ($20 in those days).

"You're joking! That part costs ten shillings [$1] in Nairobi!" I said. And then the inevitable response, "Yes, but this is not Nairobi!" I knew enough about tradesmen in East Africa (whether Somalis, Ismailis, Sikhs, or Swahili) to say, "Look, why don't we have some *chai* and talk this over?"

"Excellent idea," replied Mahmoud.

We went to a *hoteli*, a single-room building with a dirt floor, a few tables, and a cooking hearth outside in the rear. I knew these restaurants were filthy, but I have to admit I loved them. I knew what was on the menu, since there were only two items on any menu from Maralal to Ethiopia at that time: *chai*, the spicy sugary tea, and *karanga*, a goat meat stew with potatoes served with flat bread that I hoped would be soft and fresh. I sat down with Mahmoud and Dapash and we all ate our stew. We knocked back a few Fantas (warm, of course) and then a round of tea (with steamed milk and thick with sugar). After the good fellowship of eating a meal together, Mahmoud gave in and let me have the metal nut for fifty shillings ($5), with a used cotter pin thrown in, since the loss of the pin was the reason the nut had come off in the first place. Not a bargain price, but it ensured that I would get to Nairobi and return to find Lonyoki's son and make it back to Lukumai.

My visit to Nairobi was short. I had been gone three months and needed only to collect mail, buy some spare parts for the Rover, and buy enough food supplies to last another three months in Lukumai. Usually I would stay two weeks or more, do several loads of laundry, see a film or two, type up notes on my portable Olivetti typewriter. But I only planned to stay one night this time. I went to the institute at the university to pick up my mail. There was a letter from my mother and father reporting nothing sensational, but it was pleasant to hear from them. I was always worried that a family member or someone close to me might die while I was away, and in those days before the Internet, news traveled very slowly.

As I was reading the letter, a tall young man with blond hair approached me in the front lobby of the old institute building. "Are you Fratkin?" he asked in a distinct German accent. He told me his name was Guenther and that he was a graduate student in anthropology intent on studying the Rendille in northern Kenya. Small world. I told him I was preparing to return the next day, and if he wanted, I could take him as far as my village of Lukumai, from which he could make his way to Naiborr, a center for the camel-herding Rendille. I asked him if he would mind a detour through Maralal and Barsaloi where I needed to pick up a Samburu family that I was bringing back to Lukumai.

"I don't mind at all," he replied, "this should be interesting."

And interesting it was. The next day, the three of us—Dapash, Guenther, and I—got into the Land Rover and drove northwest into Samburu District. Leaving the broad plains of Laikipia District, we ascended up the mountainous Leroki Plateau where the town of Maralal was located. The air got cooler and it felt good to get out of the hot Rift Valley. As we climbed into the highlands, the vegetation changed to forests of hemlock and juniper, fragrant with their sweet and pungent smell. We saw Grevy's zebra, whose stripes are narrower than those of common zebras, and caught our breath when a rare bongo, a highland antelope, bolted across the road. But we did not see any lions or leopards; they usually wait until night to hunt.

From Maralal we turned east on a narrow and twisting road through the forest toward the town of Barsaloi. We reached the town around five o'clock; it was a sleepy place of only a few shops with a large shade tree in the center. It would be dark in an hour, and we decided to go directly to Lembalen's mother's village, if we could find it. We stopped briefly, and Dapash asked an old man to show us where the manyatta was. In a relatively short time we made our way to a small circle of houses made of timber and mud in the more permanent highland Samburu style; there were a dozen or so cattle in their enclosures and more were being brought in by a herd boy.

Several elders emerged from the manyatta and approached us. We greeted each other formally and I offered them some tobacco, my pro forma gesture any time I visited a new community. The elders told Dapash that the mother and boy had gone to town to shop and would be coming home shortly. We waited about twenty minutes until we saw a tall woman and a boy about eight years old walking up the path toward us. The woman was about thirty years old with a pretty face. She was clearly frightened when she saw us and shrieked when her son happily ran toward us, telling him to stay away from us. Her son, Lembalen, had his mother's face but without her fearful look. He had a huge and beautiful smile. Paying no heed to his mother, he ran to the truck and hugged me around the waist. He then climbed into the Land Rover, made himself comfortable, and to all appearances looked like he was ready to go. His mother was crying now, her hands on her face, saying "Wo, wo, my son, no!" hysterical with fear. I don't think she had ever seen a white person before, or a vehicle for that matter. I doubt the boy had seen these things either, but he wasn't at all afraid. The elders told the woman the reason for our visit and she stopped crying, although she still looked worried and skeptical. Finally, I took out the tape cassette and played her Lonyoki's words. I couldn't follow all that he said, but I could recognize "Elliot . . . carry you and Lembalen . . . Lukumai."

The woman calmed down, and Dapash and I followed her inside the manyatta to her house. She sat down in the women's area near the hearth and began to heat some water in a pot. I gave her some small packets of tea and sugar, and for the first time she smiled, looking away shyly as she said "acheoling" (thank you). Lembalen was beaming, holding my hand, playing with objects in my knapsack, including the tape recorder. Dapash told me that the boy said he had dreamt we were coming and had told his mother to pack her things, as his father had sent a *mzungu* (white person) to fetch them. I asked "Mother of Lembalen" (as one called her) if this was true, and she smiled and said, "*Ey*, it is true. He is a laibon, his father's son." But then she looked serious and said to Dapash, "*Apaiya*, I do not want to leave this place. This is my home; we have lived here all our lives. I don't know this place we are going to; it is far and full of strangers. I don't want this."

Dapash, gentle as ever, sighed but did not answer her. We all knew that these were Lonyoki's wishes, and the male head of household has all the power over his wife and children. I had a huge store of questions to ask Mo' Lembalen, the nickname for her I later used. I wanted to know about her life here and her thoughts about joining her husband, but I held off, mainly out of respect for her silence and apparent heaviness of heart.

The next morning, we awoke and prepared for our trip. As before, Lembalen was smiling and happy, busily packing and helping me load up the car. Mo' Lembalen had only a few possessions to take: a leather skin bag and a few containers. I assumed that Dapash told her not to bring everything, that Lonyoki would provide all the things she needed for her new home, and to come directly.

We got into the car, Lembalen sitting in front between me and Guenther, Dapash and Mother of Lembalen sitting in the back of the Rover. As we were beginning to move, several women approached and one of them gave Mo' Lembalen containers of fat and a gourd of milk for the journey. Mo' Lembalen was crying and held the woman's arm tightly. As soon as we drove off, she was sick. She asked me to stop and quickly got out of the car, crouching to throw up. After a few minutes, she climbed back into the car, weak and weary, and we drove on. This must have been her first time in a vehicle, I thought.

Things got bad for us in Barsaloi. As we were driving slowly through the town, an angry Samburu elder approached us and thrust his hand through the car window, trying to grab Lembalen by the arm. I pulled away, but four elders jumped in front of the car, hitting it with their cattle sticks and crying angrily, "*Wo, wo*, stop!" One man looked apoplectic, his veins pulsating on his temple and neck.

"*Taicho!* Stop! You are not taking our laibon away from us." One man tried to open the door on Mo' Lembalen's side, causing her to tremble and cry again. Lembalen looked up at me and pleaded, "Let's go, let's go." Although he was only a boy, the elders felt they had already lost one laibon when Lonyoki had left and now they would be deprived of his son.

I was getting angry now, and in my limited but righteous Samburu, yelled, "*Mara, Mara* [No, no!], this boy is coming with me. I am here for his father,

Lonyoki, who has sent for his wife and child. It's not any of your business, so bugger off!" (or something to that effect). Dapash, in the back, tapped me on the shoulder, and said, "Just drive, let's go." I slowly moved forward and the men cleared out of the way, although Guenther warned us that another elder had picked up a rock and was getting ready to throw it at the Land Rover.

We drove north, stopping briefly for *chai* and *karanga* stew, and then turned east onto the road leading to Ker'ngera and Lukumai. We arrived at the manyatta around three o'clock in the afternoon to a tumultuous greeting—women, children, and elders clamored around the car to meet Lembalen and his mother. Lonyoki and Dominic were standing there smiling and greeting Guenther, Dapash, and me, but I could see that Lonyoki was anxious to see his son and wife. I was surprised when he embraced Mo' Lembalen, as public displays of affection between men and women were almost never seen. Then Lonyoki turned to his eight-year-old son. He did not embrace him but touched his head in the Maasai manner, while Lembalen bowed his head deferentially. We all went into Naiseku's house for tea.

I Am Adopted by the Laibon

The day after I brought Lembalen and his mother to Lukumai, the women helped Mo' Lembalen construct her house, bringing long round poles of the *sigteti* tree to serve as the house frame and donating woven sisal fiber mats to use for the roof. Leather skins from cows and goats lined the floor and inside wall, and the tall narrow door had two large hides on either side as an entrance. When the house construction was finished, the women went to their homes, put on their ritual *sara* aprons (with bells and strings of cowry shells), and returned carrying wooden containers filled with milk.

Singing loudly, they prayed for Mother of Lembalen to have many children in this house, both boys and girls, and to always have animals with milk in the *bo'o* (fenced livestock enclosure).

Mother of Lembalen was genuinely moved, smiling and holding back her tears. The long journey with strangers, packing up her belongings and moving with her son from the highland home she had known her whole life to Rendille country in the lowland desert, was exhausting both physically and emotionally. When the singing and ceremony were over, she thanked everyone personally and went into her new house to arrange her fireplace, bags, and containers and to get ready for her new life.

The following morning, the laibon called me to his new house. He had a warm smile on his face as he finished tying together a string of large round blue beads with a beautiful dik-dik horn in the middle. (A dik-dik is a tiny antelope with small horns about two inches long.) The blue beads were worn only by members of the Lonyoki family, and the dik-dik horn containing *ntasim* was worn only by the immediate family members. Lonyoki gave me the beads to wear around my neck and said that he was adopting me as his son. I was stunned; this was not something I was expecting. Rather than expressing his feelings verbally, he concentrated on telling me how to use the *ntasim*.

"You must learn to use the [dik-dik] horn, not just wear it," he said. "You must let it 'see' for you. If a bad thing such as an enemy approaches, you should hold up the horn toward the attacker, or blow on it in the direction of the enemy. If there is danger on the ground, such as a snake, you should take off the necklace and pass it around your legs like this (twice around the legs in a clockwise direction). If you want something from a man, point the horn toward his back without him seeing it, and then ask him for what you want. With this horn, no sorcerer can harm you, not even the WaKamba, who are the strongest of sorcerers."

"What is inside the horn?" I asked.

"Very powerful *ntasim*," he replied. "It is made from two things, a ball of fur found inside the lion's stomach. It can be divided eight times and ground up. It also contains ground bone from the head of a cobra. In addition, I use the roots of two bushes from my healing *ntasim*. This *ntasim* is not to be used frivolously, but you do not need to hide it. Everyone will recognize the horn and beads, and that you are a Lonyoki."

In the evening, I was called back to Lonyoki's house. Guenther, who was planning to leave for Naiborr the next day, came with me. Lonyoki was sitting on his low round elder's stool to the left of the entrance door; eight elders, including Dominic's brothers, were sitting in a broad circle around him, and Lembalen sat at his right. All of the men had been drinking, and Lonyoki was pretty intoxicated. He had a large gourd container of honey wine (*naisho*) beside him and his eyes were glassy. When he spoke, he slurred his speech. He invited me to sit down on his left, pulled me close affectionately, and passed me the large gourd of *naisho* wine, which I drank reluctantly. (I usually tried to avoid liquids from a common container.)

He turned to the elders and said, "After five years there is only one man who could bring me my son. I knew this man would come here to Lukumai with me, and I knew he would bring me my wife and son. I dreamt it. *Kara Lonyoki!* [I am Lonyoki! Or, am I *not* Lonyoki?] Many years ago I saw this would happen. And I see peace for this manyatta, there will be no harm to this manyatta."

Lonyoki then leaned over to me, held the dik-dik horn from my neck beads close to his mouth, and spit air on it to bless it. He motioned me to take his necklace and do the same. I took the large crocodile tooth filled with *ntasim* hanging on Lonyoki's beads and blew on it, as he had done.

"Good," said Lonyoki. To the assembled men sitting outside the house, he said, "From now on Elliot is my son, as much as Lembalen whom he brought here all the way from Barsaloi. And everybody in this place, and every Samburu will know, that Elliot is my son."

He continued. "I don't want to hear anyone say, 'There goes the white Lonyoki.' There are no white Lonyokis, there are no black Lonyokis, there are only Lonyokis! And you are from Lukumai clan. And I am from Lorukushu clan. When Elliot came here, none of you knew him or where he is from. And now I know him and you know him. You cannot refuse him anything now. Because it is me who brought him here. I called him here because I know he is my son. He is the same as Lembalen. It is me who brought both of them. Because Elliot went to Barsaloi and brought me Lembalen, and I have not paid him anything! 'There is no child that eats its placenta' [i.e., they are all born to us and we care for them]. And he took me to Ker'ngera to get *naisho*, and he doesn't drink himself. Then he is my son. *Naa mara kedede?* [Is this not true?]"

"Ey," responded the elders, "*kedede*" (it is true).

"And I don't want him to forget me, or me to forget him. Here is my *nkidong*; my *nkidong* blesses everywhere, children and cattle, now and wherever they are."

I had sat there by Lonyoki's side, a little embarrassed to be the center of all this attention. I tried to say something, preparing a short speech in Samburu in my head about the honor of being included in the Lonyoki family, but the laibon told me to stay still and be quiet. I was not expected, or permitted, to say anything. I was to sit quietly by his side, like Lembalen.

Lonyoki then took his *nkidong* gourd, spat air into its mouth, and, turning it upside down, began to throw the stones and predict the future.

"There are some people who don't know there is a white man in the Lonyoki family." Looking at the stones, he said, "*Kelo l-tunguani ale na serian*" (This man will leave here in peace).

Lonyoki proceeded to throw his stones and made many predictions that evening: that Elliot would live here in peace, that there would be a raid by Turkana on Rendille ("Five of our warriors will join them, but they will all return safely"), on problems in various manyattas ("There is a girl in the Lengewa family whom I can see is in a bad condition"), and on the fate of Guenther set to leave for Rendille ("I can see that he will be in this country for a long time"). Finally Lonyoki pronounced, "There will be nothing wrong within our *nkang* or our own area. *Ke supati* [Everything is good]."

Lonyoki was finished divining. The assembled elders ended the evening with their blessings, a syncopated chorus of "*Nkai, Nkai*" (God), in which I joined.

The adoption ceremony was over. I returned to my house and talked with Guenther about the events of the past few days. It had been good to have conversations with another anthropologist, something I had missed since being here. Guenther said, "You know, being adopted by this man may cause you to lose your objectivity in your research and writing."

This was, and remains, a concern in anthropology. In those days before "postmodern, self-reflexive" anthropology, ethnographers were supposed to keep themselves outside of the story they were telling. But in truth, it was impossible to remain totally objective when doing fieldwork. You had real relationships with real people, and, as in a family, your own life and the lives of your subjects were intertwined.

I replied to Guenther, "I know, but very few *wazungu* have even been able to interview a laibon, let alone live with him and study his practices. Being adopted by Lonyoki is a great honor. Wouldn't you do the same if you were in my position?"

"Yes," he replied, "I would probably do the same."

That night I thought long and hard about my relationship to Lonyoki, to Lukumai, and to my own family back in the States. I had been raised in a middle-class home in Philadelphia with a twin brother, two older sisters, and a mother who was devoted to her family. My father, although present in my upbringing, was a distant and noncommunicative person. Like many others who had experienced the Great Depression, he wanted economic security and worked hard to achieve it, and saw his main role as providing for our economic rather than emotional needs. He was also a timid man who would never put himself or his family in physical danger. His life was complicated by his frequent bouts of depression interspersed with periods of true craziness—he was later diagnosed as having bipolar disorder. It was only later that I recognized his silence as part of his illness and not, as I thought then, a rejection of me.

As a teenager, I wanted to get away from my home and community. I rejected my family and schoolmates, most of whose goals included success and wealth through business, law, or medicine. I sought an alternative culture; in high school and college I was attracted to radical politics, protesting the Vietnam War and racism in the United States. I was also drawn to the counterculture of my generation—"sex, drugs, and rock and roll!" Still, as a young person I felt a dark hole and emptiness. I needed the attention and love from a father who was not there. This space couldn't be filled by my mother, sisters, or twin brother, and it couldn't be filled by girlfriends, even though I had developed an intense relationship in high school that carried over into college. What was missing for me was a strong father figure to be interested in me and to guide me. I was drawn to people I could look up to as mentors—the scientist who was the father of my high school girlfriend or the Mexican artist and his family with whom I lived in London while in graduate school. And now, here I was living with camel nomads in Kenya, in a place so alien to anywhere I had ever been, but a place that was comfortable and accepting. Now I was adopted by a man I respected and was fascinated by, the laibon Lonyoki. Was this the father figure I was looking for?

So in a way, Guenther was right: I was losing my objectivity. But in some ways, I had already lost it. And what does objectivity mean in the first place? The ability to stand outside and look in? I was tired of standing on the outside; I wanted to be on the inside. And I did that by joining Lonyoki's family and living with the people in Lukumai. It didn't hurt my understanding of Samburu culture; quite the opposite, it aided my understanding. It allowed me to accept them, and, I truly believe, it allowed them to accept me.

From that day on, I was known as a Lonyoki, son of the laibon. Sometimes Samburu who did not know me would say, on seeing my dik-dik horn, "Are you a laibon? Oh, you must be the white Lonyoki [*Lonyoki neibor*]!" (as they had not heard Lonyoki's words at my adoption). I didn't mind being called the white Lonyoki; a leopard cannot be ashamed of his spots. But my status was now fixed: I had a Samburu identity and a family to which I belonged.

A few weeks after Lembalen arrived, Lonyoki took him to Ker'ngera and enrolled him in the primary school in the first grade ("Standard One"). The headmaster, a Samburu from Maralal, said he would look after the boy. "I never had a laibon to teach," he chuckled, "already I can see he is a very smart boy." Lembalen beamed and was clearly excited. Lonyoki told him to study hard, that he wanted him to know both the traditional and modern ways. Lembalen looked at us longingly as we drove off. His life had obviously changed dramatically in the past few weeks.

Dancing with Warriors

I delivered Guenther to Naiborr, where he began his own long-term research among Rendille people. When I returned to Lukumai, I found that the women had built a house for me, which they blessed just as they had blessed Mo' Lembalen's house. I slept on a leather mat on the ground like everyone else, but I had a gas stove rather than a wood fireplace. Although people visited throughout the day, I needed privacy. I usually could achieve this only after eight o'clock in the evening, when I could write up my notes and read a novel. Still, whenever I lit up the gas stove to make tea or dinner, several faces would appear in my doorway. "*Sopa*, Elliot," an elder would say, quoting a Samburu proverb, "'Only the hyena eats alone,' you know!" Invariably I would offer tea and, if I had any, crackers or cookies. Still, I preferred to socialize outside my house rather than inside it. Privacy was a precious and rare commodity I was reluctant to give up.

I continued with my field research, meeting mainly with Lonyoki to discuss his *nkidong* divination and *ntasim*, but also interviewing other specialists about medicines and traditional healing practices. I developed relationships with two other healers, Lolongoi and Lolcheni. Lolongoi was the manyatta's midwife, who delivered babies and made herbal treatments for problems of the "women's stomach." She was also the person who performed the female genital cutting when young women were married. I asked her how she had become a midwife, expecting some lofty answer like, "I love children and the miracle of giving life." Instead, she told me, "I am not afraid to do these things; I know no fear. When a woman was giving birth, screaming so loudly that all the other women trembled in fear, I would go over and help deliver the baby, sometimes having to cut the mother with a razor to make it happen. I have never known fear. Even as a young woman, I was not afraid of men; I would carry my *panga* blade in the forest and no man would dare bother me!" Lolongoi did not live with a husband, although she had been married and had several children. In her words, she "would not put up with men's foolishness."

The other healer was an herbalist named Lolcheni. He was a member of the Dorrobo tribe, hunter-gatherers who lived in the forests and had symbiotic relations with the Maasai, Nandi, and Samburu herders they lived near. Lolcheni lived in the forest above Lenguas town and was known for the "tree medicines" with which he treated a variety of physical ailments. He made herbal teas and soups from the roots, bark, and leaves of trees and bushes and treated complaints ranging from backaches to "bad stomachs." With Lolcheni's help, I was able to collect and identify (at the East African Herbarium in Nairobi) 135 different species of plants used for medicines. I spent so much time in the forest with Lolcheni that Dominic started calling me "Lengirrira," which is a Dorrobo family name: "Where is your beehive, Lengirrira?" Dominic would tease me, "Why are you hiding your honey wine from us?"

Unlike Lonyoki's ritual medicines, which showed no immediate physical effects, many of Lolcheni's cures were strong emetics and purgatives that made you vomit and defecate almost immediately. Lolcheni explained that many ailments were due to poorly circulating blood that had turned "black and hard." Bad circulation was caused by "eating the wrong foods," such as animal fat and milk consumed at the same time, or by diseases such as malaria or tuberculosis. He had other medicines to dry wounds, treat burns, or soothe itches; he also made liquid broths to reduce fevers or relieve headaches. Samburu looked down on Lolcheni as a Dorrobo and as someone who dealt with human sicknesses. But I enjoyed his company, his knowledge, and his good humor.

I did not spend all my time hanging out with married adults. I also made friends with Lukumai's warriors, particularly two young men my age who became my loyal companions. Kidenye and Lalem were as opposite as night and day. Kidenye was tall, jocular, and outgoing. He had long braided hair with a leather visor attached to the front like a baseball cap and spoke with a slight stutter, which never seemed to bother him or anyone else. He constantly made lewd jokes; once he showed me the shortened tail of one of his cows, which had been bitten by a hyena, and then proceeded to stroke it as if he were masturbating, laughing conspiratorially.

Lalem, by contrast, was a quiet man. Although short and slender, he was one of the fiercest warriors in Lukumai and wore several brass bracelets on his wrist, signifying the number of enemies he had killed in battle. But with a chipped front tooth, Lalem had a loopy grin, and he enjoyed both my jokes and Kidenye's. Sometimes I would go with them when they moved their cattle to watering areas or to pastures in the hills above Lukumai. Kidenye would try to teach me the names of all the cattle colors, an inexhaustible list, it seemed to me—gray, gray-blue, blue, spotted blue, brown, spotted brown, gold, and so on—and then combine the color names with body features like low-hanging horns, highly curved horns, tilted hump, side-curved tail. I never could remember them all.

Warriors spent most of the dry season herding livestock in camps far from the main settlement, taking cattle into the mountain valleys and camels far into the desert lowlands to the east. Here they slept in the open, living exclusively on the milk and blood they tapped from living animals. Sometimes they made soup from wild plants, but they would not hunt or eat wild meat unless they were desperate, and even then they ate only those animals that resembled their domestic livestock—a gazelle instead of a goat, a giraffe instead of a camel. When the rains came and there was enough grass in the lowlands, they would return with the animals to their home manyattas, sleeping at their mothers' houses and generally lying low during the daytime. At night they wanted to be with their girlfriends, teenage girls living in Lukumai or neighboring manyattas. Some were cousins whom they were prohibited from marrying but with whom they could still have sex. This was an accepted practice between warriors and teenage girls, although no girl was permitted to get pregnant before marriage. (Birth control was strictly coitus interruptus; when that failed, midwives would perform abortions.) By the time the girls were sixteen or seventeen years old (and sometimes earlier), they would be married, always to older men and usually strangers, in marriages arranged by their fathers and uncles.

But for the brief period between puberty and marriage, girls were free to choose lovers and hang out with their friends and warriors. Lukumai's warriors and their girlfriends held dances outside the manyatta, singing late into the night when the adults and young children were sleeping. I loved these dances; the melodies were slow and mournful, the dances highly charged and sensual.

One dance was called the *mparingoi*. The warriors would line up, four across and three rows deep, shoulders touching and singing as they jumped in unison toward a receptive half-circle of girls singing their responses. The two groups alternated singing: an individual warrior would sing solo verse joined by the other *l-murran* singing a chorus, and the lead female singer would respond in a high soprano with the other girls singing their chorus. It was like an English round, but sung in a minor key slowly and forcefully. Kidenye would take me by the hand and pull me next to him into the dances. In rhythm, we would thrust our heads forward, snapping our long braided hair (or in my case, a *pilipili* ornament attached with a slim chain) as we moved toward the semicircle of girls in front of us. With each thrust forward, the warriors would twirl their long spears, letting go and then grabbing them midair. Invariably the songs were about acts of daring, of stealing cattle and fighting enemies, or they were declarations of love for their girlfriends. The girls urged the warriors to be heroic, and warriors sang of their disgust for the elders who tried to hold them back.

> Oo, wo-oh lei-yo, wo pantor-ai-lai, mama len yeyo
> Oh mother of mine, listen to me
> My spear is dangerous, lucky girl,
> We meet our enemies in the night
> I don't know the owner of the cattle
> Some sing three words and some sing two
> But we sing of the roots of the tree.
>
> The elders cannot venture far without the snuff boxes
> They can only finish off flies with their flywhisks
> They ruin their blankets by dragging them in the ground

And they ruin their blankets by playing *ndotoi* (the board game)
And by sleeping under the tree
With their blankets when talking to us
Do not tell us that ostriches are always right

Oh, you are beautiful, girl,
When you stand with your hand on your waist
You must control yourself until we return

When the men had finished a round of four verses, the young women would take over, with a single girl delivering a high-pitched solo as the other girls responded with the chorus of *Oye wo-yai* from the rear of the group.

Oh mother of mine
Oh sister of my age
The cattle are coming home
Come at nighttime to my house,
The white cattle glistening in the moonlight

Oh warrior of mine
I have gone to Lenguas, to buy a *nanga* cloth
Oh my lover, oh light of my age
Quickly, I have finished my words,
Come, let us meet this good night, my lover.

I went to the dances for the same reason that the warriors did, to meet girls. I pined for Senti, who, as Samburu would say, was as graceful as a giraffe gliding across the plains. But she wanted nothing to do with me and barely greeted me when I said hello.

Kidenye knew that I liked her. "Listen," he said, "all you need to do is go to her house late at night when everyone is sleeping. Lift up her toe, and she will wake up and follow you outside. Then you can go somewhere quiet, your house or even the bush, and 'give her the bull.'" I was skeptical, but one evening after the dancing had ended, Kidenye and Lalem accompanied me to Senti's house. He whispered, "Go inside now, while everyone is sleeping."

I hesitated but they pushed me in the door. It was pitch black. I couldn't see a thing, but I extended my arm until I felt a foot. I did as they said, and lifted the big toe. I felt the body move and then heard a thin high voice say, "Oh?" It was Timbien, Senti's five-year-old sister! I ran out of the house as quickly as possible, telling Kidenye and Lalem, who were laughing hard, that I thought they were assholes.

Nevertheless, love did come to me in Lukumai. One evening, after our dancing outside the manyatta, the warriors and girls went into a vacant house to continue singing. Here, about eight warriors and an equal number of young women sat close to each other, shoulders and bodies touching as they sang. Whenever the hearth fire burst into flame, someone would stir the fire to keep the light low. The mood was highly sexual; all the men and women moved together in unison as we sang, our shoulders and legs touching. Suddenly, I felt two small hands from behind place themselves on my stomach, and they remained there as we sang. Touching someone's stomach in Samburu is like rubbing a person's upper thighs in Western culture; it is incredibly erotic and a very direct signal. In case I missed the message, a soft voice whispered in my ear, "*Kaiyo iye*" (I want you), "*Karlo ade aa nkaji-ino*" (I'll come later to your house).

Sembara and I became a couple, pairing up at the dances, visiting each other as often and quietly as we could. She was good company and enjoyed hanging out with me at my house and at the dances. After this relationship began, the villagers treated me differently. They seemed more accepting and looked at me more as a human being and a member of the community. In time I "beaded" Sembara, meaning I bought her a large number of small colored beads to make necklaces and bracelets for herself and for me.

One night during our dancing, four warriors from Soritari clan village came, looking very unfriendly. They stood at a distance outside our manyatta, leaning on their spears. Lalem and Kidenye went to meet them. I followed, but Lalem motioned to me to stay behind them.

"*Kore Mzungu?*" (Where is the white man?), the outsiders asked.

"Why do you want him?" asked Lalem.

"He stole the girlfriend of one of our warriors, and we have come to beat him."

My heart started beating hard. I wasn't afraid of a fight, but I did not want any of us hurt with weapons. Lalem and Kidenye stood their ground. I moved to stand next to them. Lalem spoke up, with a menacing look on his face.

"The *mzungu* is one of us; he is a warrior of Lukumai. He is the son of the laibon Lonyoki. Even if he has twenty girlfriends, so what? The girl went to him willingly—she is free to choose who she wants to bead her."

The Soritari warriors were angry, but they knew they were defeated. They glared at us, and one in particular stared at me, pointedly tapping his *rungu* club into his other hand. But they turned around and disappeared into the night.

Lalem said to me, "They won't bother you again, because you are our friend and because you are Lonyoki's son. But those Soritari can be very dangerous."

We walked back toward the dancing. Kidenye added, "*Ey*, a Soritari girl got pregnant by a Lukumai warrior, and the Soritari *murrani* who had beaded her wanted to beat her and her boyfriend. The elders heard about it and called a meeting. Her Lukumai lover said, 'If you want to beat her, you will have to kill me first.' The Soritari *murran* backed off, just like tonight. There is a lot of blood spilled between *l-murran* because of girlfriends."

I said to Kidenye, "Sembara really is a brave person to be my girlfriend. And I want to thank you for being here tonight and standing firm when these warriors came looking for me."

"That's what age-mates do for each other," Kidenye replied.

Lalem agreed, "*Ey*, that is what we do."

Shivers, Fever, and Body Aches

A few weeks after the confrontation with the Soritari warriors, I woke up with uncontrollable shivering and an intense pain in my head and shoulders; I felt as if I were being crushed in a vise. I imagined that my shoulders and upper arms had become an open-pit mine divided into a hundred small rooms. In each room was a little devil with a pickax hammering away at my body; I had become a fifteenth-century inhabitant of a Dutch hell by Hieronymus Bosch. Although I was feverish and could hardly move, I managed to lift myself up and crawl next door to Naiseku's house, where I collapsed on her skin mat. When I awoke, Naiseku had made tea and poured a cup for me. "Here, drink this," she said. "You have *nkerugwa* [the 'fever']" Yes, I nodded, and fell back asleep.

When I awoke, Naiseku had more tea prepared for me. She was a godsend, an angel of mercy. I managed to return to my house and find my chloroquine pills for malaria; I crawled back to Naiseku's and stayed there for the next four days.

There is no vaccine for malaria. Unlike a bacterial illness that can be treated with antibiotics or a virus preventable by a vaccine, malaria is caused by an amoeba-sized protozoan (of the genus *plasmodium*) delivered by a female *anopheles* mosquito. It enters and destroys red blood cells during its life cycle, and its waste products cause fevers, chills, and sometimes death. I probably had *Plasmodium falciparum*, which is the deadliest form and is common in East Africa. Malaria was and continues to be responsible for many of the deaths of adults, children, and infants in Africa.

Everyone in the manyatta was worried about me; visitors poked their head into my house nonstop asking me how I was feeling. Sembara came regularly, bringing me soup and tea. Sometimes she lay down next to me, but she would leave when a married adult came into the house. A week later, I was paid a visit by Lolcheni, the herbalist. He had heard I was ill and wanted to help me. He came into my house clicking his tongue, assessing my situation. I remembered a treatment I had witnessed in which he had administered an enema to a man using a hollowed goats' horn. I told Lolcheni, "No, thank you, I am much better now and don't need any treatment."

With a look of "We'll see about that," he motioned for me to lie flat on my back. He placed his thin strong hands on my abdomen and began to strenuously knead my belly, as if he were trying to pull the sickness out of my body.

"Ow, that hurts!" I said.

"Of course it does," Lolcheni replied, "it's supposed to hurt!"

I told him to leave his bark medicine by the cookware, and I would have Naiseku make it later on. Lolcheni was agreeable, and made his departure laughing.

I recovered, aided in no small part by my chloroquine pills, but appreciating the concern shown to me by the community. There were now few people in the manyatta. It was the dry season and there was not enough pasture for the livestock to stay in the settlement; the warriors had taken the animals into the mountains to graze and had been gone for almost a month. Late one evening I heard a distant trumpeting coming from the direction of the Lenguas wells. I realized they were elephants roaring long into the night.

"Did you hear what happened last night?" Usana asked me when I arose the next morning. "A baby elephant fell into one of the wells, and the elephants stayed up all night digging it out."

"How did they do that?" I asked. Those wells were three-men deep and chiseled out of the hard calcium rock of the riverbed.

"They used their tusks and created a slope for the baby to walk out. Those damned elephants, they ruined our wells!"

"And you say elephants aren't clever," I exclaimed. "That is the most clever thing I have ever heard!" I wished I had been there to see it.

The next morning I awoke to heavy rainfall on the roof. This was unusual, and I hadn't seen it rain this hard before. It was cold outside and I had to find my cloth rain jacket hidden away in my duffle bag. Despite the weather, people were in a cheery mood. Rain meant grass and grass meant milk; it also meant that our warriors and animals would be returning to the manyatta.

A few evenings later, Lalem quietly entered my house. I hadn't seen him or the other warriors from Lukumai in more than a month. We smiled in greeting, but he kept his voice low as he did not want the village to know the warriors had returned.

"*Sopa, murratai*," Lalem greeted me. "I heard you were ill with *nkerugwa* [the fever]. Are you better now? Listen, we need *sabuni* [soap]." I knew he wanted some Omo detergent so that the warriors could wash their *nanga* clothes; they wanted to look their best when they entered the village the next day. The following morning at around nine o'clock, the manyatta heard and saw the singing warriors as they approached the village. There were about fifteen men in all, resplendent in freshly ochred red hair and clean red cloths (thanks to yours truly), twirling their spears as they skip-danced into the village. Behind them came several hundred cattle herded by two warriors. Everyone came out to greet the *l-murran*; even the elders who were resting under their shade tree got up, although I suspected they were more interested in seeing their cattle than their sons. The women were beaming with joy. Paker, my pretend mother-in-law, said to me, "Aren't our warriors beautiful?" Small children ran alongside the *l-murran* as they moved inside the manyatta, some holding the hands of their older brothers and uncles.

Kidenye came over to greet me. "You should have come with us this time; we chased some Turkana trying to steal our cattle. I almost got to kill one of them, but they got away."

The elders helped bring the cattle into the manyatta, whistling and raising the cattle sticks to keep the livestock moving. There were about five hundred cattle of every color—white, brown, "blue," or gray; some mottled, some single-colored—kicking up dust and moaning as they entered their pens. The *nkang* felt whole again, and I knew there would be joy as people could drink the cow's rich milk, having lived on their camels' thin milk and *posho* meal these past months.

That evening, the warriors danced with the *nkang's* teenage girls, who were dressed in their finest with blackened scalps and red ochre and grease on their neck beads and breasts. I joined the warriors as we sang late into the night outside the village with our *nkerai* (sweethearts), our melodies serving as lullabies for the old folks and children sleeping in their houses. It felt good to have our warriors back home again.

Photo 1.   The laibon Lonyoki

Photo 2. Naiseku, Dominic's first wife

Photo 3.   Lonyoki, with Mother of Lembalen and Lembalen

Photo 4.   Warriors dancing with their girlfriends

Photo 5.   Elliot dispensing first aid outside his house, with Lonyoki on left

Photo 6. Lonyoki throws his *nkidong* divination

Photo 7. Usana with two new born camels

Photo 8. Langata the Dark Valley

Photo 9. Lonyoki marks *ntasim* medicine on warrior at new settlement location

Photo 10. Marty Nathan and AnnaMarie weighing a baby in Maternal Child Health study

Photo 11. Leah and Lembalen write down their names

Photo 12.   Lembalen as a warrior

CHAPTER THREE

The Dark Valley

Fear events that come simultaneously.

I had been living with Lonyoki and Dominic in Lukumai *nkang* for eight months. I was fairly fluent in Samburu and was now treated as a regular member of the community. One evening, Dominic, Lonyoki, Lalem, and I were sitting and chatting outside my house. The wind was blowing strongly and I swore I could hear a distant wailing from the direction of Baiyo Mountain; it was a cross between people singing and people moaning.

"Do you hear that sound? What is it?" I asked.

"Ey, I hear it," Dominic said. "Those are the ghosts [*milikas*] of the *shifta*, the ones we fought at Lorrien swamp. So many of them died there. Maybe eighty men."

Dominic described what happened.

"It began when Somalis and Sakuye people attacked Rendille near Kargi. It was a big raid that took a lot of animals, and Rendille and Samburu counter-raided them. So the Samburu and Ariaal manyattas around Baiyo all moved to Lorrien swamp. We needed to stay close together because we were afraid of the *shiftas*. One day, women with baggage camels were returning with water from Lorrien and they saw the raiders coming. A few of them had guns. They moved on but we knew they would return, so we posted sentries and sent scouts to find them. Most of our warriors stayed with the animals near the manyattas. Around nine o'clock in the morning, the *shifta* came back to Lorrien, many of them, to steal our animals at Lorrien. Our warriors came running from four manyattas; we fought until the early afternoon."

I said to Lalem, "You participated in this, didn't you?" Lalem wore three narrow brass bracelets, and I knew he had killed men in battle.

"*Eẙ*, I was there," said Lalem. "The Somalis came. How many? Perhaps one hundred, even one hundred and fifty, and we killed them. Yes, a lot of people died, I think eighty *shifta* were killed. And of our people, only one Samburu died. It was not just Lukumai; it was Longieli, Lorukushu, Lturia. Even my father was there, and you know my father. All Kishili age-set warriors were there, perhaps two hundred *l-murran*. Those people had come to take our cattle. They had guns. They came to take cattle which had come to drink at Lorrien. And all the warriors came running to the swamp. We had spears, and the Somalis had guns, and we fought and killed each other that day. Many *shifta* were trapped in the crater of Lorrien; some drowned in the water. Even if they surrendered or begged for mercy we killed them. Only one wasn't killed—he was wounded in the leg and hid behind a rock. But he caught Dominic by the waist and begged for mercy."

Dominic said, "Our *l-murran* wanted to spear him, but I said 'Don't kill this man, he is begging for his life.' But he was the only one who survived." After a moment or so of silence, Dominic said, "That is why sometimes on nights like this, when you hear the wind whistle, you will hear the *milikas* [ghosts] singing their Somali songs at Lorrien swamp."

A Hyena Attacks, a Lion Stalks

The drought was setting in again and hungry predators were lurking about. One night a hyena jumped into the manyatta, alarming the dogs but making off with a baby goat before anyone could respond. I heard the women screaming "*Ku-tey! Ku-tey!*" (Get away! Get away!). I ran out of my house with my flashlight and grabbed my spear, but the hyena was long gone.

The following day around dusk, as I was walking outside the manyatta, I saw Naiseku returning with her pack donkey from shopping in Lenguas. Suddenly a fast-moving object, low and gray, appeared from the right. It was a hyena, possibly the same one from the previous evening, and it banged directly into the donkey's side, disemboweling it on the run. Naiseku waved her stick in the air, shouting "*Ku-tey!*" I ran over and saw the donkey's intestines hanging from its belly, nearly touching the ground.

"Quick!" Naiseku told me, "Help me get the donkey home." I pushed the intestines into its belly, holding it closed as we hurried into the manyatta. We got through the thorn bush gate and into the animal enclosure. "Help me, Elliot, you must help fix the donkey," she cried. Help fix the donkey? What did she expect me to do? "Fix it!" she said.

I went to my house to fetch my first aid box and a sewing kit. While Naiseku and Usana's wife held the donkey by its nose ring, I squeezed Neosporin into the wound, pushing the guts back into the cavity. Usana and another man came to help, and while they held the animal still, I proceeded to sew up the torn skin. The donkey's hide was thicker than shoe leather, and I had to use the waxed cobbler thread and large needle I kept to repair shoes. Five large stitches later, we let the donkey free. She ran around the *bo'o* a few steps, then stopped and stood still, as if nothing had happened. The donkey miraculously lived.

But the hyena incident worried people. Women talked about it in small groups outside their houses, and Usana and the other elders spoke about it under their shade tree. It was always worrisome when a wild animal came into or close to the manyatta. While attacks on livestock by wild predators were not in themselves unusual, they typically occurred at night or while herding animals away from the village. But for a hyena to attack in daylight (or dusk), with a human holding the animal as Naiseku did, was highly unusual. And unusual events involving wild animals, or other strange mishaps such as occurrences of lightning, floods, or fire, made the people of Lukumai worry.

What happened next startled even the old-timers in the village. It was early evening, and I was resting on a cow skin outside of my house reading *The Brothers Karamazov* by flashlight as the dusk set in. My house was located at a bend in the circular perimeter of the manyatta, and something moving, something large, caught my eye. Incredibly, it was a lion, moving slowly in a crouching position down the thoroughfare between the houses and the animal pens, about three houses away. It was a young male with a short black mane and mangy skin; it did not look healthy. I saw immediately that it was stalking Nkitari's three-year-old son, who was playing in front of their house. The boy glanced up and saw the lion, and with remarkable speed jumped up and cried, "Wo, wo, wo" as he ran into his mother's house. Nkitari rushed out immediately and threw her arms up in the air to frighten the lion, yelling loudly, "*Ku-tey! Ku-tey!*" Then she yelled for the warriors, "*Loi-yei! Loi-yei!*" (Boys! Boys! Come quickly!)

In a sudden flurry of movement people ran out of their houses, warriors and men grabbing their weapons. A woman ran toward me and yelled, "Get your spear, quickly!" Lonyoki, who had been napping, came rushing out of his house, tying his cloth around his waist. He told me, "Quick, grab your flashlight! Lions hate flashlights!"

The lion had escaped by jumping over the manyatta's outside thorn fence. In a rush, I ran after him, jumping over the fence in unison with two other warriors. It was exciting and terrifying at the same time. I was outside the manyatta now, quite alone and enveloped in increasing darkness. I held my flashlight in one hand and long spear in the other. Heart-beating reality was setting in. I heard a voice—it was my own—"Elliot, what are you going to do if you see this lion? You don't even know how to throw this spear!"

I yelled out, "*Murratai* [age-mates]! Do you see the lion?"

"No," was the distant response, "it is gone. Let's go back; we will hunt it tomorrow."

The incident upset everyone in the manyatta. Dominic said, "This lion is crazy; it is a man-eater. It happens when a young male is chased out of its group; he has no luck hunting antelopes or goats, so he starts to hunt humans. Usually lions have sense enough to stay away from people. But once they have killed and eaten a man, there is no other meat they will eat."

Later, we heard that warriors from Longieli had trapped and killed the lion in the hills above Lenguas town. They first killed a goat and stuffed it with poison from the *pirantai* tree (the desert rose). The lion ate the bait and struggled on for another day, roaring in pain and leaving its white poisoned spoor behind. I later saw the hide of the dead lion after it was skinned. It had eleven spear holes in it.

The day following the lion incident, Usana and Dominic visited Lonyoki's house. Usana asked the laibon, "What can you tell us about this lion?"

Dominic spit on the ground, and before Lonyoki could reply, he spoke up. "It's him, isn't it?"

Lonyoki answered, "We need to throw the *nkidong* to see if it is this man or not."

No one said his name, but I knew they suspected that the lion had been sent by sorcery produced by Lobata, the laibon of Soritari clan. That evening, four elders came to Lonyoki's house, including Dominic, his older brother Usana, Lepere, and Lemeti. They were anxious to learn what Lonyoki's divination would reveal.

Lonyoki took out his divination gourd, and the men sat around the blue cloth. Lonyoki asked, "Who will open this *nkidong*?"

Usana answered by putting two shillings down on the cloth. Lonyoki passed him the *nkidong* gourd, and Usana spat air into its open mouth.

He threw three times onto the cloth, and a total of eleven stones came out. The last throw included a large canine tooth from a lion.

There was a soft murmur among the men. Lonyoki continued, unperturbed. "Will this lion come back? Tell me about this lion."

He threw again. Twenty-nine pieces appeared, including a cross-shaped piece of leather made of lion skin. The lion skin concerned Lonyoki, as did the number of objects thrown. Dominic and I knew that nine was not a good number; in fact, it was the most dangerous number from zero to nine.

"Will we be harassed by this lion?"

Lonyoki counted out nine stones and passed them around to all the elders, who spat on them.

"Are we fearing anything? Is there anything wrong with our manyatta?" He vigorously shook the gourd and out came eight pieces.

"These eight show there is nothing wrong. Is it true? *Serian ake?*"

He threw more objects including an ivory piece, a broken piece of thermometer, and a blue bead. I knew that these objects meant, respectively, Lukumai, a hospital, and the presence of Turkana enemies.

"The Turkana have put their shoes on [they are coming to raid]. The cattle disease *lodua* is coming soon. Someone will be taken to the hospital, but I will not say who it is." Looking at the stones, the laibon asked, "What is wrong?"

He studied the layout of the stones on the blue cloth for some time. Then he said, "Some warriors will be eaten by hyenas [they will die], but they are not from here. What about Lukumai? How are the warriors? Are they in peace?"

Lonyoki threw again and twelve pieces emerged, including the hyena's tooth again, an iron bracelet, and red ball.

Everyone was quiet, but you could feel the tension. We all knew the meaning of the red ball—it meant the presence of sorcery. "There is someone 'looking the wrong way' at Lukumai," said Lonyoki. "I know about this person."

Lonyoki passed the gourd to Usana, as elder of Lukumai. Usana spat into its mouth, and Lonyoki threw the gourd two times.

"It is true? Is it Lukumai? You are cheating me, *tu tum menye!*"

Lonyoki shook the *nkidong* again and out came several pieces, including a white shell and a small leather knot made of lion skin.

"This is good. Who needs this *ntasim'l-ke'ene* [*ntasim* of the lion skin]?" asked Lonyoki, half to himself. "Yes, it is true. Lukumai will be given *ntasim*," Lonyoki said with certainty.

Lonyoki spoke to the group. "We have problems here; we have enemies on this side. But it is not the Boran I worry about, or even the Turkana. Our warriors will be eating Turkana cattle in Baragoi, I can see that. But we have an enemy near us, someone I know. This is too disturbing now; I need to think about all this."

Outside, I asked Dominic how the laibon would protect Lukumai from harm.

"He will make *ntasim* for the entire village. I've seen him do this before. Lobata will see who the stronger laibon is."

The next morning, Lonyoki called the elders and announced that he had dreamt of a terrible illness coming to the manyatta; it was measles. Measles was, and remains, a devastating disease to those who are not vaccinated, and no one in Lukumai or any of the nomadic manyattas in Marsabit District were vaccinated in the 1970s. Lonyoki said he needed to prepare an *ntasim* ceremony for the whole village, which he called "the *ntasim* of *l-ke'ene*," the *ntasim* of the lion skin.

Lonyoki set up a "rope" under which all of the village's inhabitants would pass. The laibon with several elders suspended a long leather and rope cord from the *na'abu* ritual center to the outer fence. One half of the cord was made of lion's skin, the other was a woven rope called *nokore* woven from the inner bark of the *lokore* tree. Lonyoki wiped yellow and black *ntasim* on the lion cord, which he called the male side, and red and yellow *ntasim* on the *nokore* rope, which was the female side.

Everyone in the manyatta had assembled in the area of the cord; they had been told that the laibon would be giving *ntasim* to protect them from the approaching epidemic. Lonyoki had the men go first, led by warriors, then elders, then boys and small children, who walked single file under the male side of the cord. Then the women came and passed on the female side, led by adolescent girls and followed by married women and then young girls. As they did so, Lonyoki marked the men one at a time with yellow *ntasim* on the top of their head, right ear, and twice on their right shoulder; he did the same for women but marked them on their left side. "Never wash this off," he told folks as they emerged.

Lonyoki repeated the procedure the next morning. This time, he tied *nokore* strings coated in *ntasim* around the right wrists of the men and boys, and over the left shoulder and under the right arm of all the women and girls. Lonyoki told each person not to wash off any of the *ntasim* and to leave the *nokore* strings tied on until they fell off. No visitors were allowed to stay in the *nkang* that evening, and no one was to leave the manyatta for the next four days, until the eighth day of the moon.

Lonyoki told me later that he had "tied" the string around people to protect them, just as he had "tied" the whole community by having everyone pass under the cord of lion skin and *nokore*. Tying was an important principle of Lonyoki's medicines; it sealed and protected people from external threats, particularly sorcery. After the event, Usana said to me, "Thank you for bringing Lonyoki here. He has prevented a great illness from happening. May God protect us all."

The dry season had set in, the period between the October and the April rains that the Samburu called the "short hunger" (*lameyu dorrup*, compared to the "long hunger" between April and October). Most of the large live-stock were in distant *fora* camps—the camels to the northeast in the desert lowlands, the cattle to the west in the Ndoto Mountain highlands. The man-yatta was left with very few milk animals, mainly nursing camels and goats. People were living on *posho*, corn meal made into a bland porridge. It was a monotonous diet, and people missed fresh milk terribly.

Lalem and Kidenye had asked me to go with them and the livestock. "We will take the cattle to the Arsim wells," said Lalem, "and then through the mountains to Baragoi. We will be gone a long time. Won't you come with us, *murratai?*" he asked me.

"I don't think so; I need to stay here with Lonyoki," I replied.

Kidenye laughed, "Elliot is lying. He wants to stay here with his girlfriend, Sembara. And I heard there is another girl he fancies." He paused, and then with a grin said to Lalem, "Your mother!"

"*Tu tum menye,*" Lalem laughed.

After the warriors and cattle had left, life in the manyatta became as bor-ing as the diet. The women had little to do except sit outside their houses, chatting with one another while they repaired old containers or leather skirts and cared for their small children. Men lay under the shade tree outside the manyatta, playing the *ndotoi* board game, swatting the flies away with their donkey-tail flywhisks. One evening I was summoned to Dominic's house, where he and Lonyoki were having a conversation.

"*Karibu*, Elliot," said Dominic. "Lonyoki wants to visit his father, Longo-jine, in Langata, a valley east of here in the mountains. We want you to help us. Can you drive us to Langata?"

"How long will you stay there?" I asked. I hoped it would be for a while, as there was little happening here in Lukumai.

"I don't know," Lonyoki said. "I want to convince my father to move here to Lukumai. He is old and all alone."

Dominic piped in, "*Ey*, he's outlived his four wives, and now he lives in a tiny house, not big enough for a dog."

Lonyoki added, "Also, there are families in Langata that are asking me to visit. There are many people who need my *ntasim*."

Dominic added, "The laibon also wants to see Lobata, to see clearly if he is harming our village with his sorcery."

This sounded interesting but a bit frightening. I could see Lonyoki furrow his brow and did not want to talk about this rival laibon. I changed the subject.

"Did your father teach you how to be a laibon?" I asked Lonyoki.

Lonyoki replied, "No, Longojine did not teach me about being a laibon; he was a mean person. I think he thought I was not his true son. He did not trust his wife, my mother, who was a beautiful woman. When my mother was pregnant with me, my father chased her away. My mother went back to her home in Barsaloi where I was born. My mother stayed there for four years until Longojine came to take her and his son home. But I was so unlike him, he was convinced I wasn't his son, and he started to fight with my mother again. I think that because my father's father [Kocheke] died before his son was born, Longojine thought he would die if I was born. Kocheke was the most famous laibon we had. His real name was Charrar, but people called him 'Kocheke' [stomach] because he was the center of our family. He came to Marsabit from Laikipiak Maasai when he was a young man. Kocheke dreamt he would have a son with six fingers, which he did. But Kocheke did not believe Longojine was his true son; he had chased away Longojine's mother, who he thought was unfaithful. He died before my father was born. And that is why my father chased me away."

"If you grew up without your father, how did you learn to become a laibon?"

"Despite my father's rejection," Lonyoki replied, "I knew from a young age that I had the power to predict [a-ibon]. People said that my mother had vivid dreams that came true when she was pregnant with me, and I had dreams and visions that foretold the future even as a young boy. This is the same with my own son Lembalen—his mother also had dreams that came true when she was pregnant with Lembalen. That is how people knew I would be a strong laibon, and how I know Lembalen will be strong.

"When I was about to be circumcised [in 1948], I joined other Lorukushu [clan] members near Maralal to be circumcised and initiated into the Kimaniki age-set. But my father refused to give me the ox for the first mugit [age-set rite], and I had to beg an ox from another man, my uncle. I refused to herd my father's animals because I knew he would never give me any animals in return. After my initiation, I left my father and moved away. I went to Naivasha and worked on a white man's farm, the Delamere farm, for five years. Later I took a job with another white named Janeck in Rumuruti. I worked in his storeroom. I even learned to write numbers in a book and to write my name. The white man was kind to me; he knew I was smart and he tried to teach me to read, he wanted me to read the white man's Bible. With the money I saved from working for Janeck, I married a girl from Masula, and had my son Lembalen.

"When my son was small, still at his mother's breast, I was called back to my father's village by the elders there. They said Longojine had become too old and frail, and they needed their laibon. I refused them five times, but, finally, on the sixth time, my father sent a message and said, 'You must be the laibon now.' I went, and he gave me the nkidong gourd, the blue sheet, and some sugar. He blessed me and the *nkidong*, and the elders blessed me in the house. People sent me messages from Barsaloi to return there, but I knew if I went back, the people in Barsaloi would not let me go. And I liked this place in the desert very much. The people wanted me to stay because I prevented so many bad things, and predicted so many good things."

Sorcery in the Ndotos

The next day we loaded up the Land Rover and headed toward Langata. We drove toward Laisamis, then turned onto a small track that went into the Ndoto Mountains. As we drove, we talked.

"What's Langata like?" I asked Dominic and Lonyoki.

Dominic responded, "It's all Lukumai there, *Lukumai lol nkishu* [Lukumai who keep cattle], rather than *Lukumai lol ntamesi* [with camels]. There is no town there, only a small shop at Langata. But there are many manyattas there, mainly Lukumai clan."

Lonyoki added, "The place is full of people cursed with *nkurupore*, that's why I am called there."

"What exactly is *nkurupore*?" I asked.

"It is like *ntasim*, something you can make or buy from those who know how to make it," said Lonyoki. "But when *ntasim* protects you, *nkurupore* is used to hurt someone. You can put *nkurupore* in someone's tea, or mark his house, or even mark the tracks people walk on. *Nkurupore* can drive a man mad, it can kill his cattle. It can cause his wife to be barren, it can make you blind or lame. Even someone can die—he'll fall sick, be attacked by a lion, or meet with madness and kill himself."

"Why do people use *nkurupore*?" I asked.

Dominic responded this time. "Some people hate; they have bitterness in their heart. A man has a brother with many healthy cattle, and he is jealous. Or another person slights him a favor and he revenges with *nkurupore*. If a *lairuponi* [witch] becomes too much of a nuisance, the elders will ask the laibon to curse that person, and then that person—man or woman—is finished."

I asked Lonyoki, "Who makes *nkurupore*, where can one find it?"

"People can buy *nkurupore* from other laibons; there are many Maasai laibons who sell it."

Dominic added, "Lonyoki's cousin Lokili makes *nkurupore*."

I had heard of Lokili; he was Lonyoki's older cousin, the laibon living on Marsabit Mountain.

Dominic continued, "Of all the laibons in all of Samburu, no one has stronger sorcery than Lokili. He is a killer, really. You might think he is a kind old man, but he is like steel, and his heart shows no mercy. If Lokili joins you in battle, your enemy is finished! Once Lokili killed a Boran witch by pressing sorcery poisons in her hand in the Marsabit town market."

"How did she die?" I asked.

"She died of fright," Dominic said. "She had been brought to Marsabit by Boran to attack Rendille who lived there. Lokili sought her out and he killed her, completely."

Lonyoki said, "I won't kill a man; I just prevent his *nkurupore* from harming anyone else. I protect people with my *ntasim*, which is very strong. I am not a sorcerer like Lokili. But I do know how to make sorcery poisons—Lokili taught me. He would mix the ashes of burnt cobras, chameleons, nightjars, and spider webs with the burnt roots of *l-kukulai* and *l-paramunyo* bushes, the same plants I use in my *ntasim*. We can place these substances on objects where our enemies were located—we can toss it on a stick it into a cattle enclosure or place it on the path where the person walks.

"These medicines can make someone inactive, weak, and insane; they can make an enemy shit himself to death with diarrhea. Sometimes *nkurupore* will see to it that your neighbors are never friendly so that person is disliked by everyone around him. But you can also use *nkurupore* to secure a good price for cattle, to keep your spouse sexually faithful. Sometimes we give it to warriors to attract girlfriends."

"That's how you were able to meet Sembara," Dominic said, and we all laughed.

I asked Lonyoki if he had ever been cursed with *nkurupore*.

"Yes, I was cursed during my initiation as a warrior with the Lorukushu clan *l-murran*. They put *nkurupore* in the blood I was to drink. This was done by my clan brothers."

I was shocked. "Your own brothers would do this?"

"Yes," Lonyoki replied, "these were not great laibons; they were not selected by the people. They were jealous of me. They were the sons of the man who cursed my father. After I drank the blood, I realized they had cursed me. It was during the time of our circumcision, when we go off to shoot birds. [During their ritual isolation, initiates wore all black skins and shot birds with blunted arrows to avoid blood. The dead birds were then worn from their cloths until the circumcision.] When they returned to the camp, I said, 'Come, have some of this blood with me.' But they refused.

"I drank the blood, but it did not affect me. A Maasai laibon told me it was true, that I had been cursed by my kinsmen. The same person who cursed me at the circumcision tried to curse me again when we were warriors. We were eating a goat, and the man had *nkurupore* under his fingernails, he was flicking his fingers at me when we were eating. But I had dreamt this would happen, so I was prepared. I had prepared very strong *ntasim* and had made a new dik-dik horn to wear on my neck beads. I knew who these men were, and I knew that my medicine was stronger than theirs."

As we drove toward Langata, I thought about sorcery and what it meant. Beliefs in sorcery were widely held throughout Africa, even in cities. But neither Samburu nor Maasai were known for their sorcery, certainly not to the degree that groups such as Kamba and Swahili were with their renowned healers and sorcerers. Yet here I was, driving with perfectly pragmatic and rational Samburu men who were talking about the problems of sorcery. Spending the next two weeks in Langata confirmed my impression that more than a few people were concerned about sorcery. It seemed to thrive in isolated places like Langata, far from any police post, hospital, or road.

We were getting close to Lonyoki's father's homestead, which lay near the Lengare Mara River, now a dry sand bed. We came upon a large number of manyattas on the sloping hill above the river. The word *langata* means "river crossing" or valley in Samburu. But I dubbed this community the "Dark Valley"—I found it a fearful and lonely place whose residents were unfriendly and aloof. As Lonyoki had said, "This place is full of sorcery."

We spent the night in the house of one of Dominic's relatives, falling asleep quickly after our long ride. The next morning we walked up the valley to Longojine's manyatta. Lonyoki was apprehensive about meeting his father; he didn't expect that the old man would want to return with us to Lukumai. "He likes to do things for himself," Lonyoki had said. I pictured a stubborn old man, and I wasn't mistaken. We reached Longojine's community around ten thirty in the morning. The manyatta was fairly large, not quite as big as Lukumai, with about twenty houses surrounding animal enclosures. There were no camels here, only cattle and goats.

We found Longojine living in a small house no larger than a doghouse, as Dominic had said. Longojine came out to greet us; he did so warmly, which surprised me, given everyone's description of him. He was short like his son and he wore a green cloth like other laibons, but otherwise he was indistinguishable from other old men in Samburu and Ariaal. He was old and bent over from arthritis, with skin shriveled from a life in the sun. He had incredibly long ears, pulled even longer by his heavy brass earrings. And he did indeed have six fingers, with an extra half-digit, complete with a fingernail, on his left thumb. It is said that six fingers are not uncommon among laibons.

Longojine pulled a cow skin from his house, and we sat down. Dominic began with small talk. "Ah, your grandson asks, 'Where is my *akuya* [grandfather], bring him to our *nkang!*'" The old man and Lonyoki said little as Dominic chatted away.

Longojine was a frail old man in his seventies; he was of the Merisho age-set initiated around 1912. But he was not without his wits. He turned to me and said, "I've heard about you, and I wanted to see you. Now, I've seen you, and I am pleased."

A woman from a neighboring house brought us hot tea. After we finished, the four of us sat under a shade tree outside the manyatta. First Dominic and then Lonyoki made impassioned pleas for Longojine to return to our manyatta.

"*Mai-yo*" (I don't want to), the old man said to his son. "Where were you five years ago? You didn't ask me then. I do not want to go."

He said this without rancor or bitterness, but it was clear that the old man was adamant and could not be persuaded. After a half an hour or so, we departed. As we walked down the hill, I was surprised that Lonyoki was upbeat.

"Last time it was *tu tum menye* [abusive words], but he's not angry now. He'll come with us. We just have to keep encouraging him."

We made our way across the valley to one of the larger settlements on the opposing hill. These were all Lukumai settlements, and Dominic spent little time finding us a house to stay in. We expected to stay about a week while Lonyoki did his divination for various clients.

"Why don't people use Longojine as a laibon?" I asked.

Lonyoki replied, "He is too old; he does not perform his divination any longer or make *ntasim* for people. He only dreams now."

Lonyoki's Divination and Healing

This place had more business for Lonyoki than I had ever seen. He was visited by elders, women, and warriors and performed one or more divinations every day. Almost immediately, a warrior asked for divination to see how his marriage negotiations would turn out. As in many of the divination sessions, I turned on my tape recorder so that with the help of an assistant I could transcribe and translate the conversations later on.

During the divination, Lonyoki said, "Yes, I can see you have a problem. It came to you while you were in the bush, on the way here, and not in the *nkang.*" Throwing his stones, Lonyoki said, "This problem has been brought to you by another warrior, and by another laibon. Someone has put *nkurupore* in two *l-tepes* [acacia trees] on your way here."

The warrior stiffened, as did his friends.

Lonyoki shook the gourd and threw seven objects. He shook again and threw ten more.

"I can see many girls come to search for you." Everyone laughed. I am sure Lonyoki said this to relieve the tension.

"You are preparing to marry," he continued, "but I see quarrels in the girl's family, brought about by gossiping of other people. You want to ask whether the girl is from a good family, but you are afraid to ask. But these two stones show you have no mother, that this is your stepmother with whom you live. And someone wants to bring conflict between you and your stepmother." He threw more stones. "I see people fear you because of your bravery, and they gave you a nickname. Is that true?"

"*Ey,*" smiled the warrior, but he did not say his nickname.

Then, addressing the stepmother, Lonyoki asked, "What happened to this man's baby mat where he lay as a child? [The woman did not answer.] I see that it's been stolen, taken by a blind woman. I see more quarrels. This yellow stone shows that there's a hill where warriors are eating meat and where quarrels started. Who dislikes this warrior?" Lonyoki asked his *nkidong.*

He threw the gourd several times.

"There will be a Turkana raid, but no relatives will be hurt. I see old men dying as a result of this raid. Camel people [Rendille or Ariaal] will die in large numbers. Very many of them. Also some people will be bitten by snakes, but only one woman will die.

"What about this man's life? Will he see peace?" asked Lonyoki to his gourd. He handed the gourd to the warrior, who spat air into it. Lonyoki threw three more times, and a total of ten stones appeared.

"Is there peace [*serian*]?" Lonyoki threw again and then said to the warrior, "Go with people and don't travel alone. The name you have used before should not be used anymore." Then Lonyoki addressed the stepmother again, "You are crying, saying you are not being cared for. You be careful, mama, to say you are not being cared for by this warrior."

The warrior asked, "Do you think she's not being cared for?"

"Yes, it is true," Lonyoki replied. "You are not taking care of her well. Your father is gone, your own mother is gone, and you are the oldest son. And now you are preparing to marry. And this girl's family is saying, 'If this man is not taking care of his mother, how will he take care of his wife?'" But Lonyoki said this with a smile and slapped the warrior's knee affectionately. Then Lonyoki turned serious.

"You were cursed by a man called Kiriman. Also there is a trouble with your future *lauton* [brother-in-law]. You must chase this brother-in-law away from your family; he only wishes to make quarrels."

Lonyoki finished his divination and proceeded to prepare *ntasim* powders for the warrior. He poured yellow *ntasim* from one of the small gourds and told the man to sniff it. Then Lonyoki mixed some of the ground red ochre powder that warriors use to paint themselves with black *ntasim* and water. He poured the solution into his left hand and, using his right thumb, marked the warrior's face, neck, shoulders, chest, arms, hands, palms, thighs, and legs and finished at the feet. Drawing on another small container, he mixed some *ntasim* powders with honey in a long spoon and gave it to the warrior to swallow. When the marking of *ntasim* was complete, the warriors gathered their weapons and departed from the house. Later the client would pay Lonyoki for his medicines. This could vary from a few goats to a cow, depending on both the seriousness of the attack and the means of the person to pay.

Outside, Lonyoki told Dominic and me, "The warrior knew he was cursed by a laibon before tonight's *nkidong*. It was done by his future brother-in-law, who paid another laibon for the *nkurupore*. I don't know why he cursed him, but this was powerful poison." We headed back to Dominic's relative's house, and while Lonyoki and Dominic chatted outside with some elders, I went inside to write up notes about everything I witnessed.

In anthropological terms, the laibon's divination and his dispensing of *ntasim* medicines constituted a "rite of affliction," a ritual aimed at curing illnesses or misfortunes believed to result from spiritual attacks, in this case sorcery instigated by human enemies. The laibon's *ntasim* medicines commanded the same sort of spiritual power that the sorcery did, but did so to protect and heal individuals and their families from attack. I had the sense that people lived in a day-to-day world of cattle, pastures, and villages but were surrounded by invisible spiritual forces, like radio waves in the air. These forces could be mobilized for good through the prayers of elders to bless the community, but also for evil, particularly when people were angry or jealous and wanted to cause someone harm.

An interesting feature of beliefs in sorcery among the Samburu—and this seemed true throughout the African continent—was the notion that sorcery was caused not by strangers, but by close neighbors and family members. The person who meant to harm you was someone you knew—a greedy brother, a jealous co-wife, a spurned lover, or a neighbor denied a favor. As Alfred Hitchcock was fond of saying, "Murder begins at home."

A Cursed Family

After treating the warrior who was cursed, Lonyoki was approached by a man named Lengidi, who was the same age-set as the laibon. Lengidi came to visit well after dark, and I assume that he was fearful of being seen consulting the laibon. Sorcery was not a topic that people addressed openly. Lengidi had a worried look; he seemed a person beaten down by events. I learned his story after the divination. Lengidi was a married man with two wives: Nkadume, a woman in her forties, and Malepen, who was fifteen years younger. Nkadume had given birth to three children, but two had died in infancy, and the third one, now nearly twelve years old, was not "normal in the head." This daughter, who was called Nkueny (which means bird), did as she was asked, but she had no joy, no energy; she could barely milk an animal. The other children teased her and called her *maduup*, a flightless bird.

Because Nkadume had problems bearing children, Lengidi had taken Malepen as a second wife. Within one year of marriage, Malepen gave birth to a healthy girl, and a second child, a son, was born three years later. Now Malepen was pregnant with her third child, but she was uneasy. She worried that her senior co-wife might be jealous of her, and indeed Nkadume had ceased being friendly after Malepen's son was born.

When Malepen learned that she was pregnant with her third child, she kept it to herself, not even telling her husband. But now her pregnancy was becoming visible. One evening, as she passed her neighbor's house, she heard Nkadume talking to a neighbor inside. "God may not protect her next birth as he has the first two. God did not protect mine, and one's luck does not last forever." It was a terrible thing to speak of an expectant mother in this way; it could only result in harm to her unborn child. Malepen did not say anything, but she grew increasingly fearful.

One day, Nkadume asked Malepen's young daughter, Septima, to fetch water from the wells at Lenguas. But Septima was only five years old and too little to do this task; this was something you sent teenagers to do. Malepen asked herself, "Why would Nkadume endanger my daughter this way? Did she want to see harm come to her?" On another occasion, Malepen entered her house to fetch her young son, who was napping. She gasped when she saw Nkadume leaning over the child, patting him on the head. "What are you doing here?" Malepen cried, trying to control her fear and anger. Nkadume replied, "I came in to borrow a cooking pot, but sat down to talk to your son as he was waking up. He is such a beautiful boy, isn't he? Is it so terrible for his *yeyo* to say hello to him?"

That night, Malepen spoke to her husband. "She was in my house, without telling me or waiting for me to return. Why was she touching our son if not to harm him? I worry she had something bad in her hand that she was wiping on him."

Lengidi replied, "Surely Nkadume meant no harm. She loves your children as her own, she really does." But he, too, was worried, although he did not share his concern with Malepen. Several of his milk cattle in the *nkang* had contracted udder disease, and he had heard recently that one of his heifers was killed by a lion while being herded by warriors near the Lengare Mara River. There were many cattle herded that day, Lengidi thought, but only his was killed by the lion. In addition, he was not feeling well. His stomach was bothering him, and he was feeling tired and weak. These things can happen to anyone, of course, but why did they happen all at once to him?

For these reasons, Lengidi sought out Lonyoki for a divination and intervention. He had to resolve this problem before losing another of his cattle, or worse, the child Malepen was carrying. His worst fears were that he would lose his young wife or even die himself.

The next afternoon, Lonyoki, Dominic, and I entered the house of Nkadume and Lengidi. The younger wife Malepen was seated inside with her small son on her lap. Lonyoki seated himself on a cow skin mat, spread out his blue cloth, and began his divination.

He asked, "Who is going to open the *nkidong?*" and Lengidi placed a one-shilling coin on the cloth. Lonyoki spat into the mouth of his divination gourd and said, "This *nkidong* knows my truths and my lies. And now I want some news from Lukumai." To Lengidi, Lonyoki asked, "What are your problems?"

Lengidi replied, "My cattle are sick and I am unhappy about this person not having children," nodding toward his first wife. "We want you to tell us about this."

Lonyoki went to work, throwing the stones from his gourd. After some consideration he turned to the family.

"This man has two wives. The first is bad because she lies, and the second is good, as she does not cheat. There were once twins in this family," he said, pointing to a leather ring object, "and both were girls. If not from this house, then from this family [i.e., the patrilineage]. Let's continue the *nkidong.*"

He spat again into gourd again.

"I have this *nkidong*, and God will help me do it. This will not come quickly, and it will not come badly. Every throw is new. I say *serian* [peace]; *serian ake* [is there peace]? What is this meat for? Is there a fight for this meat? Tell me truths, not lies."

Several throws resulted in fifty-three pieces. Lonyoki and Lengidi divided these into piles of ten, placing fifty pieces to the left side of the cloth and leaving three stones where they fell.

Lonyoki said, "I see a quarrel over the wedding ox." To the first wife: "Was there a quarrel on your wedding day?" She replied, "I don't know."

Lonyoki said, "Is it true?" He threw two pieces. "Is it true," he asked again, and threw four. "Is it true, this fight over meat?" He threw seven stones. "Try to remember what happened that day."

To the husband he said, "There was a problem over meat on that day. Do you remember? Try to work hard; otherwise, these women will never give birth." To the *nkidong*: "Is it true there was an argument?" He threw three large groups of stones, which he and Lengidi added up. There were ninety-two pieces.

Lonyoki continued, nodding to the first wife, "It was the woman's problem. They did something to the meat, arguing over shares."

Lonyoki spat and threw nine stones. "She will be taken to another laibon," he said, and threw again. "This seventh stone shows it is not a problem of cattle; it is a problem of the wedding ox [*l-kuret*]. I see a cow must be taken by a laibon [i.e., this calls for *ntasim*, to be paid for in cattle]. What about the *ntasim*?"

He threw again and out came a piece made of black iron.

"No, there is peace here. But the blacksmiths will come together. There will be a pregnant girl and they will try to abort the baby and the girl will die."

Lonyoki asked the *nkidong*, "What about this woman? Can *ntasim* help?"

He threw and four objects came out. "Yes, it will be all right."

Lengidi asked, "Does my wife need *ntasim*?"

"Yes, the stones say yes."

Lengidi asked, "What about the cattle?"

Lonyoki threw fourteen pieces. "Yes, the cattle as well. We are done now."

Lonyoki put the stones and objects back in his gourd. To Lengidi he said, "Go and collect for me the tail hairs of twenty-seven cattle from your herds and we will make the *ntasim*."

After we left the house, Lonyoki confided, "This family has been cursed for some time. Someone from Lukumai clan cursed the first wife with *nkurupore*, someone who was later arrested and beaten up by the police. He had marked a small stick with *nkurupore* and threw it near her gateway where she walked over it. Later when her daughter died, and her cattle died, she knew she was cursed. She has one child who is *madai* [crazy] and who will never marry. There were problems between her and her husband's family. But that was not the cause of her troubles. This woman lies, while the second wife is good and does not cheat. This woman is the cause of these problems; she has brought on this badness herself."

Thoughts about Divination

While Lonyoki and Dominic spent the evening outside chatting with local elders, I went into the house where we were staying and wrote up my notes. I had watched enough *nkidong* rituals to grasp some of its basic principles, and many clients and followers of the laibon, including Dominic and me, had some knowledge of the meaning of the objects thrown. A hyena's tooth could mean death; a particular bead signified a Rendille clan. Eight stones meant peace, while nine stones meant danger, often the danger of sorcery. But only the laibon could understand the totality of meanings that the stones revealed, based on his power to see, interpret, and understand what he threw.

Lonyoki had explained to me, "When I throw the nkidong, every stone comes out for a certain reason. When I see how the stones fall out, how they lie on the blue cloth, it's like looking in a mirror; I see what it means. But I can't take out one stone and say 'here is what it means'—it only means something in how it falls. A stone may mean something in one throw, and something completely different in another throw—it depends on how it lies next to other stones, plus the number of all the stones, plus the particular stone it lies next to."

Dominic explained this in a different way. "When the laibon sees the stones, it is like a hunter reading animal tracks. He can see movement and can tell what is happening. We who follow the laibon know how to read the stones a bit, but only the laibon knows what will happen."

Lonyoki's nkidong gourd contained more than five hundred objects including polished pebbles, glass marbles, seeds, cowry shells, teeth, horns, pieces made from leather and bone, and metal objects including coins and bullets. There was even a toy metal car from a Monopoly game. Many of these pieces had explicit meanings that were easily recognizable—two leather rings tied together meant twins; a glass thermometer meant hospital; a lion's tooth meant the presence of a lion; a brass bullet shell showed enemies and the possibility of a raid. Most important were the stones that signified sorcery: a red glass ball meant sorcery against humans; a ring of cow-tail hair wrapped in leather signified sorcery against livestock. Sorcery acts could be specific: the large seed of the se'eki tree revealed that someone had died or was about to die; a piece of a simanderi tree branch appeared if a murder was involved; and particular stones indicated death by fire or drowning.

Particularly treasured by Lonyoki were five highly polished black and white stones. "These come from an ostrich's stomach and were given to me by my father," he said. The stones had acquired their shiny patina from tumbling inside the ostrich's sand-filled gut. They did not mean anything in themselves but acquired significance when they appeared in relation to other stones. Lonyoki said the colored marbles in his gourd had specific meanings when they appeared in pairs, such as red and yellow or white and black. He told me that the Maasai laibons only used polished stones in their gourds, while he used many different kinds of objects. "Sometimes, I dream of a particular object for my gourd and look for it to use," he said.

In addition to the specific type of stone thrown, the *number* of stones that were cast had specific meanings. Each digit from zero to nine had a name and meaning. For example, if several throws added up to thirty-two objects, two was the meaningful number, holding the same value as two, twelve, twenty-two, and so forth. Much attention in the divination ritual was paid to counting the objects, and the laibon often had the participants help in their count. Numbers had the following meanings:

0—Nothing (*me-ata*)—a negative response, can also mean evil
1—The ear (*n-kiok*)—news, information
2—The leg (*n-keju*)—journeys, someone visits
3—Cattle stick (*e-seti*)—cattle herding, going and coming
4—Strength (*n-golon*)—good fortune, also a journey
5—Preparing—for a journey, work
6—Meeting (*n-kiguana*)—an important discussion or argument
7—Meat (*n-kiri*)—ritual feast or reconciliation
8—Peace, laughter (*n-kueni*)—peace, safety, joy
9—Danger (*bata*)—sorcery, the need for *ntasim*

Many times during a divination session Lonyoki would periodically make statements whose truth was difficult to verify. Lonyoki said, "I see a fight over the wedding ox," to which the first wife replied, "I can't remember." Lengidi, the husband, responded, "I heard no quarrel that day. After I killed the ox, I left the slaughter site."

But people are more likely to remember the predictions that came true than the ones that did not. Moreover, Lonyoki often said, "These stones sometimes lie. Don't lie to me! Tell me the truth!" Sometimes the laibon knew the personal situation of his clients, sometimes not. During the *nkidong* for Lengidi, for example, Lonyoki had explicitly mentioned Lengidi's two wives and the deceased twins. Other "facts" might not be specific to a particular household but could very well be true for the larger community. Often Lonyoki saw events that had nothing to do with the particular problem at hand. "I see that the blacksmiths will come together. There will be a pregnant girl and they will try to abort the baby and the girl will die." These statements all reflected realistic possibilities.

Ntasim for Lengidi

A divination informed the laibon about threats or actions that had been directed to his client and also revealed the type of protective medicine that was needed to ward off the sorcery. That evening, after the meeting with Lengidi and his wives, Lonyoki returned to Lengidi's house; inside were Lengidi, his two wives, his sister, and his sister's husband. As requested by Lonyoki, Lengidi had brought tail hairs cut from twenty-seven cattle.

On a blue cloth placed in front of him, Lonyoki laid out his *ntasim* paraphernalia—the large white half shell in which he mixed the *ntasim* powders, two large tiger shell cowries filled with *ntasim*, and the black and white stones. All of these items were encircled by the lion skin cord and were called *l-maneta* (the tying ones).

Lonyoki took the hairs from Lengidi's twenty-seven cattle and divided them into eighty-one separate strands, which he then placed into nine separate groups. He soaked each group in a solution of yellow and red *ntasim* mixed with milk and honey, and formed each into small rings bounded by a leather strip. The nine rings were presented to all the assembled adults in the house to tie on their neck beads or to place on their personal milk gourds and containers.

To Lengidi, Lonyoki said, "Never give away these cattle whose hair you cut, although you may continue to milk them or slaughter them for the *l-mugit* [age-set rites]. Do not bleed any of these cattle for four days." To the women, he said, "Do not borrow or lend any of your hearth fire for four days." These prohibitions were meant to enhance the strength of the cattle hair amulets.

When the *ntasim* amulets were completed, the laibon and Lengidi went outside to prepare a ritual fire (*ntasim laisar*, "of the burning") to protect the man's cattle. Lonyoki placed two cut branches of the *l-seki* tree across the path of the enclosure's thorn branch gateway for the cattle to walk over. Outside of the manyatta, he prepared a fire with branches of four sacred trees, *l-tepes*, *silipani*, *sucha*, and *larasoro*, on which he sprinkled *ntasim* powders. The fire was quite large, and we men all stood around until the fire had burned down. The *ntasim* ritual was complete; later Lengidi would pay the laibon one heifer cow for his services.

That evening, as I wrote up my notes, I took some time to think about the *ntasim* ritual I had just witnessed and its abundance of symbolic elements. The first concerned purification. Lonyoki mixed *ntasim* with milk—an important symbol signifying the life and future of the manyatta, its people, and its livestock—and with honey—a symbol of fertility and longevity.

He prohibited the tapping of cattle blood for four days and prepared a ritual fire using four species of sacred trees. All of these actions were intended to purify the house, family, and livestock and prevent them from future sorcery attacks. These were symbols that all Samburu acknowledged and recognized. But Lonyoki also introduced his own particular symbolism to the process, particularly the meaning inherent in his *ntasim*. Immediately I could see that he concentrated both on color categories and on numerical combinations.

The basis of Lonyoki's *ntasim* medicines were the ground roots of two plants—"yellow" *l-paramunyo* (*Toddalia asiatica*) and "black" *l-kukulai* (*Rhamnus staddo*). When burnt, *l-paramunyo* was sweet smelling while *l-kukulai*, its opposite, was pungent and bitter. Mixed together, they harnessed powerful spiritual forces, and they were used in nearly all of Lonyoki's *ntasim*, to which he also would add other substances for specific purposes. For women, he used red-colored scrapings from the inner bark of the fig tree (*l-reteti*), a powerful symbol of menstrual blood; for warriors he used white chalk representing semen, strength, and purity; for elders he mixed yellow *ntasim* with tobacco; for women or children he often mixed in honey. *Ntasim* medicines could be applied to one's body as a paste, ingested, snorted as snuff, or worn inside leather bags as amulets; in all cases, the *ntasim* was worn for protection. Lonyoki wore a dozen *ntasim* amulets around his neck made from dik-dik horn and large crocodile teeth. In Lonyoki's words, *ntasim* "tied" a protective barrier around an individual, making him or her impervious to sorcery.

The numerology used by Lonyoki in reading the divination stones and preparing *ntasim* was also significant. Twenty-seven (the number of cattle from which hairs had been harvested), eighty-one (the number of pieces that resulted from their division into three parts each), and nine (the number of amulets made from those pieces) are all odd numbers divisible by three, with the number nine the most important. The number three was associated directly with the laibon; I believe that it served to distinguish him and his practices from the more commonplace social rituals of elders and clanship that typically were associated with even numbers, particularly the number four. Prayers of the elders were repeated two or four times ("May God grant you children—*Nkai*! May God grant you children—*Nkai*!"), ritual fires contained four types of wood, rites of community like *soriu* were held on the fourth, eighth, or fourteenth (full moon) day of the month, and so on. Even numbers, in this way, represented the moral order of Samburu society, whereas odd numbers represented supernatural power. In Samburu, one did not journey on the fifth day of the week (Wednesday) or hold life-passage rituals (birthing ceremonies, circumcisions, marriages, funerals) on odd-numbered days of the month. By "owning" the numbers three and nine, the laibon demonstrated his ability to manipulate and control these dangerous forces, a capacity that he alone possessed.

Thinking about Sorcery

The Samburu I knew did not seem overly concerned with sorcery; they certainly did not attribute every misfortune to supernatural causes. Common health problems including malaria, chest colds, or bone fractures were said to be due to "God alone," meaning they just happened and were natural occurrences. But misfortunes involving pregnancy or childbirth, or unusual deaths such as those caused by drowning, fire, or animal attacks, were almost always attributed to sorcery. As Dominic said, "Some people hate; they have bitterness in their heart."

This was an interesting way to view the world, albeit a paranoid one. While one's community—family members, friends, and neighbors—helped nurture and protect you, there also were some individuals who wished you harm. Formerly, anthropologists working in Africa distinguished sorcery from witchcraft, where sorcery involved the use of substances or incantations, while witchcraft was an innate ability possessed by an individual who could release destructive power toward an adversary. These days the words are used interchangeably by anthropologists, and to Samburu they both imply a mystical power used by humans to harm you. Sometimes a witch wasn't even human, but rather a malicious spirit posing as a human who could harm you simply by fixing you with an "evil eye." Samburu acknowledged that there were witches (lairuponi), but they were more likely to fear an ordinary person they personally knew who had managed to acquire sorcery poisons. These individuals either knew how to make these substances themselves or, more often, bought these substances from sorcerers who knew how to make them. These substances could be placed in food or on a stick thrown into a doorway or animal enclosure. Laibons were one source of sorcery poisons, but so were specialists from Maasai, Kamba, or Swahili societies.

Beliefs in sorcery were embedded in the Samburu worldview, in which spirituality was central to Samburu life. A creator spirit (Nkai) formed the world; she (it is a feminine word) was all-powerful and was appealed to regularly in large community rituals, including formal prayers for blessings, rain, and fertility. Clans and lineages also had guardian spirits; if not exactly ancestors, as in some other African cultures, then at least a shared idea of the spiritual integrity of the kin group. Certain families from Rendille, the laisi, commanded particularly strong blessings and curses. Curses from clan elders had to have a moral justification to be effective. Clan elders could threaten to curse warriors if they misbehaved and violated social norms. But the spirit world in itself was not benign, and certain individuals could harness these forces for the immoral purpose of destruction and injury.

"Why are my babies dying and no one else's are? Why do my cattle have *lodua* (rinderpest) when my neighbor's herds are healthy?" a Samburu woman or man might ask. If they suspected sorcery, they needed to consult a laibon to see if this was true and, if so, to obtain *ntasim* medicines to protect themselves.

Anthropologists have explained sorcery beliefs in a variety of ways. One view is that they serve as a pressure valve for social tensions in small-scale societies that lack formal courts and institutionalized means to resolve conflict. Others have said that sorcery functions like other religious beliefs to "explain unusual events or the inexplicable mysteries of life," providing both intellectual explanations and psychological soothing to overcome grief and fear. And sorcery accusations help keep the community together by driving out, and sometimes killing, individuals who disrupt the social order.

There is of course another explanation: that sorcery is real. Anthropologists are, on the whole, an agnostic and skeptical bunch. Many prefer to hold our opinions about the existence or nonexistence of the spiritual world to ourselves, confining our role to transcribing and translating cultural ideas and beliefs without imposing our own judgments. But there were a few anthropologists who came to accept beliefs in the spirit world held by the people they studied. Michael Harner, an anthropologist who studied the Jivaro Indians of the upper Amazon, shared in their ritual use of a hallucinogenic plant (*ayahuasca*) and ultimately become a shaman himself. Leaving his career in academic anthropology, he established the Foundation for Shamanic Studies, which continues to teach shamanistic practices to interested students. A review for the *Shaman's Drum Journal*, published by Harner's foundation, critiqued a book edited by Michael Winkelman and Philip Peek called *Divination and Healing: Potent Vision* (which includes a chapter from me on Samburu laibons) and asked:

> Why do some Western academics seem so recalcitrant when it comes to accepting the existence of spirits? Why—if they claim to treat other cultures respectfully—can't they accept the validity of those culture's central beliefs? Could it be that taking seriously those beliefs would threaten the comfort they find in their own culturalbelief system—that of scientific materialism?

An interesting thought. But, in truth, as much as I respected Lonyoki and Dominic and the people of Lukumai, I could no more accept the existence of sorcery and spirits than I could the Judeo-Christian notion of "God the Creator" or an afterlife in heaven—what George Carlin calls the "invisible man" theory. Some of my American friends were disappointed to learn this, suggesting that I had the opportunity to witness sacred and spiritual forces directly and refused to see these. And yet, I did see certain things in Kenya for which I really did not have satisfactory scientific explanations.

A Meeting of Laibons

We stayed a total of ten days in Langata, during which Lonyoki performed a dozen divination and *ntasim* rituals. Dominic missed being at home and was ready to return to Lukumai; I was fine as long as I was with my two friends. Lonyoki was still hoping that his father would return with us, although that did not happen. But I also knew that Lonyoki was worried about his laibon rival, Lobata, and how he was going to deal with him. At the end of our stay, Lonyoki received a message telling us that Lokili, Lonyoki's older cousin, was in Laisamis and wanted to see him. I suspected this was not an accident but was designed to be a meeting of laibons.

We packed up the Land Rover for our journey home. Lengidi had come out to say good-bye. He said to me, "If it wasn't for Lonyoki, you would see a very different man today. This man has saved my family and property. I thank God that you brought Lonyoki to our community. Go with God's blessings."

As usual, Dominic did not return empty-handed. He bought several bundles of sisal fiber to give to his wives to make roof mats, and we tied these up on the roof of the Land Rover. As we were getting ready to leave, one of Dominic's relatives appeared with a large white goat, and Dominic tied it up in the back of the vehicle. I could just imagine the urine and pellets that would be there when we arrived home.

We drove off to Laisamis to meet with the laibon Lokili. Laisamis was a dusty and hot town on the main road from Marsabit to Isiolo, consisting of a few shops and several dozen houses. Across the road was the Catholic mission, with a large church, hospital, and elementary school. We drove into the town section and learned that Lokili was waiting in a restaurant nearby. Perhaps restaurant is too dignified a term. It was a small Somali establishment, one room with a concrete floor and five or six bare wooden tables and chairs with a separate kitchen out back. It served tea, *mandazi* (fried dough), and, of course, my favorite goat-and-potato stew. A few people glanced at us as we entered, but they did not stare.

We were a group of men that included a young *mzungu* they had possibly seen before, a short older Samburu wearing a green robe with a necklace of crocodile teeth and dik-dik horns, and a thin Ariaal elder with a bald head and long earlobes. But the town was full of odd characters—Samburu warriors with their red braided hair and spears, a few Boran elders in their white turbans, and Somali shopkeepers wearing checkered cloth *shukas* around their waists, Western shirts, and embroidered *kefir* hats.

In the back of the restaurant sat Lokili, a large man with a serious demeanor. He was wearing a long green cloth, a black army beret, and a blue beaded necklace with dik-dik horns like the one worn by Lonyoki and myself. So this was the famous sorcerer, I thought. Lokili rose to greet us, shaking my hand formally and saying, "Ah, you are the white Lonyoki I have heard about. Welcome, kinsman." He greeted Lonyoki and Dominic pleasantly and exchanged news about their villages. Lokili lived near Marsabit town in one of his daughters' houses. She was married to a policeman and Lokili had arrived here in a police truck.

Lokili spoke quietly. I could not understand all of the Samburu phrases, but I got the gist of it. They were speaking about Lobata. Lokili said, "Lobata is causing mischief and people are growing wary of him. Some are fearing that he is 'looking far' in the district."

Lonyoki replied, "I am not afraid of this man; my *ntasim* protects me from any harm Lobata could do."

Lokili smiled and said, "We have no need to fear Lobata." And then Lokili turned to me, as if he knew I was studying the laibons. He said, "You know, Lobata is not really from a laibon family. He was nursed as a baby by one of our aunts after his mother was given *ntasim* to help her have a baby. That is how he got his powers. But the true laibons are descended from the Kidong'oi clan in Maasai. All of our family are descended from Charrar, our grandfather, who came from Laikipiak Maasai. Lobata is not really one of us."

I used this opportunity to interview Lokili. He answered my questions straightforwardly and, I believe, truthfully. I began by asking him if he would tell me how he became a laibon.

"When I was a child," he began, "I would dream powerful dreams. My father, Samanga, would ask 'What did you dream about?' each morning. My father was the oldest of four brothers, all born to Charrar, who came here from Laikipiak Maasai. The other brothers were Ngaldaiya, Kaldeya, and Longojine, the father of Lonyoki. Ngaldaiya was the strongest of them all; he was the strongest laibon outside of Charrar. But the British took him away to prison, where he died."

I had heard that Lonyoki's uncle had been arrested in the 1930s for his alleged involvement in the murder of a white ranch manager, Theodore Powys, committed by Samburu warriors. The warriors were acquitted for lack of evidence, but Ngaldaiya was deported to the Kenyan coast, never to return.

Lokili continued, "I learned everything I know from Ngaldaiya; he was more of a father to me than Samanga was. We all lived in the same manyatta near Maralal. It was Ngaldaiya who gave me the *nkidong* divination gourd, who taught me *ntasim* medicines, who taught me *nkurupore* sorcery. Ngaldaiya was the most powerful laibon then, and I am the most powerful laibon now."

With that, Lokili stood up and took Lonyoki by the hand and led him out of the restaurant to a *naisho* house (local bar). I feared that Lonyoki and Lokili were going to drink and that we would be there for hours. I suspected they were going to discuss Lobata and come up with a plan to deal with him. I believe Lokili had brought actual *nkurupore* powders to give to Lonyoki to use on their nemesis.

Dominic and I remained in the restaurant, drinking our third cup of tea, prepared the Somali way with hot milk, cloves, cinnamon, and sugar. I asked Dominic about Lobata; I wanted to understand this tension.

"Soritari clan is not bad, only Lobata is bad. He's crazy. The elders of Soritari would like him to go away, but they cannot do anything about it. He causes trouble wherever he goes. Before Lonyoki came, our village was in great danger. Since Lonyoki joined us, not one bad thing has happened to us. Not one person has died, no warrior slain, no cattle or camels stolen."

We finished our tea and decided to go find Lonyoki and extricate him from the bar and Lokili. We drove up to the bar—really just a house where women made home brew—maize beer—and saw Lonyoki and Lokili standing outside. Lonyoki got into the car and nodded good-bye to Lokili. The old man came around to my window and with a large smile gave me his hand to shake. "It was good to meet you, kinsman," he said. "I know we will meet again."

We drove away and onto the small road that led to Lukumai. After a few miles we came upon a smaller track into the mountains. Lonyoki commanded, "Turn here, we need to find Lobata's *nkang*."

I was growing anxious about this meeting; I worried there might be a physical confrontation. Lonyoki had grown increasingly quiet during the journey from Laisamis, and I could feel a mounting tension. I asked the laibon, "How long have you known Lobata?"

Lonyoki replied, "Lobata and I lived in the same manyatta as children, where my cousin Lokili lived in Samburu. Lobata was older than me; he is a Mekuri [age-set], the same as Lokili. He always thought he was superior to me; we quarreled and competed for my father's attention and blessings. I told you that Longojine did not think that I was his son and he favored Lobata. He gave his *nkidong* gourd to Lobata and not to me, although later he gave me my own gourd."

(What was it between laibon fathers and sons? I wondered.)

"Lobata became an active laibon among Ariaal and Samburu living here in Marsabit District. It was his medicine that was used to defend Lukumai and the other manyattas from the big *shifta* attack at Lorrien [as described by Dominic in his explanation of the ghostly voices I had heard in the desert]. But when I moved here from Samburu a few years ago, a rivalry developed between us over who would be the *ol oiboni kitok* [the greater laibon] in this region. Lobata became *kagol* [meaning strong but also fierce]; he stopped doing good and increasingly did bad things." (That is, he became more involved in sorcery than in healing.) Lonyoki did not say why he avoided his cousin Lokili in Marsabit, but I could see there was a rivalry between these two men as contentious as the one between Lonyoki and Lobata. These laibons seemed to have carved out separate niches for themselves—Lokili in the highlands of Marsabit Mountain, Lobata near Laisamis town, and Lonyoki along the base of the Ndoto Mountains.

We finally reached a small manyatta where Lobata lived. A tall man, robust and talkative, came out to greet us; it was Lobata. He had only one good eye; the other was gray and opaque, either from an injury or trachoma. Like Lonyoki and Lokili, he wore a green cloth and black beret (he also wore the blue bead that Lonyoki wore). He invited us to sit on a leather skin that his wife brought out and placed next to the house. I presented her with some tea and sugar; she smiled and thanked me and went back inside the house to prepare it.

Lobata and Lonyoki sat next to each other, their backs against the curved wall of the house. About a half dozen elders from this village, as well as Dominic and me, sat in a semicircle in front of them. Lobata laughed loudly and often, encouraging others to laugh with him. He carried himself with authority and power, like a local headman.

After drinking some tea, Lonyoki announced to Lobata, "I have dreamed of a great illness. Do you know of this disease? Will it enter the right or left side? You tell me now, who between us two will prevent this disease?"

Lobata laughed at Lonyoki's question but did not answer. This was Lonyoki's way of asserting his superiority, I imagined. Lonyoki continued, flicking his fingers in the air and lecturing to all the elders assembled around him, "There is a terrible disease that will enter our lungs. I have seen seven things, including a war. What have you seen? I know each of us thinks we are better than the other; let us see who will stop this disease."

Lobata laughed loudly, pretending it was a good joke. But another elder spoke up and said, "Let us not talk about such things here; let's say *serian* [peace and good health]."

All the men became serious—Lonyoki stopped boasting and Lobata stopped laughing, and all said "*Ey, serian.*"

Lobata set out a blue cloth and threw his *nkidong*. It was a short divination, but I could see Lonyoki and Lobata looking very carefully at the objects thrown out. The tension could have been cut with a knife. After the third throw, Lonyoki widened his eyes and Lobata took a deep breath. Both a red ball and a lion's tooth had appeared. Neither said a word.

Lobata suddenly ended the *nkidong* and put the stones back in his gourd. He did not look at Lonyoki, but folded up his blue cloth and, without saying a word, rose and went into his house. Lonyoki stood up and with anger in his voice, shouted, "Where are you going? To get your *nkuruporen* to curse me?"

Dominic tried to calm Lonyoki down, holding him by the arm.

"*Tigerai murrata*" (calm yourself, age-mate), he said, "let us leave this place."

But Lonyoki would not be placated. He shouted at Lobata's house, "You can hide in that house, but my head can see everything, near and far away. You have been revealed, do you hear me? You have been revealed!"

With that, Lonyoki allowed himself to be taken to the car and we drove away. I had never seen elders in Samburu talk this way to each other. Normally people tried to keep their voices down and their emotions under control; they feared that an angry person was capable of both mystical and physical harm. I had been a witness to a great battle going on between these two laibons, carried out in a spiritual space separate from the world we ordinary mortals moved in. I had watched closely during the divination interchange to see if either laibon had tried to press *nkurupore* powders on the other, but I saw nothing. But now, in retrospect, I realized that both men had been flicking their fingers at each other as they talked. I wondered, did they have sorcery powders under their fingernails? Were they assaulting each other while we sat and watched?

Lonyoki said thoughtfully, "Laibons can do great mischief. They can use their medicines to help, or they can use their medicines to harm. Lobata used to be a very good laibon, but something happened that must have turned his heart black. Now he just makes *nkuruporen* and tries to harm people."

I feared we had not seen the last of Lobata. We drove on in silence, each of us lost in our own thoughts. I realized on this trip that sorcery was the stock and trade of laibons—only laibons could detect its presence, and only laibons could combat and prevent sorcery attacks. But then again, only laibons could make sorcery substances. A Maasai elder had remarked to the anthropologist Paul Spencer, "If we did not have *Lo'onkidIng'i* [the clan of laibons], we would not need *Lo'onkidong'i*."

Out of the blue I asked Lonyoki, "Did you ever wish you weren't a laibon?"

"*Ey*," said Lonyoki. "When I lived in Barsaloi as a young married man, I stopped being a laibon; I just carried on with running my shop."

"Why did you stop?" I asked.

Lonyoki replied, "It made me too sad to be asked by someone what would happen in their future, when I knew that they were going to die or face some other problem. It was terrible, because there was nothing I could do about it. I felt like I carried a curse, the curse of prophesy, and I could no longer be a laibon."

Lonyoki continued, "In any case, I had lost my powers. I had lost my powers at that time, because I had slept with a woman who had had an abortion. This is something that a laibon can never do, and it took my powers away. To become a laibon, as a boy or even a circumcised *l-murrani*, a laibon can never have sex or marry an impregnated girl. If you do that, you will never be able to give *ntasim*. Even if you are grown and you sleep with another woman, she must never have been aborted."

"How did you become a laibon again after losing your powers?" I asked.

"I needed to be purified and made a whole laibon again," he said. "So I went to Maasailand to visit their laibons called Lembatian [the 'family of Mbatian,' the famous laibon of the nineteenth century]. They made me stand in a burning house to regain my powers."

"A burning house?" I asked.

"*Ey*," said Lonyoki. "The laibons had built a very small house with grass on a stick frame, way out in the bush [*awulo*] away from settlement. I was told to go inside and take off all my clothes. They said, 'Remove everything you are wearing—beads, shoes, *ntasim*—and leave them there.' They had instructed me to bring a new *nanga* cloth, new shoes, and new beads, which were placed outside the house. I had also brought my *nkidong* gourd, which I placed in the house.

"This house had two small openings; you went through one side and out the other. They lit a fire completely around the house and waited until the whole house was burning, then I had to run out. Many people were watching, all the elders from the Lembatian clan. When I left this house, naked and trembling, I was given a new *nkidong*, new clothes, new medicine beads. All the elders prayed and asked blessings [*Nkai, Nkai!*]. After the burning, I wore a new green *nanga*, new shoes, and had new *ntasim* put inside the dik-dik horns. They gave me the blue beads I wear around my neck, and the red ball earrings [something worn by Maasai but not Samburu].

"After the *laisar* burning I was purified. I was reinvigorated with the powers to see the future and make *ntasim* medicines. With my new *nkidong* gourd and *ntasim* medicines, I returned to my father's homestead in Langata. I never returned to Barsaloi."

I Am Cursed

People were glad to see us back in Lukumai, and my life returned to its routine of conducting interviews, censusing, tape recording, and photographing people in and around the manyatta. But, as the Samburu proverb says, "The wood in the wood pile laughs at the one in the fire." One night, while I was deep asleep, I was awakened by a noise of somebody, or something, bumping around inside my house. I reached for my flashlight and shone it around until I saw the back of a man who was bent over the steel box in which I kept items such as sugar, tobacco, and batteries. It was Meron, a tobacco addict who was always pestering me for chewing tobacco. Meron was a *lais* (pl. *laisi*), a member of a certain family who had strong blessings and curses because of a special relationship to God. Most *laisi* didn't try to abuse their powers, preferring to use them for the benefit of the community by leading prayers at community rituals.

But Meron was not that sort of *lais*. He was struggling with the catch on the box.

"What are you doing?" I demanded angrily. My initial fear had turned to annoyance at being awakened.

"*Cho'oke l-kambau!*" (Give me tobacco!) Meron turned and demanded of me.

I had never refused Meron's requests for tobacco, or those of any other elder, but I always gave it to them in public when I could put a pinch or two of *l-kambau* (the nasty hard clumps of tobacco old men liked to chew and women ground up into snuff) in their outstretched palms. Nearly all elders and women would thank me for the small gift and were generally satisfied until the next time I visited them. But not Meron. He would always "tsk-tsk" me for not giving him enough tobacco, smiling and keeping his hand outstretched, even after my second dip into the tobacco bag. I kept a large bag of tobacco in my steel box for social visits and formal interviews, and I should never have let him see where I kept it. Meron was known as the great beggar in the manyatta, always asking for sugar, tea, and particularly tobacco. Meron could get away with this because it was almost impossible to refuse the request of a *lais*, for the same reason that it was hard to refuse the request of a blacksmith—both possessed powerful curses and an ability to endanger someone with their spiritual powers.

Still, I was mightily annoyed at being awakened. "You want tobacco? If you want tobacco, you come and ask me for tobacco. You don't come rummaging in my house late at night like a thief!" I yelled.

"*Cho'oke l-kambau*," he repeated, his eyes glaring at me with anger and need.

And then I did something I shouldn't have done. I spoke to Meron as a mother does to an annoying child.

"*Mu tum! Tshombe iye!*" I said, meaning, "You can't have any! Go away!"

"*Mu tum?*" he answered slowly, his eyes growing wide. "You say '*mu tum*' to me?" Then standing fully erect and pointing his finger at me, he declared, "You will never see the sun set tomorrow! You will only see fire!" and stormed out of my house.

The next morning, I went over to Lonyoki's house and told him what happened. "I think I was cursed last night by the *lais* Meron. He told me I wouldn't see the sun set today." I explained about the box and tobacco.

Lonyoki responded with a weary look, "Don't worry about Meron. His curses cannot hurt you, certainly not for refusing him tobacco. Anyway, my *ntasim* protects you from all that."

I soon forgot about the incident and got back to the routine of my fieldwork. A month or so had passed when one day, as I was sitting in a house chatting with Naiseku, we heard wailing and crying from some distance away. "Quick," she said. "Run, Elliot, there's trouble!"

I ran out of the house and joined several other men who were running toward the large rock known as Tunguar, located about three hundred yards from the village. Tunguar was a freestanding rock about forty feet high and one hundred feet long. During and after the rainy season, it held a temporary body of water near its top, in a depression about twenty-five feet long and three feet deep that collected rainwater. I could see several people on top of the boulder. I scrambled to the top and saw four warriors waist deep in the pool, feeling around with their arms.

Fearing that someone had drowned, I jumped into the pool but could feel nothing with my feet. I went underwater and found a small opening deep down on the left side, leading to an underwater crevasse. I surfaced and told the warriors to hold me by my ankles and push me into the hole. "But pull me out when I kick!" I shouted, frightened that I, too, would become stuck in the crevasse.

The warriors did as I asked. I felt around and around and then, finally, felt something soft—a human foot. I grabbed the leg by the ankle and signaled the others to pull me out. I pulled out the body of a young girl; she was about nine years old. Her eyes were gray and half closed, and her tongue was hanging loosely from her mouth. Women were wailing below when they saw me emerge with the body. I placed the girl on her back next to the pool and initiated mouth-to-mouth resuscitation, holding her nose while I forced air into her lungs. I did this for about five minutes. Some water came out of her lungs, but the girl was flaccid and still. She was dead. I continued with the CPR until Usana, who had joined the other elders, pulled me away. "*Taisho* [Stop now], that is enough," he said.

I was devastated. I had never seen a dead person before, let alone tried to save a drowning person. The warriors carried the body down the rock, and I followed, trembling and shaken up. When we reached the bottom of the rock, Lonyoki was there and he put his arm around my shoulder. He said, "There was nothing you could do. Her family was cursed for a long time."

It was then I realized that the girl was the daughter of Meron, the *lais* whom I had refused tobacco.

This seemed to me a terrible way to curse someone—why take the life of an innocent child? I was baffled and upset. I was also considered quite toxic after "breathing in the death" of the girl. No one in Lukumai had seen anyone do this before. The elders took me to a house and forced me to drink a very strong herbal emetic—a medicinal broth that immediately induced vomiting and diarrhea. They kept this up well into the evening, telling me I needed to cleanse my body of the girl's death. I did this until I passed out.

CHAPTER FOUR

The Long Hunger

Jackals follow lions, lions do not follow jackals.

The April rains came but they were not sufficient. The bushes and grass were green for about three weeks, but by May everything was turning brown and yellow. It appeared that the "long hunger" (*lameyu la'ado*) between the spring and fall rains would be lengthy and difficult, and no one knew if the fall rains would even come at all. The cattle were getting thin and their milk yield had nearly stopped; the warriors were waiting impatiently to take them to new pasture. People were living on *posho* (corn meal) bought on credit from the shops in Lenguas. The social scene in Lukumai was disrupted as well. It seemed that everyone was angry with everyone else. Lonyoki was spending more time in Ker'ngera away from the manyatta, visiting the bars, I feared. Dominic, usually calm and even-keeled, was irritable and quarreling with his wife Naiseku. As for me, I was annoyed with everybody. I had been here for nine months now, and I was growing tired of the lack of privacy, the constant requests, and my perpetual anxiety about running out of money and gasoline.

We heard that four Lukumai *l-murran* had been jumped by eight l-Turia warriors while herding cattle. The Lukumai *l-murran* fought back and one of our guys, La'amo, had clubbed an l-Turia with his *rungu*, seriously injuring him. To avoid escalating the fight or bringing in the police, the elders of the two communities came together and forced the warriors to make peace. A fine was paid—four goats from Lukumai to l-Turia—and the two sets of warriors were told to stay away from each other. But hardships seemed to follow.

La'amo, who had injured the l-Turia warrior, began losing goats to *l-pus*, a disease affecting the respiratory system. A lion had attacked one of Lepere's camels, although his son had amazingly driven the lion off. Lukumai's elders discussed the matter at length and suspected that the laibon Lobata was giving *nkuruporen* sorcery to the l-Turia clan to use against us.

This also meant that while Lukumai needed the laibon's presence, they also had to tolerate Lonyoki's increasingly troublesome behavior, particularly when he came home drunk. Although Lonyoki never asked me for money directly (he never requested anything of me except to bring his son and wife from Barsaloi), I still offered him gifts of cash whenever I knew their supplies were running low.

"None of this money will go to *naisho* [literally honey, but also honey wine], I promise," Lonyoki said often enough. He had me figured out pretty well, the liberal *mzungu* with Puritan values who disapproved of his drinking. When Lonyoki once asked me if I had any medicine to help with his chronic liver pains, I told him that the problem was alcohol and that his drinking would kill him one day. He laughed this off, and I knew that he would continue drinking.

Eventually Lonyoki stopped coming home altogether. I learned that he was staying in Ker'ngera with a young woman named Nkarami. She had been married but had deserted (or been thrown out by) her husband and hung around the bars in town seeking money from men.

Unbelievably, Lonyoki brought Nkarami home to move in with him at Lukumai, telling everyone she would be his second wife. Worse still, he parked her in Mo' Lembalen's house. Mother of Lembalen was furious but said nothing, as there was little she could do about it. She often looked beaten down and submissive these days, with a sad and depressed expression about her. Dominic was also angry about this development.

"This woman [Nkarami] is very bad," he told me. "Lonyoki should not have brought her here. But as the saying goes, 'You can't advise a man who is after a woman.' Nkarami asked Lonyoki for his beads [i.e., the beads of a laibon—in other words, to marry him], and Lonyoki refused, so I guess he knows what he is doing."

Nevertheless, Lonyoki announced that he intended to marry Nkarami in Lukumai manyatta, and he set about making plans to hold a ceremony in one week. The elders held a meeting and told Lonyoki, "It is a bad time. There are no cattle here, no sheep, no camels. There is no milk and meat for a *sikukuu* [festival]."

But Lonyoki did not agree: "We can do it! I can get the ox for sacrifice, we can do this!"

Usana, Dominic's older brother, argued with Lonyoki, "No, the elders have met to advise on this. Most of the elders [*payiani*] are out with their herds; there are no girls here, no warriors, just the married women."

Lonyoki had asked Dominic to lend him four hundred shillings for tea and sugar for the wedding feast, but Dominic said he only had two hundred. "You don't have any money," Dominic said, "and I don't have any money, and Elliot doesn't have any money. There is no way you can do this."

Lonyoki was forced to concede. "OK, leave it for now," he said. "We will postpone the wedding." He didn't seem very angry or perturbed, and I wondered how serious he really was about marrying Nkarami; perhaps he was asking for a wedding to assuage her.

Mother of Lembalen bore the burden of Nkarami's company. I never saw Nkarami cook or help her with the house or livestock; she preferred to spend her time preening or making beadwork for herself or her laibon boyfriend. One afternoon, when Nkarami had left to buy goods in Lenguas, Mo' Lembalen took me into her confidence.

"Lock your box up tight, Elliot! She steals, you know. I saw her reaching into my own leather bag where I keep some money, and she took it. I confronted her about it, and she said 'You're crazy, I didn't take anything. You're a crazy old bitch, and that's why your husband is going to marry me.' I don't know what to do," she said with tears in her eyes. "I can't take much more of this."

I had in fact caught Nkarami stealing from my box already. I had come into my house at one point and found her bent over my steel box. "What do you want, Nkarami?" I asked. I never honored her with the term *yeyo*, or mother. I do not hold much malice toward people, and particularly not toward an unfortunate person like Nkarami who had been divorced or chased away by her husband. But she truly was manipulative, deceitful, and hard to like.

"That woman will ruin Lonyoki," Dominic said to me bitterly. "She sees to it that he has *busa'a* [strong drink] all the time, and then when he is not looking or asleep, she tries to steal his money from his purse. That man is blinded by love. But it is not love; it is lust, because she is young and will do what he wants."

Because of Lonyoki, everyone, including me, put up with Nkarami.

Sometimes when Lonyoki drank, he became sentimental and maudlin. One evening when Nkarami was elsewhere, he sat crying in his house with Mother of Lembalen close by. He said he would not marry Nkarami. "I didn't know how bad she is and how good the mother of Lembalen is," he said, leaning over to hug and kiss Mo' Lembalen, who sat still with an uncertain and unbelieving look on her face.

One day Lonyoki received a visit from two elders from Langata, who brought a message from his father, Longojine. The old man wanted his grandson Lembalen to live with him in Langata to herd his goats and donkeys. But Lembalen was in school in Ker'ngera, and by all accounts he was doing well. His school headmaster told me, "It's not every teacher who gets a laibon in his class. One day, you drove here from Baragoi, do you remember that day, Elliot? No one knew you were coming to Ker'ngera. I certainly didn't know. But Lembalen knew. He woke up and said to me, 'Mwalimu [teacher], you have to kill a goat and prepare a meal, because Elliot is coming today.' Kwale! [Truly!]"

I thought it a very progressive move on Lonyoki's part to enroll Lembalen in school, but Lembalen's school days seemed to be coming to an end. Longojine had asked Lonyoki once before to take the boy out of school, but Lonyoki had resisted. Now the old man said he would curse Lonyoki if Lembalen returned to school, and Lonyoki had to comply. As the Samburu proverb goes, "He who has a father is not yet circumcised."

Now Lembalen was going to leave school and enter a very different life, herding goats for his grandfather in Langata. He was smart, focused, and determined, and I really believed he would have gone on to secondary school and even university, and he possibly would have become a Western-trained doctor. He wouldn't be the first Samburu to go to university, but he would be one of a very few in those days.

This was just one more piece of disappointing news that we received. I was becoming irritated and losing my patience at the never-ending stream of requests from people I hardly knew. One man in particular, Lesikeri, seemed insatiable. I heard him approach my house as he called "Hodi?"(Anyone home?) Despite my silence, he came inside and sat by the door. He was eyeing everything greedily—touching the shoes on my feet and my steel box, holding my flashlight, telling me he needed these things.

"Elliot," he asked, his eyes glistening, "will you be going to Nairobi? You know, you are a son of Lukumai clan, even though your father is a Lorukushu; you are really one of us. I need some things. Kaiyo paren [I have a favor to ask]. I need shoes very much. Look at these sandals of mine, they are finished. And a cloth, I need a new cloth. And Elliot, if you go, I need a flashlight, I don't have one." On and on he went, eyeing everything in my house. And yet this particular elder was one of the wealthier men in the community, with at least twenty camels and a large flock of goats and sheep.

I was getting fed up. I went over to Dominic's house to escape. I could see Dominic was also in a bad mood; perhaps Lesikeri had paid him a visit as well. People bothered Dominic a lot because they knew he was my close friend and I always brought tea and sugar for his family. When I entered, Dominic told his wife Naiseku to make some tea. She balked—it was the height of the dry season and there was not much water. The task of fetching water was a huge undertaking—it meant loading up camels or donkeys and trekking twelve miles to the Lenguas wells, and it was always done by women. I told Naiseku, "Please don't bother, I am fine. I don't want any tea right now."

Naiseku lit up and said to Dominic, "You see, he doesn't want any."

Dominic's voice was harsh now. "Then make him some meat" (i.e., heat up some meat from the recent *soriu* goat slaughter).

I stupidly, but honestly, added, "None for me, please, I am very satisfied right now." I was not that hungry and I also knew they had little to share. But I was being insensitive because one should not refuse hospitality when offered.

Again Naiseku argued, "See, Elliot doesn't want any meat now."

Dominic was really angry now. In a low but menacing voice he said, "I want some meat. When I tell you to do something, just do it."

But Naiseku was nonplussed; she was no shrinking violet like Mother of Lembalen. She argued back spiritedly, but by no means in a hostile way, trying to use reason to temper Dominic's irrational and stubborn pride.

"Why should we make something nobody wants to eat?" I could not follow all that she said but I heard words like "drought," "Lenguas," "shops," and "donkeys," and then she detoured into an argument about one of her children, Misilon, who needed money while herding.

I watched Dominic become angrier. I could see that his pride demanded that he give me a gift without expecting anything in return, that he distinguish himself from beggars like Lesikeri. I also knew Dominic was humiliated because his wife was defying him. A man who could not "manage" his wife likely could not manage his livestock well either and would be a man of little consequence. Yet Dominic had married two very strong women, Naiseku and Rendille, both of whom had always stood up to him and had clear compasses about what was necessary and what was not. Dominic had once said, "Rendille is a bad wife; she doesn't do what she is told." But it seemed to me that these two women had an impressive ability to do what needed to be done, even with very few resources. The men provided their wives with very little money to feed their families, and the women could not buy or sell livestock (at least not back then) or earn extra income selling milk, the way women who lived near Lorubai or Marsabit did.

I liked Dominic. I admired his honesty, modesty, and effervescent good nature and high spirits. But he focused a lot of his wound-up energy into get-rich-quick schemes that did not usually pay off, and I could see how disappointed he often became. We had lived together almost a year and I now sensed that Dominic was growing distant from Lonyoki. It occurred to me that he had attached himself to the laibon for the status and power the connection offered him, however small those rewards were. Now Dominic had attached himself to me, and the manyatta saw him as a repository of wealth with a pile of money, tea, and sugar hidden in his house.

As if cued to make this point, Dominic's son Parengi came into the house and said, "The mother of Karmon wants some sugar."

"Tell them *meti* [there isn't any]," Dominic said with finality.

"Is that the wife of Lesikeri?" I asked. "That man was just at my house. He is always begging despite his wealth. His wife came to my house twice this morning, begging. I gave her a little sugar, and when she came back again, I told her, 'Don't come back here again. *Mikin togor!*' [Don't annoy me!]"

Dominic laughed at my Samburu idiom. But quietly, he said, "You know, that family is a bit crazy [*madai*, foolish]; they don't know any better. Rendille people only know 'i-yau' [bring me], not 'ng'o-na' [here, take this]."

But I think Dominic was gently admonishing me not to be too critical of the begging. This was a way of life here; people constantly asking favors of each other. Goods like tea and sugar were in constant circulation, and people relied on their neighbors to get through hard times. I was the getting the feeling that what he really wanted to say was, "You have a ton of stuff compared to us, Elliot. You will never truly go hungry. So what does it matter if someone begs a little sugar or tobacco off of you?"

Dominic went on, "The people who make me angry are the ones who should know better, not Lesikeri. Today I asked the mother of Senti to take the bags of *posho* [corn flour] to Rendille [Dominic's second wife now living in Lenguas with their small stock], as the woman was going there anyway to fetch water on the camels. 'Maiyo,' she told me, 'I don't want to do it.'

"So I asked the old widow of Losapo to bring the bags to them, but she said, 'I don't want to do it.' Bastards! A while ago, the mother of Senti came to me and asked me for money: 'I have no food for my children, my husband is away.' So I gave her some money. And the old widow Losapo came to me for money, and I gave her some. Three shillings for *posho*. And the mother of Senti five shillings. One small favor, I ask, take the bags to Lenguas. Small bags, not even ten shillings of flour. And they won't do it. That's why Lolcheni is coming here tomorrow with a donkey, to get his food and bring some to my wife. They all come to me, everybody in the manyatta, every day, just like they all come to you. 'Give me tea, give me *posho*, give me money,'" he said in a high voice, chuckling now that he had vented his spleen.

Shadows on the Land

The drought that was scorching northern Kenya in the mid-1970s was not a local event, but part of a much larger desiccation extending from Senegal clear across the Sahel region (Niger, Mali, Chad, Sudan); it was known as the Sahelian Drought. Droughts had been appearing with increasing frequency and severity in Africa since 1968. Before then East Africa had had higher-than-average rainfall. Old man Usana once chuckled, "I wish the British were still ruling Kenya. When I was a child, the grass was this high!" he said, raising his hand to his mid-chest. The grass probably was indeed that high, though I doubt it was due to the British.

World attention was beginning to focus on Africa's climate problems. In the 1970s, the international Conference on Desertification was held to launch the new United Nations Environment Program (UNEP), whose headquarters were in Nairobi. One of their first projects was to launch the Integrated Project in Arid Land (IPAL) sponsored by UNESCO's Man and the Biosphere Programme. IPAL's agenda was to conduct environmental research in Marsabit District to understand "why the Sahara Desert was moving south," in the words of its first director, a British wildlife biologist. I attended a meeting of UNESCO (as it was called by Ariaal) held on top of Mount Kulal, a desolate and cold location where the African Inland Mission had its northern Kenya headquarters. This seemed like an odd place to study desertification as no Africans lived up there (unless they worked for UNESCO or the AIM) and it was far from the pastoralists living in the desert below. Nevertheless, the well-funded UNESCO built prefab housing and offices for their expatriate experts (i.e., white people) who regularly flew in from Nairobi. Plant, veterinary, and wildlife biologists made up the core of the research team, although they did invite a few anthropologists and historians, including me, to attend their opening meeting on Mount Kulal. But I had the impression they did not really want to hear what we had to say.

"Can't these nomads see this is not cattle country!" declared the director at the meeting. He was convinced that pastoral overgrazing was the principal cause of desertification, that the Rendille and other herders were following age-old and irrational practices of maximizing their livestock herds at the expense of rangeland conservation. He showed aerial photographs that supposedly pointed to the decline in vegetation cover, although they were in fact views of the lowland towns of Naiborr and Kargi, which had been created by the Catholic Diocese to distribute famine relief foods. Several of us tried to argue against him. Neal Sobania, a historian, talked about how traditional pastoral practices actually conserved environmental resources through no-madism and livestock mobility, but these movements were severely restricted by "tribal boundaries" imposed by colonial rule. Jürgen Schwartz, a camel biologist, described the natural adaptation of camels to desert environments, calling them superb converters of patchy and scarce resources into a steady food supply for their herders. And I protested the vilification of human herd-ers as the agents of environmental degradation. I argued that the increased population densities were caused by political and economic factors that en-couraged former nomads to settle, and I disputed the director's Malthusian assumptions that high birth rates were a threat to the environment, a popular view then as now. As Jürgen Schwartz remarked, "The desert is moving south because the desert is moving south." This meeting took place long before ideas about global warming were widely disseminated.

Still, the Kenyan government liked the German-funded UNESCO proj-ect, in no small part because of the money it brought into the district and country. The UNESCO-IPAL director had concluded that the pastoralists needed to reduce their herd sizes to save the environment, but he had few proposals about how to achieve this. In time, the British director was re-placed by a Kenyan biologist who proceeded to develop water points and livestock auctions to reduce livestock numbers in Marsabit. Ten years later the UNESCO-IPAL program ended, leaving little in its wake for the Ariaal or Rendille save a few water catchment areas made of stone to collect rain runoff. But UNESCO did open the door to several government offices and nongovernment organizations (NGOs) that remained to monitor "desert encroachment."

I asked elders at Lukumai about the impact UNESCO-IPAL had had on their lives. Usana replied, "What UNESCO? They are like shadows on the land. You see them fly over us, or sometimes drive their cars across the desert. But they never stop for us. They never ask us, 'What is good for the Rendille?' They buy our goats and cattle at very low prices, then drive them to Nanyuki or Nairobi and sell them for much more money. But they do nothing for us, so don't speak to me of UNESCO. That is all I have to say."

For my own part, I was becoming increasingly disgusted at what the in-ternational community (meaning the Western powers) was doing to Kenya, as well as to the rest of Africa. Yes, colonial rule had ended for most African countries in the 1960s. But I could see that European, American, and Japanese corporations and interests were all over the place, from Barclays Bank and American Express to Toyota and Motorola. In Nairobi there were billboards advertising Nescafé instant coffee sipped by a young professional African couple and selling for four times the cost of local coffee beans. The members of the growing middle class were taught to value manufactured goods imported from overseas, even if the raw materials originated in the hills behind Nairobi. Not just imported manufactured products, but also the so-called development assistance provided by wealthy donor countries seemed to benefit the donors more than the poor countries they were supposedly helping. For example, the United States government provided loans for the Kenyatta Hospital in Nairobi to purchase a million-dollar CAT scan machine, manufactured by General Electric in the United States. While CAT scans were important, they served only a small number of people, yet Kenya had a much greater need for primary health care, which was largely neglected.

And it wasn't just the United States who behaved this way. The French won a bid to smooth out the Marsabit road. God knows it was needed, but not surprisingly all the technicians, engineers, heavy equipment, and vehicles were French. The Germans, British, Italians, Canadians, and Japanese were no better. To be fair, the Soviet Union was exerting its influence on its post-1975 client states, including Ethiopia, Angola, and Mozambique, and China had built a large railroad in Tanzania to gain influence.

I was becoming politically radicalized as a result of living among poor people in a developing country. I began to read and think more about global poverty, and I listened to arguments that claimed it was not caused by any internal deficiencies of African countries (or Latin American or Asian countries), but by the exploitative activities of capitalist countries of the North and West. Radical critics had labeled these policies "neocolonial" and "underdevelopment," while Western capital and businesses that dominated the development of the poorer countries after European colonization had ended called it "modernization."

This became more widely apparent years later with the development of the General Agreement of Trade and Tariffs (GATT) and the World Trade Organization (WTO), which, along with the loan policies of the World Bank and International Monetary Fund, sought to integrate all economies into a single globalized market. While globalization advocates talk today about a "tide that lifts all boats," these policies for the most part benefit the developed countries more than the poor countries they were aimed at. Most African countries in the 1970s depended on one or two crops or minerals such as coffee, cotton, copper, or gold to provide all their foreign income revenue. Today, these products are still important but have been joined by other valuable exports—coltan (for mobile phones), oil, or the beauty of the land itself for tourism dollars—yet the exploitative relationship remains. And African states have increasingly come to rely on foreign aid, including from the World Bank, to keep their governments going.

At that time I was becoming convinced that African countries needed socialist revolutions like those that had occurred in China, Vietnam, and Cuba in the 1950s and 1960s. In the 1970s, the African continent saw armed liberation struggles in Mozambique, Angola, and Guinea Bissau against Portuguese colonial rule, and in Zimbabwe and South Africa against white settler regimes.

But how could this obscure corner of northern Kenya occupied by nomadic pastoralists participate in such a struggle? I didn't know the answer, but I was convinced that real development would occur only at the hands of people like those in Lukumai and countless other poor communities in African countries. Increasingly, I sought out books on revolution and socialism in the Nairobi bookstores, finding classics like Edgar Snow's *Red Star over China* and Frances Fitzgerald's *Fire in the Lake*, a history of the Vietnam War, as well as critical histories of Kenya including the memoirs of Mau Mau fighters. But, as always, the day-to-day tasks of survival, logistics, and fieldwork occupied most of my time.

Where to Move the Manyatta?

By July, Lonyoki's mistress, Nkarami, had built her own house next to Mother of Lembalen, and Lonyoki spent nearly all of his time there. I expressed my dismay to Dominic.

Dominic said, "Lonyoki can be a foolish person, especially when he drinks. It is easy to be led by a beautiful woman. But Lonyoki is not a bad person. His *ntasim* is beautiful [*ke-sidai ntasimi lenye*]."

Dominic was always pragmatic. He weighed choices and acted in the direction of the general good. And he genuinely believed in Lonyoki's powers as a laibon. Dominic felt deeply that the world was made up of unsavory characters like the unscrupulous laibon Lobata, and one had to defend oneself with all available means.

It was hot and dry, and the vegetation was brown; there was not enough pasture for the milk animals that remained in the settlements. We feared that it was no longer possible to keep all the animals and people together in one large *nkang*. Most of the cattle were already in the highlands, but the camels needed to go farther into the desert, and the settlement needed to move someplace where they could find enough grazing and water for the small stock.

Several warriors, including Lalem and Kidenye, had been called back from the livestock camp in the mountains to meet with the elders and the laibon and plan what to do next. Lonyoki had advised earlier that the elders should move the settlement toward Ker'ngera and the Arsim wells and that the warriors should take both the cattle and camels west to the l-Barta plains in Samburu District. But the warriors feared the large presence of Turkana warriors in the l-Barta area and preferred to go south toward Langata in the mountains, where there were many Ariaal and Samburu settlements. The elders, too, wanted to stay where they were or, at the most, move closer to Lorrien swamp. But the laibon was determined not to let Lukumai go south. Although he did not say so publicly, he feared that Lobata would be able to curse Lukumai's animals and warriors if they moved too close to his manyatta.

I visited with Lalem and Kidenye at Lalem's mother's house. The two warriors were not happy. Lalem said, "The laibon says we should go to l-Barta. But that place is full of Turkana. You know they recently raided Longieli manyatta near Mount Nyiru. The Turkana surrounded the manyatta at night; there were probably two hundred of them. They hooted like hyenas— 'whoo-oo, whoo-oo.' What could the few warriors there do? Nothing, and the Turkana took all of their cattle away."

Kidenye added, "If we go to l-Barta, there will be many Turkana, and some of them have guns. That is why most of the Ariaal manyattas are down near Laisamis and Langata. It is safe there, and it is green, very green. Lonyoki told the *payiani* [elders] to move Lukumai manyatta toward l-Barta, in the direction he wants us to move our cattle. But the elders are content to stay here near Lorrien swamp."

Lalem added, "The elders are lazy, because they would have to dig new wells at Arsim if they move in that direction."

That evening, a delegation of elders went to visit Lonyoki, bringing a case of beer to help him "make accurate predictions." We sat outside where other members of the community could listen. Lonyoki sat on his elder's stool outside of Nkarami's house. Dominic, his brother Usana, and Lepere sat to Lonyoki's right, and I sat with the two warriors to the left. I brought my tape recorder because I knew that the oration would be complex and I would need help translating it later.

Dominic began the meeting. "Now we are going to make predictions about our own manyatta, but let's not jump to it quickly, without reason. We are here to discuss this together, because only God knows what will happen in the future. 'Homes are made from lungs,' so let us begin to speak."

Lonyoki, who had been drinking steadily, spoke forcefully and dramatically.

"So we will try to find a way to keep our camels, cattle, goats, and sheep together. Because you have refused what I told you, you want to go to the Lengare Mara River (to the south). I said to go west to Baragoi and you refused, so where am I going to put you? Do you want an empty manyatta [without animals]?

"So we need to find what to do, because the drought is coming. Tell me the place you wish to shift and I will see if it is a good place or not," Lonyoki said. "And if I tell you it is not a good place to shift to, you can choose a better place."

To the warriors, the laibon asked, "Boys, are you so fond of the green soup you drink in the mountains that you want to go to the Lengare Mara River?"

Warriors in cattle camps make soup out of wild plants when their milk supplies have run low. It is considered a pretty poor substitute and hard duty away from home.

He continued, "Is it the soup you prepare in the buckets that is keeping you from taking the cattle to Baragoi?"

Kidenye answered wryly, "Why should I leave my green soup prepared in the buckets?"

Lonyoki said, "Because you say we should take the cattle into the mountains when I told you to take them west; otherwise you will blame me later, saying it was me who prevented the cattle from getting the bull [i.e., growing]. So let's do this—we will try to find a solution because there is a proverb which says, 'An elephant cannot miss carrying his own tusks' [i.e., we can't be ashamed of who we are or the mistakes we make]. Is this true or not true?"

The elders responded, "It is true."

Turning to Kidenye and Lalem, Lonyoki asked, "Boys, are there any cattle who died where you drank soup?"

"No," they responded.

"Why didn't they die when the warriors said they would all die there?" he asked, implying that it was his medicines that protected them.

Kidenye laughed sarcastically and asked, "Does it mean we were cursed to die?"

Lonyoki got excited and said, "Ooh! What about when you took the cattle for a week to Lengare Mara River and returned back for *soriu*? What did you see that was not good? And don't count the cow taken by the lion, because cattle of left-handed people are always eaten by lions!"

The warriors laughed, for the cow lost had belonged to La'amo, who was left-handed.

Kidenye said, "Nothing bad happened up there."

"Did any warrior die?" asked the laibon. "Then you will go to Baragoi and die there, because 'there is no place that is chosen for you to die' [you can die anywhere]. So let the cattle pass here, and pass Ker'ngera until they reach Baragoi, because you are warriors. And if the cattle are taken there, then you will die with them, because if you die, it is only a warrior doing his duty. I tell you, if you don't like that side [Baragoi], then go to the side you want, and watch your cattle being taken by *shifta*!"

Kidenye asked, "And you say we will get Turkana cattle at Baragoi?"

Lonyoki replied, "Yes, you can even ask a *lais* to tie you from bringing back cattle, and you will still capture them from Turkana."

Dominic said, "Let's tie Elliot instead so he will stay here with us!" (I was flattered.)

Lonyoki laughed, "He is not going away; he is just going to visit his people and then return to us. I have fixed it so that he will continue to return to us, because this man has helped us a lot. So *loyei* [boys], let the cattle go where you wish. Let them go to Lodosoit [near the Lengare Mara], and then you will have to shave your hair" (i.e., an act of mourning; someone will die).

Lonyoki continued to drink and was becoming more maudlin. To the elders as a whole, he said, "Thanks, thanks to God, for seeing what was to happen during *soriu*. Because Lukumai manyatta did not lose a single child, and I say thanks to God. Because the day it was said I curse people with *nkurupore*, when I came only to stay with Lukumai. God didn't ignore me then, and will not ignore me now. God did not ignore me. What about you with a different heart [who did not trust me]? Because I, Lonyoki, know what is good for you, because this person who stays with you is your brother. God will not leave you, and he will not leave me. And what happened to those warriors at Marsabit Mountain [who didn't listen to me]? Poisoned [*nkurupore*], that's what happened! Are you listening, my brother?" (He directed this question to Usana, who replied, "I'm listening.")

"Of what clan am I?" demanded Lonyoki. "Lorukushu!"

"Lorukushu!" replied the elders.

"And when I left Lorukushu, who did I come to live with? Lukumai clan!"

"Lukumai," agreed the elders.

"I did Lorukushu a great favor when I protected their hair [warriors]." He was referring to *ntasim* he had given to the warriors in Lorubai when I first met him.

"They said, 'Ache oloiboni' [Thank you, Laibon]. And when I needed shoes, I was given shoes!"

"Shoes!" repeated the elders.

"When I needed a cloth, I was given a cloth!"

"Cloth," repeated the elders.

"They knew how to say, 'Thank you, Laibon!'" Lonyoki paused and changed his tone, speaking softly now. "And here at Lukumai, they have many things to be thankful for. And how many animals did Lorukushu clan give me for protecting their hair? And they did not give me sheep and goats, they brought cattle!"

Lonyoki stood up to urinate in back of the house. The elders and warriors were murmuring among themselves, wondering perhaps if Lonyoki would ask them to pay him a large number of animals for his *ntasim*. Lonyoki returned and said to Usana, "How many animals did they give me? Many!"

"*Ey*, many," said Usana.

"How is it now with your herd, Lemeti?" asked Lonyoki. "They're fat and large, and free from disease, aren't they?"

Lemeti responded warmly, "*Ey*, they are."

Lonyoki then asked the elders, softly and intimately, "And your cattle, are they suffering *lodua* [rinderpest] as the other manyattas?"

"No, they are fine," replied the elders.

"Now tell me truthfully, to what do you attribute this? And the health of your warriors, who faced all the hazards of Langata, which is full of *nkurupore* and *shiftas*? Were any one of them harmed?"

"No," replied Usana.

"Have you ever known the peace we've known here? What have the people of Lorubai faced since I left that place? Thieves, war, hunger! And what has Lukumai suffered since I've been here? Nothing! Tell me truthfully, to what do you attribute this? For the cattle of Lukumai, what have I done? In Langata, how many women have I helped have babies? Eight! It was I, Lonyoki!"

The oration continued for some time. At about eleven o'clock at night the gathering broke up, and the elders gave a formal prayer and blessing to the warriors and manyatta.

The next morning, the warriors agreed to move the cattle to the west, toward l-Barta, as Lonyoki had dictated. I asked Lalem if he was satisfied with this plan, as he had advocated the move south. He told me, "We warriors had already agreed to go west to l-Barta, but do you think the people will say yes to the first thing a laibon says? People must argue with the laibon, to understand his reasoning, to find out what he really knows. Lonyoki knows what the dangers are, but we won't give him immediate authority and power without a fight. We listen to laibons, but men can think too."

Lukumai manyatta itself was breaking up. Over the next week those families with camels began to move northeast to the Rendille lowlands, and those with goats and sheep moved closer to Lorrien swamp. Nomadic communities like Lukumai periodically separated and later rejoined when the climate and grazing conditions improved. The community was in a major state of transition, and I sensed that I, too, should get ready to move on.

That night, Sembara came to my house; this would be our last meeting together. She said, "My father and uncle have arranged for me to marry a man from Mount Nyiru."

"How do you feel about that?" I asked. We both knew this would happen sooner or later; it happened to most young women as marriage alliances were formed by elder men and girls were separated from their warrior lovers.

"It is good," Sembara said without any sadness in her voice. "It is time for me to marry and start my own family," she said with a smile.

"What! You don't want to get on an airplane and come live in my country?" I teased.

"Yes, I want that," she replied earnestly. "But that is not to be."

It was a bittersweet moment. I was always amazed at how confident and comfortable Sembara was when she was with me. She did not treat me as a foreigner, but genuinely enjoyed my company, as I did hers. I was a young man, with a young person's heart.

Lion and Ostrich's Children

On our last evening before the move, I went over to Dominic and Naiseku's house. Naiseku was sitting on her mat and organizing her household goods, putting small containers of tobacco and salt into her leather bags, getting ready for the following day. Dominic was resting, sitting against the wall and playing with his youngest daughter, Naisaba. Mikilan, Naisaba's cousin and best friend, was lying next to her. The house had a relaxed atmosphere, a welcome relief after a week of intense dialogue between Lonyoki, the elders, and the warriors.

"Sit down, Elliot, I am telling a story to the children," Naiseku said. "This is the story of how Lion tried to steal Ostrich's children. Do you know it?"

This was a popular folk story and I did know it, but I didn't mind hearing it again. The children leaned forward in anticipation as Naiseku began.

"Long ago, Lion's children fell sick to a terrible disease, l-tipo [smallpox], and they all died." This seemed like a terrifying way to start a story, but the kids seemed nonplussed. Their smiles told me they had also heard this story many times before. She continued,

Sad at his loss, Lion went out and saw Ostrich's children, which he gathered up and took to his home. The baby ostriches were on their own because their father had left them to find food. When Ostrich came home, he saw his children were missing. "Where are my children?" he cried, and the other animals in the manyatta told him that Lion had taken his children away. Ostrich went immediately to Lion's home and demanded his children back.

"These are not your children, they are mine," said Ostrich to Lion.

Lion sat there calm as could be. He said, "These children are not yours, they are mine of course. Just ask anyone."

"No," said Ostrich. "These are not your children, they are mine, anyone can see that." But Lion refused to give over the children. Ostrich became very angry and said, "Tomorrow we shall have a big meeting with all the animals to judge whose children these are!" and he left.

The next morning, a meeting with all the animals was held. Giraffe was there, and Elephant, and Antelope, even Sesuk the Squirrel was there. Every animal was asked to determine whose children these were.

Elephant spoke up first and said, "These are Lion's children, of course."

Antelope spoke up and said, "I believe these children belong to Lion."

Giraffe said, "These are Lion's children, anyone can see that."

On and on, all the animals supported Lion's claim, because they were all afraid of Lion. No one would say that these children were Ostrich's.

Finally, little Sesuk the Squirrel was asked to tell whose children these belonged to. Sesuk stood up and said, "Because I am small, find me something tall to climb, so you can all see and hear me."

The animals found a termite hill, and Sesuk the Squirrel ran to the top of it.

Squirrel said, "I cannot speak an untrue thing. Since when have you heard it said that something with hair gives birth to something with feathers? And when have you heard it said that something with feathers gives birth to something with hair? These children belong to Ostrich, and not to Lion!"

Ostrich quickly gathered his children and took them away. Lion was very angry and looked around for Squirrel. Seeing Lion so angry, Squirrel jumped right down into a hole in the termite hill. Lion was in a rage and sent Elephant to catch Squirrel.

Elephant pushed his long trunk into the termite hill, until he finally found Squirrel, who he grabbed by the legs. But clever Squirrel said, "Oh, you stupid elephant, you think you have me? You are only catching a root!" So Elephant let go and felt around until he caught a real root. Squirrel screamed "Oh, please, you're hurting me, don't kill me, let me go!"

Elephant pulled up his trunk and saw that all he held was a root. Clever little Squirrel had gotten away.

Ostrich took his children back to his home, never to leave them alone again until they were fully grown.

I laughed with everyone after she finished. The children had grown sleepy and curled themselves up next to each other on the sleeping skin, covered with a *nanga* cloth. I rose and went back to my house to pack up my own belongings and, as always, write up my notes. This was a wonderful story and children delighted in hearing it. But like many folk stories and fairy tales, this one had origins in something real, something unpleasant, whose retelling held morals and lessons for its listeners.

I believe this story goes back to *Emutai*, the period of famine and disease that included smallpox and rinderpest at the end of the nineteenth century. The story of Lion, Ostrich, and Squirrel capture that period of death and loss.

For Samburu, Lion was the most powerful of all animals. He was beautiful and powerful, but he was also a killer who threatened all living creatures; he was the only wild animal that could rule over human beings. Ostrich also was a beautiful animal—in Samburu its name, *sidai*, meant "beautiful" because of its pure black and white colors. But it was a wingless and powerless bird; warriors in their songs called elders "ostriches" who could only "drag their blankets on the ground."

This was a story about life and death, but it also expressed a conflict between the all-powerful supernatural world (Lion) and the natural, mortal world of human beings (Ostrich, beautiful but stuck on the ground). But this opposition and inequality in power was not static, and the time of one's death was never certain. Death might not be prevented, but it could be delayed. In this story, small and puny Squirrel was able to mediate between Lion and Ostrich, between supernatural power and the everyday world of people. This was the significance of the termite hill—it transcended boundaries, as one would argue in the terms of structural anthropology developed by Claude Lévi-Strauss. Squirrel outwitted Lion, climbing high up the termite hill to speak and return Ostrich's children; he escaped his own death by diving into the depths of the termite hill and pretending he was a root, tricking Elephant who was sent to kill him.

The Lion and Ostrich story had several variants among Maa-speaking people, with the role of Squirrel sometimes played by the jackal and sometimes the rabbit. All three of these animals were small, quick, and clever. A similar figure existed in Native American folklore in the form of coyote, sometimes called the Trickster. In West Africa this figure was sometimes Anansi the Spider, or sometimes the jackal or, again, the rabbit. Americans may recognize from African American folklore the character Br'er (Brother) Rabbit, who could "outfox" even the fox.

In my thinking, the laibon was the squirrel in the story, someone who was clever and who could mediate between the world of the supernaturally powerful and world of mortals. The laibon could sometimes delay death, like the squirrel outwitting the lion; he could do this with his *nkidong* divination and *ntasim* medicines. But the laibon was never as powerful as God: "Jackals follow lions, lions never follow jackals," goes the proverb. Not unlike the shaman of Siberia and Native America, Lonyoki was a mystical intermediary, who could communicate with the unseen spirit world. The laibon did not go into a trance like the Siberian shaman, although he could go into an altered psychological state with the aid of alcohol. Still, the laibon could "see"—through his divination, prophecy, or dreams—events not visible to ordinary human beings.

Samburu laibons were not holy men who speak for men to God; for this, Samburu consulted their *laisi* or elders. Lonyoki played no leading role in the public rituals of Lukumai, nor could he speak from the *na'abu* ritual center, although he did provide *ntasim* to warriors at their *mugit* ceremonies. Laibons more closely resembled prophets, those who speak from God to men. Lonyoki did play an essential and irreplaceable role in Lukumai affairs—he could predict and protect the community from attack, both mystical and real. Physical attacks by Turkana and *shifta* were a frightening reality that periodically occurred. Similarly, sorcery and witchcraft were believed to be real; they were the means through which jealousy, fear, and social conflict were manifested. They were also spiritual weapons that laibons could provide warriors going on raids. Laibons could be difficult to live with, but Samburu communities needed them for the protection and security they provided in the dangerous world in which Samburu lived.

Laibons were outsiders; they were not ordinary members of the society. Indeed, the first laibon appeared mysteriously to the Maasai and led their warriors to water that suddenly appeared from the ground. Lonyoki and his kin—Kocheke, Longojine, and Lokili—stood apart from the other elders. They wore green instead of white cloths; they were excluded from the community prayers held inside the *na'abu* ritual center; they were represented by odd numbers rather than even numbers in Samburu numerology and symbolism. These laibons did not behave like other elders; they liked to drink, chased after women, and were not constrained from abusing people in public. Women and children generally avoided them, and they were held in awe and fear by most of the community.

But the elders needed the laibon. Lonyoki had asked the Lukumai elders, "Have you ever known the peace we've known here? What have the people of Lorubai faced since I left that place? Thieves, war, hunger! And what has Lukumai suffered since I've been here? Nothing! Tell me truthfully, to what do you attribute this?"

And, truthfully, the elders of Lukumai could not disagree with Lonyoki.

A Trip to Mombasa

As Lukumai was separating into different camps, Dominic and I made a special trip to Mombasa on Kenya's Indian Ocean coast. We had been invited to the wedding of our friends David and Joan in Nairobi, and Dominic never missed an opportunity to visit new places and meet new people. I needed to return to Nairobi, and this would be a good opportunity to travel with Dominic alone. David was a Canadian doctor who had been working at Kenyatta Hospital in Nairobi; his fiancée, Joan, was a U.S. Peace Corps volunteer who worked with the Ministry of Health. Both had come to Marsabit to develop a primary health care program for nomadic peoples in the district, and through me they had become friends with people in Lukumai. Dominic, in particular, connected with David and Joan the same way he did to me; he enjoyed our company, appreciated our activities, and shared our sense of humor. When Dominic was invited to the wedding, he insisted on bringing a goat.

"You're joking," I told Dominic. "I am not taking a goat in my car for twelve hours."

"Come on," said Dominic, "we've got to take this goat to David and Joan's wedding. This is what we do for weddings. I will clean up its mess, I promise."

"All right, but you sit in the back with it, and don't let it jump to the front while I am driving." Dominic put the goat in the Land Rover and, with a broad smile on his face, got into the truck.

The wedding in Nairobi was a big *sikukuu* [festival] with an outdoor barbecue (courtesy of Dominic and his goat) and guests that included Kenyan doctors, Ministry of Health workers, U.S. Peace Corps volunteers, young American adventurers, and David's and Joan's family, including Joan's brother who lived and worked in Kenya. We drank, played music, and danced the day away. David and Joan had planned to travel to Mombasa, and they invited Dominic and me to join them for part of the trip. Dominic had never seen the ocean and wanted to see what people did there.

We drove down to Mombasa on Kenya's main road to the Indian Ocean coast, 350 miles from Nairobi. As we traveled, Joan asked Dominic, "So what did you think of the wedding?"

"*Ke sidai oling n-kiama lol Tayfid and Jon* [the wedding of David and Joan was really beautiful]," said Dominic. He went on, "I liked the food, the music, the *naisho* [wine]. And there was even *bhangi*—I saw people smoking *bhangi* [marijuana] from a pipe!"

I asked Dominic if he got along with the Kikuyu and Kamba guests, as these were considered enemies by Ariaal and Samburu.

Dominic responded, "Tribes cannot love each other, but people can love each other. You remember when we went to Maralal that time, and I stayed with my lady friend. Do you know where she is from? She is Boran, and Rendille and Boran hate each other. But I love all people. Do you remember when we stayed in Baragoi, and I visited a woman there? She was Turkana, and Samburu hate Turkana!"

"Dominic, you have a girlfriend in every town we travel through," I said. "Did you have a girlfriend in Nairobi?

"I do have a girlfriend in Nairobi, a Kikuyu," he laughed, "but I did not visit her this time."

"Have you ever had an American girlfriend?" Joan asked with a smile.

"American? I love all people, but I have never known a white woman. What are they like?"

"They're the best!" said Joan. "American girls like romance, and they are not afraid of men."

"Do you know why they like romance?" I teased. "Because they are not circumcised, and they can enjoy sex more."

"Just like the Turkana!" Dominic said, laughing heartily. He went on, "I like all women, it is true. Any two people can like each other. But tribes cannot like each other. They cannot like each other because each one wants what the other has. Look at the Kikuyu. Kenyatta [who was then still president] is a great man, he led our country to freedom. But the Kikuyu people are not so good, they want to control everything—the government, all businesses—even the cattle business which we Samburu know better than they do. But the Kikuyu really understand *biashara* [business], like the Somalis and *Wahindi* [Indians]. Samburu are not very good businessmen, because we are always eating our animals or giving them away to our friends," he laughed.

I thought to myself, "I wish everyone in Kenya could just say, 'We are Kenyans first, and Samburu or Kikuyu second.'" But I knew that what I believed would not happen for a long time. Ethnicity, or what some people call tribalism, was not just blind loyalty, but rational identification with a group that would look after and protect you. This is why patronage was so important, why everyone, from politicians to shopkeepers to cattle herders, would find jobs for or receive favors from kinsmen or fellow tribesmen. As one politician put it, "If I don't give jobs to my people, who will?"

We reached Mombasa in the early evening and headed to the old town area to find a hotel. Unlike Nairobi with its tall skyscrapers, supermarkets, and people dressed in European clothes, Mombasa was an African city with a multicultural population of Swahili, Kikuyu, Luo, Somalis, Arabs, Omanis, East Indians, and even Persians (Iranians), with many fewer whites than in Nairobi. The old town in Mombasa was a maze of small streets and alleys with shops, mosques, and marketplaces.

I was pretty worried when Dominic disappeared and failed to return to our hotel room that night; he didn't show up until early the next morning. At first I thought he had gotten lost, but then I saw by his weary but intense look that he had been up all night chewing khat (called mira'a by Samburu), a green plant (Catha edulis) whose stems were chewed as an amphetamine-like stimulant. It has long been consumed by people in northeast Africa and Arabia, particularly by Muslim men who are not permitted to drink alcohol. If Dominic could get his hands on khat, he would chew it all night, "like a camel grazing" he admitted to me.

I let Dominic sleep while David, Joan, and I walked around the old town's narrow streets, visiting its large mosques and the imposing Fort Jesus, built by the Portuguese and now a museum. By the afternoon, we had roused Dominic and headed to Tiwi beach to be near the water. Tiwi was a resort area with several expensive tourist hotels, but at that time of the year most of the Indian Ocean beaches were quiet, particularly as you moved farther up the coast. We decided to camp under some palm trees close to the ocean, where the breeze was strong and the deadly mosquitoes were kept at bay.

The ocean here was shallow and protected by a long coral reef, accommodating gorgeous snorkeling in water too shallow for sharks. Here one could see brain coral inundated with colorful fish, including the scorpion fish with its long and venomous spines. But these fish were shy and slow moving, not as dangerous as the sea snakes and electric eels that also lived there. We even got Dominic into a diving mask. He stood in about two feet of water, put his head under the water for about three seconds, and immediately shot up, "OK, I saw it, I'm getting out now!"

That evening, we made a fire to cook dinner. I had caught an African lobster (without claws), which I looked forward to eating. Dominic was so revolted that I was going to eat a "scorpion" that he took some of the fire and moved ten feet up the beach, making his own fire to cook the beefsteak we had bought earlier in the market. But we all sat together as we ate, Dominic still wincing over our choice of food. While we were eating, two Giriama men, local Swahili dressed in *kikoi* cloths tied around their waists, stopped to greet us. The men had been tapping the palm trees along the beach, cutting off upper palm fronds to collect the sap, which they made into palm wine. They had been climbing the trees during the afternoon, whistling and singing as they did their work. They lived on the farms behind us and had brought us some wine to drink. We thanked them and each took a sip. It was sour but definitely alcoholic. Dominic and Joan started chatting with the men in KiSwahili, laughing and telling stories, while Dominic translated their KiSwahili into Maa so I could understand.

One of the Giriama men asked Dominic, "What kind of *mzungu* is this who doesn't speak KiSwahili, but speaks your language?"

Dominic responded, "He's a crazy *mzungu*. He's so crazy, he even eats scorpions from the sea. He even eats fish!"

"You don't eat fish?" the Giriama asked incredulously. "Where are you from? Are you Maasai?"

"*Ey*, like the Maasai, I am Samburu from Marsabit District, near Ethiopia."

The Giriama took this in stride and asked, "So what's it like in your country?"

Dominic replied, "It's like here, only instead of milking trees like you do, we milk our cattle."

Dominic and the Giriama talked for a while in pleasant conversation. I was totally struck by the affability between the men and their curiosity about each other's backgrounds and customs. As Dominic said, "Two people can love each other." I only wished different tribes could love each other as well.

A Final Meeting of Laibons

After spending an extraordinary three days together at the beach, Dominic and I left for Lukumai via Nairobi. In Nairobi, we stopped for supplies and Dominic shopped for cloths and kitchen utensils for his wives. In town, Dominic liked to wear Western trousers and a shirt rather than his *shuka* cloth. Before leaving, we made a trip to the Ngong Hills, a beautiful formation that separates Nairobi from the vast Rift Valley below. This was the place where the original laibon Kidong'oi is said to have appeared, and it was still a sacred place for Maasai.

We walked along the hills, looking at Nairobi fourteen miles away, a modern city with skyscrapers on one side and the vast plains and savannas of the Rift Valley on the other.

"What will happen to this place?" I half asked Dominic and half asked myself. I worried that the city would expand and envelop everything around it, absorbing and assimilating traditional cultures including the Maasai.

As if reading my mind, Dominic replied, "Nairobi is not a bad place. Our country needs *maendeleo* [progress] if we want to grow strong. We need hospitals and schools and roads—those are good things. *Mara e-torronu*, Nairobi is not a bad place."

But I worried that those schools, hospitals, and roads would not go to the rural places, certainly not the ones occupied by nomadic pastoralists. I worried about the future of Lukumai and Dominic's family.

We left Nairobi and drove north for five hours, reaching the hard dirt road from Isiolo to Marsabit. After several hours we approached Laisamis town. Along the road we saw a Samburu elder who flagged us down. Dominic knew the man.

"*Serian?*" greeted the elder to which we replied, "Ey, *Serian*."

"The laibon Lonyoki is in Laisamis waiting for you. He said to stop you if I saw your car."

This was a pleasant surprise, I thought. It was about four o'clock in the afternoon as we drove into the town. We went to the bar where we had met with Lokili the time we had gone to see Lobata, the rival laibon. Here we found Lonyoki, who was pacing about nervously. He had his bag with his *ntasim* and *nkidong* gourd, and he had a stern look on his face.

"*Serian*," he said. "I am waiting for Lobata; he is inside the bar."

We didn't know how long Lonyoki had been here or if he had come specifically to meet with Lobata. We could just see that he was very angry.

In a short time, Lobata emerged from the building. He was taller than I remembered, a bit drunk but steady on his feet, wearing his black beret and green robe and carrying his divination gourd. As he came forward, he threw his cloth over one shoulder and glared at Lonyoki. They obviously had been quarreling.

"*Wey* [You], Lobata, you have your divination gourd, did you bring your *nkuruporen* with you as well today?" Lonyoki demanded.

Lobata, who towered over Lonyoki, glared down at him. "*Tu tum menye*," Lobata shouted back, "Get out of my way!"

Lobata tried to push past Lonyoki, but Lonyoki stood in his way without moving. Lonyoki yelled at him, "Lobata, you are a fraud! You stole your gourd from my father through deceit and lies!"

Lobata retorted, "You are a bastard, you are not even Longojine's son. And yet you have always thought you were better than me! Leave me alone!"

Lonyoki glared at him, and exclaimed, "I curse you, do you hear me, I curse you to die!"

And with that, Lonyoki raised his own *nkidong* gourd high over his head and threw it with all his might at Lobata. The gourd hit Lobata in the head and it broke into many pieces; all the *nkidong* stones spilled out on the ground. Lobata fell backward but stayed on his feet. A trickle of blood came from his left eyebrow. Lobata was clearly frightened.

"You are crazy! Crazy! Leave me alone!" he said, and turned around and went back into the bar.

Dominic and I stood there in astonishment. We had never seen Lonyoki so furious before. We bent over to help him pick up the pieces from his broken *nkidong*. His body was shaking.

We gathered Lonyoki's bag and helped him into the Land Rover. When we were on the road, Lonyoki spoke up, calmer now.

"That Lobata had given *nkurupore* to the Soritari *l-murran* to use against our warriors. I knew this. I saw this in the *nkidong*. And he tried to deny it. That man is crazy. He lies and makes trouble, especially against Lukumai. He is jealous that Lukumai came to me to be their laibon and not to him. But I have known about him for a long time. He is a terrible man [*Ke e-torronu l-tung'ani*]!"

Dominic clicked his tongue and said, "Brother, that was something. That man had it coming, you are right about that. What will happen now?"

Lonyoki replied, "He will leave this place and not bother anyone anymore."

Farewells

Lukumai had fractured into several smaller manyattas. Lonyoki was moving his family closer to the road to Ker'ngera. Lepere and Usana were taking their camels toward Naiborr, and Lemeti and La'amo were moving their goats and sheep to Lorrien swamp. Dominic said he would go to Naiborr for a while, and then move to Langata with his cattle and goats. My fieldwork was drawing to a close. I had lived with Dominic, Lonyoki, and the Lukumai community off and on over an eighteen-month period. I knew it was time to wrap up my research, although I wasn't sure if it was because I had accomplished what I wanted to accomplish or simply because I was worn out.

Before I took Dominic to Mombasa, my friend Lolongoi, the midwife, had said to me, "Elliot, you now know how to speak our language; you know how to milk a cow, kill a goat, dance the *mparingoi* with the warriors. Don't you think it is time for you to marry and settle down?"

She said this half in jest, but also out of concern for me. I was in limbo; my identity had become confused. Was I the son of Lonyoki, a warrior of the l-Kishili age-set, a member of Lukumai community? Or was I a young American graduate student, someone who would leave this place and build a career and family back in my own country? I acknowledged that it was time for me to move on.

As I delivered Lonyoki and Dominic to Dominic's *nkang*, I said, "It is time for me to go back to my country. I have finished my work here and need to go back to my home."

"Yes," said Lonyoki. "It is important for you to visit your father; you have been gone a long time. I have dreamt of you, Elliot, and I can see you will have no problems. But you will return to us, again and again."

Dominic laughed, "The laibon made medicine to keep you coming back to us."

"Well, then I will return. And I would do so whether you made this medicine or not. I want to thank both of you for being such good friends to me."

In the following few days, most of the houses had been disassembled and people had moved to their new locations. People had departed without much fanfare, stopping only to give each other blessings. When I was ready to leave, I hugged Naiseku closely. I would miss her and Dominic's family very much. I shook hands with Usana, and hugged Mother of Lembalen; I even hugged Lonyoki's mistress, Nkarami. I was sad not to say good-bye to Lembalen, who was now living with his grandfather and herding his goats in Langata. I told Mother of Lembalen to please greet him, and that I would return one day.

As I was leaving, Lonyoki came to the car. He said, "I want to give you something to give to your father from me. Here, take this."

Lonyoki had brought a beautiful walking stick. It was made of African ebony and had carefully carved curves running up the shaft and ending in a circular handle. It was indeed a handsome gift.

"Tell your father this is from Lonyoki the laibon. Tell him how grateful I am to him for sharing his son with me."

I thanked him, and then said good-bye to Lonyoki and Dominic, my two closest friends.

"You are really my family. I pray to God to bless you [a formal farewell], and I know I will see you both again."

"*Ey*, Elliot, we will see each other again," said Dominic. "*Miki-tajapa nkai*" (May God carry you).

I drove to Nairobi slowly, taking my time and in no particular hurry. I knew I was done with my fieldwork in Kenya for now, but I wasn't sure what I was returning home to. A Joni Mitchell song, *California*, played on my small cassette player.

> Oh it gets so lonely
> When you're walking
> And the streets are full of strangers,
> All the news of home you read
> More about the war
> And the bloody changes
> Oh will you take me as I am?
> Will you take me as I am?
> Will you?

In Nairobi, I managed to sell my Land Rover to a young Finnish development officer; he paid me nearly the same amount that I had paid for the car two years earlier. I was ready to leave Africa, but I was still moving slowly. I traveled through Sudan into the Sahara and Egypt by truck, train, and barge; it took several weeks of moving without stopping to finally reach Cairo, where I found a cheap air flight home. My weariness was not just psychological; when I reached New York I was diagnosed with hepatitis. Besides damaging your liver—it turns your eyes yellow and urine the color of Coca-Cola—hepatitis is a very depressing disease. "Bad blood is going through your brain," I was told by Barbara Jones, a neuroscientist, when I stayed with her and her husband, the anthropologist John Galaty, in Nairobi. Perhaps my blood had turned black, as the herbalist Lolcheni would have said. But I recovered, and managed to return to Kenya and Lukumai many times over the next thirty years. Perhaps Lonyoki had truly made medicines to bring me back. But I was never to experience again the intimacy and total immersion in a different culture of that first fieldwork.

CHAPTER FIVE

Epilogue: The Gourd Is Passed

Daylight follows a dark night.

I returned to Kenya in 1985, ten years after I had left. I was a social scientist now, funded with a research grant from the National Geographic Society to study household labor and pastoral production in a drought-prone environment. I was also a married man with a six-year-old daughter, and I brought Marty and Leah with me for this second round of fieldwork in the north. Marty was a medical doctor who intended to volunteer at local health clinics while I continued my research among the nomadic pastoralists. In an old beat-up Land Rover, we made the long journey to the north. Everything was an adventure for our young daughter, Leah. She wanted to sit in the spare tire bolted to the Rover's hood, something we let her do when we finally reached the smaller roads of Marsabit District. Leah was always in good spirits.

In many ways, the district looked the same as it had when I left it—one saw nomadic settlements of Rendille, Samburu, and Gabra people herding camels, cattle, goats, and sheep. But the district as a whole was changing. The mid-1980s was the period of the Ethiopian Famine, caused by a combination of drought and widespread civil wars in neighboring Sudan, Ethiopia, and Uganda. Kenya was relatively peaceful, although an attempted coup in Nairobi against President Moi in 1982 had unleashed a long period of repressive rule that did not end until 2002 when he was finally voted out of office. In the north, many pastoral nomads had moved to famine relief camps, small towns, or agricultural schemes. The Marsabit road was busy with large trucks carrying famine relief foods and shiny Toyotas and Land Rovers working for international organizations including World Vision, Catholic Relief Services, and Save the Children.

While many of these organizations provided essential humanitarian assistance, a major consequence of their activities—whether planned or not—was a campaign to encourage the district's nomadic pastoralists to settle down. The Catholic Diocese continued to give out famine relief foods long after the drought had ended, and both the Catholic and Protestant missionaries had developed agricultural projects on Marsabit Mountain, attracting poor Rendille, Samburu, and Boran to settle. While the missions provided health clinics and schools, I was critical of their failure to directly help the nomadic communities and their animals, with the exception of a few programs, including Oxfam, which provided goats to impoverished pastoralists. The majority of organizations, with government backing, wanted the nomads to settle down and "stop wandering about," as one official told me.

Nevertheless, pastoralism remained the preferred lifestyle for those households that had enough animals to survive, and I heard that Lukumai had for the most part stayed intact with their livestock. My research goals were shifting; I wanted to look more closely at problems of social change and development. I wanted to understand the forces that were pushing, or pulling, former pastoralists to settle; from the outset I knew there would be advantages and disadvantages to settled life.

Stopping in Laisamis, I heard that Dominic was at Naiborr; he had been taken to the hospital ill with malaria. Naiborr was a new town created in the middle of the desert, far from the main Marsabit road. Before the 1970s, Naiborr had been a dry-season watering hole for Rendille camels because of its deep wells, but it had grown as missionaries used it to distribute famine relief foods such as corn meal and cooking oil. Naiborr was now a permanent town of shops and houses, and it was home to several thousand Rendille people, many very poor, who lived around the center. But it was a barren and windswept place, with no vegetation that could support camels or small stock. At the center of the town was a large Catholic church, with a school and a dispensary close by. Nearby I found Lukumai *nkang*, where Dominic and his wife Naiseku were living with four other households.

This mini-manyatta was a depressing site, consisting mainly of women, small children, and a few old men. There were no animals, no fences, no *na'abu* ritual center—just six or seven threadbare Rendille houses with old burlap bags from famine foods for a roof. Dominic was noticeably thinner and weaker, but he came out from his house to greet us as we drove up. "*Mpirrian*" (best friend), he called me. "Where are your honey hives?" He warmly shook Marty's hands and greeted Leah, who stood behind her mother shyly. Naiseku came out of the house and gave me a warm hug. Then she invited us into her house for tea. She told Marty, "*Towana ene*" (sit next to me). "*Ng'o*," she said, giving Marty a beaded necklace as a gift. Larenbin, Dominic's young son by his second wife, Rendille, took Leah outside to show her the sights. Soon they were running around, making a collection of discarded goat bones.

As we drank our tea, Dominic brought me up to speed on what had been going on in the ten years since I had left. "The drought [*ngolan*] was terrible; most of our animals died. Everyone lost animals, even myself I lost twenty cattle and nearly all my small stock. We had nothing to eat but dirt. Then I got very sick with the fever, and Naiseku brought me here. I am feeling better, but my shoulders still hurt and my liver pains me."

"Where is Lukumai now?" I asked.

"They are still there near Lenguas. They are now in four separate manyattas: some are near the river, some near Baiyo Mountain. Most of the big animals are gone, but the goats and sheep are recovering." I knew that in time they would begin to rebuild their camel and cattle herds, as long as the rains came.

"And my father, Lonyoki, how is he?" I asked.

Dominic chuckled and said, "You know, he married Nkarami after all, and they now have a son and a daughter. They are living with Lembalen and his mother near the Ker'ngera road. And Mother of Lembalen has a new baby girl," he smiled. I was happy to hear that; she had suffered for many years as the mother of only one child. But David had treated her with antibiotics, and that may have done the trick.

"And where are my age-mates Lalem and Kidenye?" I asked.

"Kidenye moved to l-Barta in Samburu District and is married. Lalem is living in Lukumai; he is now an elder with two daughters, but his wife died last month of malaria. Two of our warriors also died of malaria. It was terrible. I think it was because we were so weak from hunger, that when it rained and the mosquitoes returned, we had no strength to fight them."

"And what about you, Dominic?" I asked. "What have you been up to?"

He replied, "Well, life had been good until this drought and my malaria. I worked as a watchman for a while with the UNESCO project; I made good money and bought cattle. I am now preparing to marry a third wife," he smiled.

"A third wife? You can barely keep one!" I said, looking at Naiseku. She raised her eyebrows as if to say, "What can I do?"

While Dominic was anxious to return to Lukumai, Naiseku was in no hurry to leave. I asked her how she found life at Naiborr.

"How do I like living here? I love living here! At Lukumai, if your child gets sick, there is no medicine or help. If you are hungry and there is no food, you must walk hours to a shop. If you need water, you must fetch it from the wells at Lenguas. But here at Naiborr the shops are close by, there are schools for the children, a dispensary if you get sick. And when I need water, it is right down the hill at the pump. I hope never to return to Lukumai!" Naiseku was not to get her wish, however, as Dominic took her back to Lukumai when he recovered a few weeks later.

We decided to stay in Naiborr until Dominic got better, after which we could all go back to Lukumai together. The Catholic priest, a man from India, let us stay at the mission guesthouse while Marty volunteered at their health clinic. Soon after our arrival, Dominic gave Marty a beautiful slender *rungu*, a combination herding stick and club, with a large round knot at one end.

"That's quite an honor," I told Marty. "It is usually only men who carry *rungus* and camel sticks."

That evening, Marty proved her worth when she, Dominic, and I walked into town. Pointing our flashlights at the footpath, we saw a yellow-brown scorpion dash in front of us. Without hesitating, Marty whacked it and killed it with her new *rungu*. Dominic chuckled, "Ey, you are a real *murrani* now."

About a week after we arrived at Naiborr, Leah became terribly ill. She woke up vomiting and her body was burning. Marty took her temperature—it was 104° F. She said we needed to drive as quickly as we could to Marsabit Hospital, which was more than two hours away. We got in the front seat of my Land Rover and I drove ferociously with Marty holding Leah on her lap. Leah was six years old; she was long and thin, with a mop of curly honey-colored hair. I was worried sick—I could not imagine the anguish of bringing my family to Africa only to lose one of them. After twenty minutes we reached a dismal area of desert known for its black soil and thin, spindly acacia trees. I looked over at Leah and saw her slowly rolling her head, talking to herself in monosyllables. I said to Marty, "She's not right; she's acting goofy."

The next moment, Leah was convulsing in a grand mal seizure, bucking her small body up and down as Marty held her tightly in her lap.

"Turn around!" Marty yelled. "Drive back to Naiborr, fast!"

My heart was racing as I floored the old Land Rover, driving as quickly as I could. When we reached the mission compound, Marty jumped out and yelled, "Put her into a cold shower, I'll go to radio for help," running into the priest's house.

I drove another hundred yards to the guesthouse, which had a shower, and carried Leah inside. As I held her under the cool water, I could hear Marty yelling into the two-way radio, "I want an airplane up here now!"

She was talking with African Medical Relief (AMREF), the medical organization made up of pilots and a mobile medical staff known as the "Flying Doctors." Amazingly, an airplane arrived in just two hours, a twin-engine Cessna equipped with a bed, an oxygen tank, and a nurse. They lifted Leah into the plane, and Marty followed her. When I tried to get into the plane, the nurse said, "Sorry, we are too full." I managed to tell Marty we would meet in Nairobi.

It took me two days to reach them. I raced my beat-up Land Rover to the next town only to find that the church's radio phone was out of order. I got back in the car and drove down the main road another three hours to Archer's Post; here the church's radio did not work as its battery was too low to transmit. I pushed on to where the paved road began and finally found a functioning telephone. I called the Nairobi hospital and spoke with the pediatrician, who reassured me, "Don't worry, your daughter is fine. In fact, she is jumping up and down on the bed right now. Whatever it was, it passed through her and is now gone."

Return to Lukumai

For Leah's health and safety, Marty decided to stay in Nairobi while I returned north to work on my research. I had hired Larion, who was a medical assistant with David and Joan's project, and his wife AnneMarie to help me with my research. He also helped as a translator, as my Samburu had become very rusty. Before reaching the nomadic Lukumai settlement, I made a short detour to greet and visit my father Lonyoki. His small *nkang* was easy to find, located on the road to Lenguas from Laisamis. There were three houses in a straight line, one built by Mother of Lembalen, one by Nkarami, and one for Nkarami's mother, who had moved in with them. Lonyoki came out of Nkarami's house even before I stopped the car. Well, he was a laibon, after all, and should have known that I was coming! Throwing his green cloth over his right shoulder and beaming with a smile, he approached me arms outstretched. We hugged each other tightly as he cried, "My son, my son; *serian* Elliot?" I greeted his two wives and mother-in-law and asked about his son, Lembalen, who was not there.

"He's living in Langata, where my father lived before he died. Lembalen is taking care of my goats and cattle, which do better in those hills than here."

"So he never went to school?" I asked with some disappointment.

"No," said Lonyoki matter-of-factly. "Longojine needed Lembalen to take care of his animals. But now that you are here, I will send a message to Lembalen to return and see you."

Inside, Nkarami made tea with the tea leaves and sugar I had brought. She had two small children, one still nursing. She had not changed much; she was still beautiful but I could see her selfish character was the same. She jealously eyed the sugar and tea packages I gave to Mother of Lembalen, although I gave them both equal amounts. It was clear that she and Mother of Lembalen had never become friends. I thought that it was a good thing my culture permitted only one wife per husband.

Mother of Lembalen seemed happier now that she had a daughter, however. The girl was about nine years old and was devoted to her mother.

As we drank our tea, Lonyoki turned to me and said, "I heard about your daughter being sick and taken by airplane to Nairobi. But I know that she is safe now. Let's throw the nkidong and see what will happen."

Nkarami handed him his divination gourd and blue cloth, and Lonyoki proceeded with the divination. "Ey, I see peace [serian]."

He threw again and held up a small metal piece. "This is an airplane," Lonyoki said. "I see that it is bringing your wife and daughter back to this place."

I smiled but thought to myself, "If only that were true, but I know that will not happen."

Lonyoki threw the stones a few more times and said, "There will be no problems for you at this place. You will know only peace and goodness."

Our visit was brief, and I promised to come back soon. But I wanted to get to Lukumai and set up my tent. I was anxious to begin this new round of research. I found Lukumai easily enough, although I still had to bushwhack across open country with large bushes and acacia trees until I reached the manyatta. It looked very much as it had ten years ago. Dominic was there, and the other married men and women came out to greet me, much as they had ten years earlier. One elder came out, hand outstretched. "Elliot, Elliot, serian? Elliot, do you remember how you once gave me a flashlight?" (Yes, I replied, not really remembering this.) "Well," he went on, "the batteries are dead!" I guess he expected me to keep the flashlight going.

I set up a camp, our own mini-manyatta, for Larion and myself outside of Lukumai's fence. Instead of cattle we had our Land Rover, from which I hung a tarp with a table and chairs underneath it. This would be a better way for me to conduct my interviews, surveys, and mapmaking. I still went to people's homes, but now my tarp became the new "shade" where the men could hang out, play ndotoi, and sleep. I asked about Rendille, and he told me that she had remained in Lenguas town and was now a caretaker of the schoolmaster's house, looking after his children and preparing their meals.

Her daughter, Ntenukwa, was now married, and their son, Parengi, my first Samburu teacher, was in school hoping to become a policeman.

An elder with a familiar face approached me. "*Sopa, murratai*," he said, with a loopy smile and cracked front tooth. It was Lalem, my old age-mate and warrior friend, but I hardly recognized him. He was now a junior elder, still slender but with a bald head where once there were long red braids. Dominic had told me that Lalem's wife had died from "the fever"; Lalem had sent his two small daughters to live with his wife's parents near Lenguas to care for them.

Within a week, I learned that Lalem's ten-year-old daughter had just died— Lalem had lost both his wife and his child within a month. Leah had indeed been fortunate. That evening, Lalem came to visit me. "*Sopa, murratai*," Lalem said to me in his familiar way.

"*Ey, sopa*," I replied.

Lalem said softly, "*Keata paren*" (I have a favor to ask). "I want to go to Arsim to pick up my daughter and bring her back to Lukumai."

Sadness was written on his face; he clearly wanted his daughter near him to show that all was not gone, that he still had a family. "Of course," I replied, even though I was down to a few jerry tanks of petrol. We left that afternoon; it was a quiet journey without conversation or our usual joking. We stopped only to wash ourselves at the Lenguas wells. We proceeded up the riverbed to Longieli manyatta where his wife's family lived; it was small with only a few houses. We entered Lalem's mother-in-law's house, but there was no one there. Soon, however, a young girl of six years entered the house. She brightened when she saw her father. Lalem softly asked her, "Would you like to come back to my *nkang*?"

She looked up at him with a big smile. "*Ey*, I would like that," she said.

"Where are your shoes? Do you have a *nanga* cloth?" he asked.

It was a tender moment, just father and daughter, and I sat quietly on a stool by the door.

Soon Lalem's father-in-law came into the house. They spoke quietly while the old man described the girl's death; "she died of sickness, sickness only." We got up to leave and made our way to my car. Lalem held his daughter affectionately on his lap, smoothing away the aches in their hearts.

After a few days, Lalem came over to my tent in the evening. Not wishing to disturb me or the people I was talking to, he just sat quietly. When everyone had gone, Lalem spoke up.

"Elliot, *murratai*. When you were here before, we were young, we were warriors together. Do you remember?

"Ey," I replied, "I remember."

"Now we are *payiani*, elders, we both have wives, we both have daughters. When you came to Lukumai this time, it was a very sad day for me as my daughter died. I was feeling very bitter. When I asked you to take me to collect my other daughter, you did so without hesitation. I will never forget such a kindness."

"It was nothing," I replied in all truthfulness.

Lalem went on, "Everyone has their own customs and regulations. In your home you do some things differently, and our ways must seem strange to you. Now you are living with us and you must put up with our hardships. Some people come around and beg from you; they think you are rich and have things to give away. Others know you and try not to bother you.

"There is a day when I will do you a big favor, when you will come to me in need and I will help you. Sometimes I have ups and downs, and I must request something small from you, like sugar. But every time you see me, it doesn't mean I want something from you. I also have livestock, and if you have a need I will help you."

I took my time to respond. This was a formal conversation, one of thanks and one of friendship. I weighed my words and said, "Yes, it is true we have different customs. But some things are the same to all peoples, important to all peoples. And these are friendship and respect. I too was very sad to hear about the loss of your wife and daughter. I almost lost my daughter before coming here. When you asked me to drive you to bring back your child, I said yes, even though I had very little petrol. If there was anything I could do to relieve your suffering, I would do it."

I went on, "In the old days, the other *l-murran* hardly bothered to know me, but only asked me for things. You were not like that. You became my friend, you taught me how to speak *n-kutuk ole Loikop* ['the mouth' of Samburu], you showed me how to be an *l-murrani*. And I am a person who values friendship, who keeps my friends, as I do with Dominic and Lonyoki. You were my friend then, and you are my friend now. If you have a need you will ask me, and if I have a need I will ask you, for we are friends."

Lalem had been looking directly at me through this, nodding in agreement at certain points, sharing a warmth that embraced both of us.

Marty and Leah Return

Marty had intended to stay with Leah in Nairobi for the remainder of my fieldwork, but in fact they stayed away barely two weeks before they decided to return north. I happened to be in Lenguas on Christmas day when the

American missionary who lived there told me that Marty and Leah were flying in that very day; he had learned this from the pilot on the radio. I couldn't believe it; Lonyoki was right in his prediction. Soon I saw the small single-engine plane swoop down and make its nerve-wracking landing in this narrow valley, surrounded on three sides by high mountain walls. Our reunion was joyous; none of us wanted to be separated by such a distance. The missionary couple, Dale and Suzanne, invited us to a rather sumptuous Christmas dinner, complete with turkey, stuffing, and the ever-present Kool-Aid in aluminum glasses. They kindly offered us their mission's guesthouse, which had a small kitchen and flush toilet, and were happy that Marty would work with their health assistant at the small clinic near the airstrip. Marty, Leah, and I stayed in Lenguas, while I divided my time between studying the nomads at Lukumai, visiting the settled Ariaal and Rendille at Naiborr town, and returning periodically to Lenguas. It was certainly a beautiful place, located in a deep forested cut in the base of the Ndoto Mountains by a flowing river. Although Lenguas had its dangers—black mamba snakes, lions, malaria—it was much more pleasant than desolate, windblown Naiborr. Few Rendille were here, as their camels could not risk the life-threatening ticks in the thick bushes, but it was an important center for Samburu and Ariaal pastoralists, as well as Dorrobo hunter-gatherers. Marty and Leah stayed in the guesthouse near the health dispensary while I commuted to nomadic Lukumai or Naiborr to continue my field research.

Anthropologists often remark how different fieldwork is when you come not alone but with your own family, and this was certainly true for me. There were certain costs—it took me away from the total immersion I had experienced as a single young person in my earlier fieldwork. But having Marty and Leah there gave me insights into aspects of Ariaal life I knew little about, particularly the world of married women and children.

At first, Marty tried joining my circle of male friends who would stop by to chat when visiting Lenguas. While polite, they did not include Marty in our conversations as we sat in a circle outside the house, and they ignored her when she tried to join in. I tried to explain to Marty that this was nothing personal, just the local custom of gender segregation. My explanations did little good, and with a big "harrumph" Marty left to join the women, who spent their time around cooking hearths and the women's "shade tree." Marty was much happier with this arrangement.

The women at Lenguas took to Marty right away. She was outgoing and friendly, unafraid to join in the women's activities. The women gave Marty an *mparua*, the married women's neck ornament made of palm fibers, leather, and red beads, although they had to adjust it to fit over Marty's large head. And as they did with me, the women teased Marty with relentless good humor.

"Ma'ati, why don't you help your husband find a second wife? Why should you have to do all the work of raising a child and preparing food all by yourself? You need a co-wife!"

Marty replied, "A second wife? What for? I think I am going to find a second husband!" and the women burst out laughing at the absurdity of this idea.

Occasionally I heard the women talk about Marty in Samburu, saying things perhaps they would not tell her to her face. "It is such a pity about Ma'ati and Elliot. They are so rich in so many ways. They have a car, nice clothes, but they are really so poor. They only have one child, and she is already getting big!" To help her solve this problem, the women presented Marty with an iron bracelet from the blacksmith's hearth and a small clay figurine of a child to sleep with, both guaranteed to help produce more children.

Leah also had a friend in Lenguas. Larenbin, Dominic's seven-year-old son, had moved in with us and shared a room with her. Larenbin had a chronic ear infection and was nearly deaf. Marty wanted to treat his infection with antibiotics but needed to make sure he followed the whole ten-day regimen of two pills twice a day. Larenbin was a delight and a good friend to Leah, jumping on the bed with her and playing outside the guesthouse. Sadly, he never did regain his hearing.

While staying in Lenguas, the laibon sent me a note written in English by a young scribe.

> To Mr. Elliot. Much greetings from Lonyoki, I hope you are in good condition as me. I am very happy that you have come with your lovely family here. But I am sad that you have not yet brought your family to meet me. I would like to know where your own children will be, for I would like to join you with a goat or something else. I am wishing you peace. Yours faithfully, Lonyoki.

Guilt is universal. I had been meaning to bring Marty and Leah to meet Lonyoki, but he lived some distance away and Marty and I were both involved in our work. We decided to visit Lonyoki the next day. As before, the laibon came out to meet us as we drove up. He shook my hand and greeted Marty and Leah warmly, stroking Leah's head and having her sit like a good granddaughter next to him on a small leather mat placed outside his house.

"Ma'ati, Ma'ati," Lonyoki smiled, "we have finally met. Now you are to call me apaiya [father], and Leah is to call me akuya [grandfather]." That seemed easy enough. Then Lonyoki asked Nkarami to bring him his bag of medicines. He reached inside and presented Marty with a gift—it was an important *ntasim*. He handed her a small yellowish ball; it was a fur ball from a lion's stomach. This was potent medicine indeed, as it was the material the laibon used to make sorcery. Marty said she knew some people she could use it against. Lonyoki then brought out his *nkidong* gourd and threw his stones for us. As he did so, he stopped and winked at me, saying,

"Didn't I tell you that you would see your wife and daughter soon?"

He had indeed, but I had not believed him. He had once told me that my twin brother was on an airplane coming to Kenya, and that did not come to pass. Sometimes the gourd told truths and sometimes it lied, Lonyoki was fond of saying. But this *nkidong* went smoothly. Lonyoki predicted that no harm would come to us and we would live a long and happy life.

A few days later, Lonyoki came to visit us at the missionary's house in Lenguas, accompanied by Dominic, Lalem, and Lembalen, who was leading a large white goat. I was so happy to see Lembalen. He was not yet a warrior, but he had grown into a tall, handsome adolescent. He was a bit shyer than when he was a boy, but he shook my hand enthusiastically and greeted Marty and Leah warmly. Our daughter of course was delighted to see the goat. Her eyes lit up and she exclaimed, "A goat, a goat! I'll name him Snowy; I'll make him clothes to wear; we'll be best friends!"

I swallowed hard and said to Leah, "I'm really sorry, but I believe Lembalen brought the goat for us to eat. It's tonight's dinner."

Leah looked disappointed, but not overwhelmingly so. When Lembalen and Lalem took the goat down to the riverbed to slaughter it, Leah followed along. After about fifteen minutes, I thought it would be a good idea to check up on her, as I didn't want her to be traumatized by what was going to happen. But Leah was a curious and sanguine kid, and I wasn't surprised when I found her holding the leg of the now-dead goat so Lembalen could carefully butcher it. Next to the goat lay the skin and the animal's intestines, which Leah had neatly piled up on a rock.

Dominic made a fire near the house and laid out long green branches to place the goat meat on. The legs, stomach, and liver were all cooked, and the smell was delicious. I felt sorry for vegetarians who visited the pastoral areas and could not share in a feast of roasted goat. Dale, the American missionary, came out to greet us. He was very respectful and shook everyone's hands, but he tightened up when I introduced Lonyoki as the laibon medicine man. Most of the American missionaries didn't like the idea of laibons, whom they called "witch doctors." Most missionaries were from evangelical denominations, and I think they believed laibons were conducting Satan's business. Still, Dale was a gracious host, and after pleasantly declining our invitation to join the feast, he went back to his house.

We sat in a loose circle on chairs and rocks, Dominic, Lonyoki, Lembalen, Lalem, and me. Marty sat with us long enough to eat a piece or two of meat but then left to join the women who were making goat stew in their cooking pots. Leah played with Larenbin outside the house. It felt good to be with the old gang again, eating meat together, telling stories. When we had finished and were wiping our greasy hands on our wooden cattle sticks and *rungus*, Dominic asked me, "Did you hear how Lonyoki saved Lukumai from a *shifta* attack after you left?"

"No, I haven't heard this," I replied.

Lonyoki smiled and his eyes lit up, and Lembalen gazed admiringly at his father.

Dominic went on. "This happened before the l-Kororo [age-set] were circumcised [around 1978]. We were living together near Lorrien swamp where we could water our cattle. Lonyoki had predicted with his *nkidong* that enemies [*l-mangati*] were coming, and they would attempt to disrupt our circumcision ceremony."

Lonyoki said, "The Lukumai elders wanted to leave that place when they heard my prophecy. They said, 'Let us shift because people are afraid of raids and attacks at Lorrien.' But I refused. My *nkidong* showed we had nothing to fear, and I knew that my *ntasim* would protect Lukumai."

Dominic continued, "After two days, reports reached the settlement that seven bandits had been seen. The elders decided to set up lookouts to check for the bandits and meet with them. Later that day, our girls, who were watering the small stock at Lorrien, came running back to the *nkang*, crying that there were *shifta* who wanted to take two goats to eat. We now knew that the enemy had come. The l-Kororo [the new warrior age-set] were still wearing leather skins [i.e., preparing for circumcision], so it was up to the l-Kishili [now junior elders] to go down there."

Lalem now joined in the storytelling. "Lonyoki worked out a plan with us. He told the *l-murran* not to go in front of him. Instead, Lonyoki walked down to the water by himself, to where the *shifta* were resting. He put tobacco in his right hand, but he also put *nkurupore* on it, and he greeted the enemies. The enemies asked for tobacco, which he gave them, but he also flicked some *nkuruporen* from under his fingernails at them while smiling and greeting them, 'How are you?'"

"Is that true, *apaiya*?" I asked Lonyoki.

"*Ey*," he nodded with a smile, "that is what happened."

Dominic said, "Now the enemies decided to have two of their people go and roast the goat, while the other five, with guns, went down to the river to rest under some trees. As they were doing so, Lonyoki gave the signal to the warriors to kill the two bandits roasting the goat."

Lalem said, "I, Lembere, and two other men came quietly from behind the two men roasting the goats. We sprang from the bushes and killed the two *shifta* when their backs were turned. I killed one with my spear, and I hit another with a rungu. He tried to run, but Lembere threw a spear into his back. We killed them both."

Dominic continued, "The *l-murran* killed the two *shifta* and left their bodies lying by the slaughtered goats. After a while, the other bandits who were waiting for the meat to be cooked saw vultures landing on the site of the fireplace. The enemy came to see what was happening, and they saw the two dead bodies of their friends. When they tried to search for the men who had killed their friends, a huge truck from Laisamis carrying police arrived and confronted them. They were chased away by police, but only those two standing by the goats were killed. When this was over, I left immediately for Marsabit to ask the Kenyan police to provide security for the clans around Lorrien who were to circumcise the boys."

This story was told with satisfaction all around. It was getting dark, and people were talking to each other softly. Everyone sitting there attributed their success against the *shifta* to the laibon's bold action and powerful medicines. I thought that Lukumai's warriors would probably have achieved the same result without Lonyoki's help, but his presence and medicines were acknowledged as ensuring their victory and reaffirmed to me the dominant role the laibon played in preventing harm from befalling their herds and herders.

Before getting up and leaving, Lonyoki called me over to his side.

"Elliot, I am going back to my *nkang* now. I don't know when we see each other again. God knows these things; sometimes we laibons can see things others cannot see, but only God knows what the future will bring. I know you will be returning to your own country soon. I hope we will see each other again, but no man knows the day he is destined to die."

This was an ominous statement. I didn't think much of it at the time, but I realize now that Lonyoki could see his own death coming. And perhaps that of my own father.

Sad News

Marty, Leah, and I returned to the United States, settling in North Carolina, where Marty finished her medical residency and I completed writing my thesis. I turned this into a book, *Surviving Drought and Development*, which described how the Samburu and Ariaal persisted in maintaining their livestock economy during prolonged drought, while pursuing new strategies, including farming and wage work in Kenya's north. Things were not falling apart, to paraphrase Chinua Achebe's novel about Nigeria, but they were definitely changing. Nor were the Samburu, Rendille, and Maasai "disappearing," as some cultural writers feared. Far from it—many were actively engaging in the tasks of nation building and economic growth. But I remained convinced that livestock pastoralism was the most practical way to exploit the sparse resources of these arid lands, and I advocated strongly for the position that development agencies should help pastoralists maintain their livestock and way of life.

One warm spring day in North Carolina in 1987, I received a letter from Dominic sent via a translator. He told me that Lonyoki had died in a local hospital from liver illness. Dominic wrote how sorry he was to send me this news and that he knew how sad I would be. I sat outside on my deck with his letter in my hand, our dog sitting close by as if he sensed my grief. My thoughts went back to Lukumai and my time spent in fieldwork. I remembered the evening when he had formally adopted me and how he told me not to say anything, that the speech was his to make. I remember looking for a moon that had disappeared during an eclipse and my ethnocentric assumptions that people would have superstitious explanations for it. I thought about our travels to Langata, where Lonyoki threw his nkidong and prepared his ntasim to deal with sorcery, and how serious and focused he could be. I also thought of those moments when he was laughing, enjoying everyone's company and trying to keep people in good humor. One time when the drought was very bad, Mother of Lembalen was loading a pack donkey to walk to the Christian mission to seek famine relief food. Lonyoki came out and pretended to be a woman, putting the saddle on the donkey himself (a woman's job), patting down the leather skin and wooden frame on its back. Women came out of their houses to watch, laughing hard and enjoying the performance. But we all knew things were very bad when one had to take a donkey to seek food handouts and charity. To beg was hard on one's dignity, but everyone was painfully hungry at that time.

Lonyoki was around sixty years old when he died. I was not surprised by the news; he drank a lot of hard liquor and it had taken its toll. Everyone knew a person could die of homemade changa'a, the corn liquor whose alcohol content could never be measured accurately. But Lonyoki's father was in his eighties when he died, and his cousin Lokili, the sorcerer, lived into his eighties as well. Lonyoki was simply too young to die. I thought about his son Lembalen, who was now truly on his own. I decided that if I could find out where he was living, I would write to him and send him some money.

Within two years my own father died, in this case from Parkinson's disease. Like Lonyoki, he was relatively young, at seventy-three years old. He had grown steadily weaker and was finally placed in a nursing facility. We managed to become closer when I returned from Africa; he admired me for doing things he would have been too fearful to do. At his funeral I spoke of how proud I was of him, how he faced his own disease and disability with dignity and fortitude, and I said that we were not so different after all. I was a grown man now with my own family, and I could let both my father and Lonyoki go peacefully.

Since Lonyoki's death, I have returned to Kenya a half dozen times. In the 1990s I developed a long-term research project with Marty and our colleague Eric Roth to study health and nutritional changes that were occurring among Ariaal and Rendille. We found that nomadic Ariaal children living in livestock-keeping households were three times less likely to be malnourished than Ariaal children living on farms and in towns, even during drought periods. They were taller and heavier, something we attributed to the greater milk consumption in the livestock-keeping manyattas. The nomadic children also had fewer respiratory and diarrheal diseases, although malaria affected settled and nomadic communities alike throughout the lowlands. This confirmed my view that livestock pastoralism was a positive adaptation that governments and development agencies should reinforce.

It was becoming more dangerous to travel in northern Kenya. Civil wars in neighboring Ethiopia, Sudan, Uganda, and Somalia had led to an influx of refugees into northern Kenya, filling the United Nations High Commission for Refugees (UNHCR) camps at Walda, Kakuma, and Dadaab. Some of the refugees were soldiers who brought guns to trade for food—a pistol for a goat, an AK-47 for a cow. This resulted in more armed raiding between the pastoralist groups and led to an increase in banditry on roads in the north.

Despite these troubles, I managed to visit Dominic and Lembalen several times over the past twenty years. Lembalen was circumcised and initiated into the l-Moli age-set in 1992, but the elders allowed him to marry early so he could practice his nkidong and ntasim for the community. When I returned in 1994, I traveled to Dominic's manyatta, which was located in the Ndoto Mountains near Langata. Although he was now a man in his sixties, Dominic was still wiry and quick. As usual, he went to his animal enclosure and picked out a goat to slaughter; another elder emerged from a house to help butcher and cook it.

As we ate, I asked for news from Lukumai.

Dominic said, "After Lukumai separated, I moved to this area to care for my goats; my brothers stayed near Baiyo Mountain. I own a farm now," he said with a broad grin. "Ey, up at Kitaruni on Marsabit Mountain. My third wife lives there with our twin daughters."

"Why aren't you there with them?" I asked.

"You know, Elliot, a farm is a good thing. You can grow twenty kilos of corn, and need only one milk cow for milk. But I can't stay there, I need to be with my animals down here."

I asked how Lembalen was doing. Dominic replied, "He is here, not far away in his own *nkang*. He is living with his mother and sister, and practices his *nkidong* divination."

"And Nkarami, Lonyoki's other wife?" I asked.

"She moved back with her own people after Lonyoki died. She had two children by Lonyoki, but they do not live with Lembalen or his mother. She wanted Lonyoki's cattle, but Lembalen said, 'Mu tum.' She was a terrible person."

Finally, I asked the question that had brought me many miles to this place. I wanted to know how Lonyoki had died. We spoke quietly, as death was not a topic Samburu liked talking about.

Laibons rarely died from natural causes, and Samburu believed that when a laibon died at a young age, it was due to the actions of a rival laibon. Marty had told me she thought Lonyoki had died from liver disease due to drinking. She added that the U.S. Occupational Safety and Health Administration (OSHA) would probably list "death by alcoholism" as the greatest risk factor for Samburu laibons. But I thought that if the Samburu had an OSHA, they would describe the laibon's greatest risk as "death by sorcery."

Dominic spoke directly. "Lonyoki was living near here in Langata while I was still with Lukumai near Lorrien swamp. Lonyoki's own father had died, and he moved to this area to take care of his father's goats. You remember Longojine's little house? It was not far from here. People came and told me, 'Your friend Lonyoki was taken to the hospital in Laisamis on a camel.' I asked what his problem was. Then people said that he was vomiting blood and that he had a problem with his liver. After a day or so, people came back and reported that he had died.

"When Lonyoki came with you to live with us at Lukumai, he did not have much livestock, and we in Lukumai had to contribute goats to give to him. He was a polite man and very friendly. Many elders and age-sets liked him because he was a sharp laibon and could give out medicines and help others."

"Dominic, tell me," I asked. "How do you think Lonyoki came to die?"

"People tried to think what disease did he have, and the elders said that when Lonyoki was in Ker'ngera, he used to drink changa'a. He would take five quarts at a go. Most of the elders thought this drink might have caused damage to his liver. But I don't think that is what killed Lonyoki. That man could drink, it is true, but it had never made him sick."

Dominic became quiet, and looked out toward the horizon for some time.

"Do you think he died at the hands of another laibon?" I asked.

Dominic spat on the ground. He looked up at me and said, "Yes, I think it was nkurupore, it was sorcery that killed Lonyoki. I don't know from where. Some say it was Lobata, because he did not want another laibon in the area. He wanted to be the most powerful laibon of all. When Lonyoki came here, Lobata told him to go back to Maralal [in Samburu District]. He chased Lonyoki away. But Lonyoki was the stronger laibon; he never told lies or cheated people. You remember when Lonyoki met Lobata in the streets of Laisamis, when he broke his divination gourd on Lonyoki's head."

"Ey," I replied. "How could I forget that?"

"You know, Lobata told people that Lonyoki gave nkurupore against the l-murran of Lukumai. These were lies, because he was jealous that Lonyoki came to live with the Lukumai and was throwing his nkidong for our clan. Lonyoki was a more accurate and perfect laibon, and even though he was Lorukushu clan, the Lukumai preferred him to Lobata. Lobata had lost popularity with his own clan, and even within his own settlement."

"What happened to Lobata?" I asked.

"He also died, not very long ago, in his village."

"Do you think it was Lobata who cursed Lonyoki?" I asked.

"Meiyolo [I don't know]," Dominic replied. "Ngai Neiyolo openy [Only God knows]. The only other laibon more powerful than either of them was Lokili, and that man is a killer. And that laibon is still alive. The ways of the loibonok are unknown to regular people, so I will never know."

Lembalen Becomes the Laibon

I had seen Lembalen transform over the years from a boy to a warrior in splendid beadwork to a young married elder beginning his own family. He had inherited his father's nkidong and learned the secrets of his father's ntasim, and he was widely accepted as his father's successor. In 2006, I was invited to an international conference on pastoralism in Nairobi, and I arranged for Dominic, Lembalen, and Daniel, the schoolteacher, to come down from Marsabit District and stay at my small hotel near the university.

The staff were curious about these visitors from the north and made efforts to accommodate their taste for goat stew and chapatis.

Eating our meal, Lembalen said to me, "My brother, my heart is so happy to see you again." (Actually he said "*kai-sham l-gosheke*," meaning "I love you in my stomach," which worked for me.)

"When my father died, I felt like I was the most alone person in the world. I had the burden of the world on my shoulders, caring for my mother and small sister, being responsible for all the herding, seeing that our household had enough food to eat. Then I heard from my brother in America, that you would visit Kenya again and help me get circumcised. You gave me an ox to slaughter when I was an *l-barnoti* [an initiate before circumcision]. I forgot that I had this brother. And when I remembered you, my heart cried for joy. I thank God that I have a brother and you are here."

I asked about his mother, and Lembalen told me she had passed away before her grandchildren were born; he said she died of "lungs," probably tuberculosis. After a few minutes' pause, Lembalen spoke of his father's death as well.

"My father's death was a very bitter thing. He taught me everything I know—how to throw the *nkidong*, how to make *ntasim*, how to understand my dreams. I was young when he died; he did not live to see me become an *l-murrani*. We did not know each other when I was very small, but then you came and brought me and my mother to Lukumai so I could live with my father. For that I am always grateful to you."

I said to Lembalen, "Yes, we are brothers and I care for you very much. Tell me, what does your *nkidong* say about the future? I see they are going to pave the road to Marsabit, and I fear the changes that may come with this, that many people will settle on the road and become farmers."

"What I am seeing now is after the circumcision of the new age-set [l-Nateli], things will become good again for Samburu. Before, during the drought, if you had one cow, that cow was enough to feed children. But for my age-set, the l-Moli, things have been very difficult and we have seen many problems. People no longer have enough cattle to feed themselves, and there has been too much fighting.

"But what I can see now is a new life coming. If you are left with one thing [i.e., one cow], that thing will become good. Even the earth will be productive for us [i.e., we will take up farming]. When the new age-set comes, we will not have trouble as we did with l-Moli. Everything you have will be more valuable. That is what I am seeing, I see goodness. There will be no drought. We shall have a big rain and things will be good. The death from illness [HIV/AIDS] will be reduced. Count what you have now, because things will be good."

Dominic, who was sitting quietly listening to all this, was shaking his head in weary disagreement. I asked Dominic what he thought, and he replied, "Laibons may see some things we cannot see, but to us, we just see things as they are. And they are a mess. You don't know if it will be good or bad; you just take things as they come, although we hope God will care for us. But now, I just see fighting everywhere; no one cares for one another anymore. Some laibons can predict things that will come, and people can have meetings to solve problems. But even in meetings, they are getting confused. The young people especially don't listen to elders anymore; they don't learn from our experiences and wisdom. These times are not good. Children are not following our customs; children are not listening to their elders. Children are even killing themselves. They go to school, and they come home and do not even sit when their elders talk. Even the government is having problems; everyone is criticizing them rather than following them. Things were better when we had a strong leader [i.e., Jomo Kenyatta or Daniel arap Moi]."

We ended our reunion on a warm note. Lembalen said, "Elliot, you are really my brother in my heart, you carried me even more than a real brother."

I knew I would see Lembalen again; he was young and strong and now an established elder in his community. But I worried about Dominic. He was as thin as I had ever seen him, no more than 110 pounds on a 5'8" frame. He was getting old, a man in his seventies, and I wanted the remainder of his life to be safe and comfortable. In the 1990s, I had provided funds for Dominic to build a house on his farmstead where his third wife and children lived on Marsabit Mountain. But Dominic did not stay in his new house. He preferred to live in the desert lowlands where he could be with his cattle and small stock, even if it meant moving around and suffering drought and hunger, predators and raiders. Dominic had once told me he would rather be a nomad living under the stars than a beggar living under a roof. In that regard, Dominic remained a true pastoralist.

Before we parted, I asked Lembalen if there was anything I could do for him, and he replied, "Yes, I want you to help me build a house as you did for Dominic. I have a vision and a plan for the future, and I want to remain in one place where I can be laibon for my community. This is the one thing I need you to do for me."

Lembalen, like his father, had never really asked me for anything, although he always appreciated and accepted any support I could provide. We worked out the details of building the house and I arranged to provide the funding.

My Own Family Grows

When Marty and I were conducting our maternal and child health research in Kenya, we learned that a married couple in Lukumai had both died of malaria, leaving behind two seven-month-old twins, a boy and a girl. Without much hesitation, we told the couple's elderly parents that we could raise the babies if they wished. Like most African families, the grandparents politely declined. "The children belong to the *nkang*. But you can help with their education if you wish."

This event planted a seed and eventually Marty and I adopted two young children from Ethiopia, a boy, Mulugetta, and a girl, Masaye. As they grew older, we were able to bring them on visits to northern Kenya to meet Lembalen and Dominic, and to Ethiopia and Eritrea when I taught at the University of Asmara in 2003.

On one occasion en route to Kenya, Marty, the children, and I were staying in Addis Ababa, courtesy of Ethiopian Airways, who put us up at the Addis Hilton. Here the kids could swim, although as seven year olds they preferred to run around the pool and lobby. The manager of the hotel, a dapper man sporting a thin mustache and wearing a suit and tie, approached me. With a serious look, he asked me, "Are those children with you?"

I cringed a little, ready to be scolded. "Yes," I replied.

"And tell me," he continued, "did you adopt those children?"

I cringed some more, ready for an admonishing lecture about white people stealing African children. Again I replied, "Yes, we adopted them."

The man then embraced me, kissed me on both cheeks, and said, "That is wonderful. I wish there were more people like you. We have so many children who need families and homes, and so few to care for them."

As the Samburu proverb goes, "You know what to say, but you do not know what you might be told."

The Gourd Is Passed

Life has become busy. For the past fifteen years I have taught anthropology at Smith College in Massachusetts, a wonderful institution that is one of the few remaining all-women's colleges in the United States. I teach courses in cultural anthropology, African health issues, and the anthropology of development. It is a real pleasure to go to work every day and meet with bright young women committed to making the world a better place. I couldn't have asked for a better job.

Through the years of teaching and writing, I have reflected on what I gained from my experiences in Africa and what lessons I can pass on to my students. I first traveled to Kenya as a young man in search of adventure, determined to build a professional career in anthropology but also to fulfill a personal quest for meaning and purpose in my life. Other young people have also chosen this path, whether by studying anthropology, joining the Peace Corps, or working with international organizations. Like me, they have experienced the kindness and shared humanity of people in other parts of the world.

That I met and was adopted by a laibon medicine man was an unexpected and fortuitous event; the relationship provided me with insights into aspects of Samburu and Maasai culture that few outsiders know about. Traveling and watching Lonyoki treat illnesses and misfortunes attributed to sorcery with his *nkidong* divination and *ntasim* medicines allowed me to think about people's beliefs in the spiritual world. While I did not share those beliefs, I respected the many Samburu who did. Their universe included a spiritual realm of invisible but powerful forces, and they relied on the power of the laibon to grapple with these forces.

I also learned that although there were pronounced differences between Samburu understandings of the world and my Western, urban notions, there were also universals found in both cultures. I could respond with empathy to the efforts of families to protect and care for their loved ones, to the community's struggles with adversity and determination to respond with dignity, to their yearnings for peace and growth. I forged deep bonds with the people of Lukumai, who shared their humor and homes even in the face of drought and hardship. Issues of ethnicity and tribal origin were important to Dominic and Lonyoki, as they were to all pastoralist groups living in Kenya. But I could see that although ethnicity and territoriality served to unite communities like Lukumai, they also led to conflict and hatred.

I learned that war was often the result of competition for land and resources, but I could also see how fear and insecurity were manipulated by individuals motivated by power, such as when President Moi and other politicians incited the Maasai to attack Kikuyu homesteads during the 1992 elections. I could see how poverty and inequality were not natural phenomena, but rather the result of conscious greed and exploitation of the weak by the powerful, and I came to believe that war and violence could be eliminated if humans learned to share fairly and equally the earth's bounty. But I also recognized our shared capacity as humans for altruism, laughter, and friendship. Surely these must be as strong as our competitive urges to fight or take what others have.

I last visited Lembalen in Kenya in January 2010. This was a period following violent clashes during the presidential elections in 2008, and Kenya was suffering its most severe drought in twenty years. But Nairobi was as energetic as ever, and I enjoyed the two-hour plane ride to Marsabit over farms and towns to the deserts and mountains of northern Kenya. Marsabit town had grown from a sleepy backwater of five thousand people in 1970 to thirty thousand people living near or around the growing capital.

The paved road that was being built from Isiolo had not yet reached Laisamis, and the dirt road from Marsabit south was still as I remembered it—bumpy, corrugated, washed out, and dangerous. Enormous trucks loaded with trade goods or livestock and carrying dozens of passengers on top roared along the road, reluctant to give way to oncoming traffic. I was traveling with my longtime friend Daniel, the schoolteacher, and we drove past a half dozen women walking with enormous loads of firewood, weighing probably seventy-five pounds each, on their backs. A bit farther we passed a small herd of camels being escorted by uniformed Home Guards who were returning the animals to their owners after they had been raided. But times had changed in many ways. We were driving in a new open-backed Land Cruiser, and we had discovered Lembalen's whereabouts by means of his mobile telephone.

Lembalen's new home was along a riverbed about three miles off the main road. It was a beautiful place with shade trees and a cool breeze, one of the most peaceful locations I have ever visited. Surrounding Lembalen's *nkang*, which included the building that I had financed were numerous manyattas with camels, cattle, goats, and sheep. The place was a vibrant community, complete with a nearby school, thanks to the efforts of their new member of parliament, Joseph Lekuton, who was developing educational and water resources around the district.

Lembalen was waiting for us as we drove up. He exclaimed, "Ai, *Lelachelai* [my brother], *ai–ai-ai*," and we hugged each other long and hard; we both had tears in our eyes. "Welcome," he said, "we need to talk and be together."

Lembalen, who was now in his forties, had matured into a tall man. He carried himself with a quiet dignity, despite his outfit of a U.S. basketball jersey and large floppy hat. "There are four *nkangitie* with about one hundred people living here, mostly from Lukumai clan," Lembalen said. "There are camels, goats, and sheep, everything," he smiled. "This is the place I dreamt about, the one I told you when we last met. I knew it would be by a river, with tall trees cooling us. It is a peaceful place; no harm can find us here."

Lembalen showed me the structure he had built, a square-shaped building with a metal roof. He used this as a storehouse and part-time *duka* (shop), where he periodically sold sugar and *posho*. Next to the shop was a large domed house, open-sided and airy, where six people sat or lay on the floor. Lembalen told me proudly that these were his patients, people he was treating for sorcery. It was a laibon's "hospital," something I had never seen before. He told me that I could watch as he treated his patients the next morning.

Lembalen then brought me to his house, which was located inside a traditional *nkang* with animal enclosures. The house was made in the Ariaal fashion with leather-skin sides and a woven sisal roof, and the whole manyatta made me nostalgic for my time in Lukumai. Lembalen's wife came out to greet us, as did his sister, who lived next door. This was Mo' Lembalen's daughter, now a young widow with two small children. She was as beautiful as her mother, but without her mother's sadness. Lembalen called for all his children to come out for a family photo. He and his wife had five children ranging in age from one year to eleven years old—the oldest two were in primary school. I was struck by how calm everyone was. The children were like their father—quiet, polite, and confident.

Lembalen said to me, "Let your companions drive back to town and find lodging there. I want to be alone with you this evening. I want you to stay with my family." This was no problem, as my driver was bored in this quiet manyatta, and Daniel worried about the mosquitoes by the river.

I was happy the others had left; I knew I had little time here and just wanted to quietly enjoy Lembalen's company. Taking me by the hand, we walked around the manyatta and visited several adjacent *nkangs*. The sheep and goats were returning to their pens, and a long string of camels was returning home in the distance. As the camels walked in I could hear their wooden bells gently tocking, and I was brought back to the sounds, smells, and sights I experienced in Lukumai thirty-five years earlier. Lembalen took a male goat from his pen and gave it to one of his neighbors to slaughter and roast for us. As it was getting dark, he pulled out a leather skin for us to sleep on outside. Remarkably, he brought out a new mosquito net, the kind that was coated with insecticide, and he suspended it with sticks over our sleeping area. He told me he also had a mosquito net in his house for his wife and children; this was a new and necessary innovation, and it showed that nomads could improve their life chances with small appropriate technology.

We ate roasted liver from the goat and saved the rest for the next day when my companions would return to collect me. Lembalen and I chatted quietly. I said to Lembalen, "Your father Lonyoki would be very proud of you, and I think he would be as pleased as I am at how well you have done for yourself and your family."

"*Ey, acheoling,*" he replied.

"You know, Lembalen," I continued, "I wished long ago that you had stayed in school. I am sorry that your grandfather pulled you away to herd his goats. You would have done very well and probably gone on to university."

Lembalen surprised me with his reply. "The elders said that taking me out of school was the best thing that could have happened for this community. They said it saved hundreds of lives."

"Because you became the laibon?" I asked.

"Yes, because I became the laibon," he replied.

We settled down side by side under the bright stars, talking long into the night until we drifted to sleep.

The next morning, Lembalen took me to his clinic. He told me that clients would come here with a family member and stay some time, even a month or so, to receive *ntasim* treatment. I asked him about the kinds of problems he treated.

"All of these people have been cursed. One young girl could not talk, could barely eat; now she is almost recovered. A warrior was brought in who had seizures so violent that we had to lock him in the storeroom when he first came. Now he is ready to go home. Come on, I will show you what I do. I have a new treatment now, something that came to me in a dream, something my father did not do. I make small cuts with a razor on the person—on his face by his eyes, or on the back of his neck. I rub my *ntasim* into the cut, and it goes directly to the blood. It is much quicker and more effective than the old way."

Lembalen then brought a young girl out to the side of his clinic. She sat quietly as he took his medicines out of his bag. Wrapping a leopard-skin strip around the girl's head, he took out a small sharp blade from his kit and cut small nicks under her eyes and on back of her neck. Only a little blood came out, and I saw these were shallow cuts. Lembalen then wiped yellow *ntasim* into the cuts and, taking off the leopard-skin strip, told her to go rest in the house. I asked him if he knew about the dangers of HIV/AIDS from making cuts, and he said, "Ey, I know about AIDS. That is why I use clean razors, I get them from the dispensary wrapped in paper."

A young warrior waiting for his treatment was standing next to the wall. He smiled at me and I asked him his name and where he was from. He was from Longieli clan near the mountain town of Lenguas and said he had been here about one month. He told me demons had possessed him and he tried to kill his mother and father. The elders tied him up and brought him to Lembalen on a donkey. As Lembalen gave him *ntasim*, he began to get better. The young man shyly smiled and said, "Lembalen is a true *l-oiboni*; he has saved my life. I don't know how I will thank this man yet, but it will be something big."

I knew my visit was coming to an end and I would soon head back to the United States. I wished I could start all over again, I thought to myself. I wished I could stay here with Lembalen as I first did with his father Lonyoki, observing him throw his *nkidong* and dispense his *ntasim* to his patients, living under the sky and stars with a nomadic community and their livestock. As the breeze blew through the trees in this small village by the river, I thought, "This would be an excellent new project." Perhaps one day I will return here. And why not? Lonyoki's medicines keep drawing me back.

List of Characters, Words, and Places

Major Characters (in Alphabetical Order)

Dominic—Elliot's closest friend in Lukumai village
Kidenye—Elliot's warrior friend, along with Lalem
Lalem—Elliot's warrior friend, along with Kidenye
Leah—Elliot's daughter
Lembalen—Lonyoki's son and succeeding laibon, Elliot's adoptive brother
Lobata—a rival laibon to Lonyoki
Lokili—Lonyoki's older cousin, a laibon and sorcerer
Longojine—Lonyoki's father
Lonyoki—a laibon medicine man, diviner, and sorcerer; adoptive father of
    Elliot
Marty—Elliot's wife
Mother of Lembalen—Lonyoki's first wife
Naiseku—Dominic's first wife
Nkarami—Lonyoki's second wife, rival to Mother of Lembalen
Rendille—Dominic's second wife

Minor Characters

Chief Lonarok—from Lorubai
Dapash, Lepere, Lemeti—elders of Lukumai
Larenbin—oldest son of Naiseku
Larion and AnnaMarie—assistants to Elliot and Marty

Lengidi—a man who consulted Lonyoki for healing in Langata
Lolcheni—a Dorrobo herbalist
Lolonogi—a midwife in Lukumai
Lengirrira—name of Dorrobo family, Dominic's nickname for Elliot
Mbatian—famous Maasai laibon of nineteenth century
Mother of Parengi—(*Moto' Parengi*) Dominic's second wife, also called
     Rendille
Meron—Lukumai *lais*
Naisaba—Dominic's daughter with Naiseku
Ngaldaiya—a laibon deported by the British in 1934
Nkitari—young second wife of Usana, Dominic's older brother
Olonana—son of laibon Mbatian
Parengi—Dominic's son through his second wife Rendille
Sembara and Senti—two teenage girls from Lukumai
Senteu—son of laibon Mbatian; rival to Olonana
Usana and Choma—Dominic's older brothers

Places Named in Text

Archer's Post—small town on Marsabit Road
Baiyo—isolated mountain in western Marsabit District
Barsaloi—town in Samburu District
l-Barta—grazing plains near Baragoi town in Samburu District
Isiolo—large town and Isiolo District capital
Kaisut Desert—in western Marsabit District, home of Rendille people
Kakuma—refugee camp in Turkana District
Ker'ngera—a small town in Marsabit District
Laisamis—town on Marsabit road
Lake Turkana—large lake in northern Kenya
Lengare Mara River—in Ndoto Mountains
Langata—a community in the Ndoto Mountains
Lenguas—a small town in the Ndoto Mountains
Lerogi Plateau—highland area in Samburu District
Lodwar—capital of Turkana District
Logologo—small town on Marsabit Road
Lorrien swamp—seasonal swamp at the base of Baiyo Mountain
Lorubai—a community on Marsabit Mountain
Maralal—capital of Samburu District
Marsabit—name of mountain, district, and district capital in northern Kenya

Matthews Range—mountains south of Ndoto Mountains
Mount Kulal—in Samburu District below Lake Turkana
Naiborr—a town in the desert
Naivasha—town and lake in Rift Valley of Kenya
Ndoto Mountains—range on eastern side of Rift Valley, divides Samburu and Marsabit Districts
Ngong Hills—outside Nairobi, sacred to Maasai
Rift Valley—large depression extending from Ethiopia to Mozambique
Rumuruti—capital of Laikipia District
Samburu District—north central Kenya
Tanganyika—former colony which became Tanzania
Tiwi beach—on Kenya coast
Turkana District—in north western Kenya
Uaso Nyiru River—large river between Marsabit and Isiolo Districts
Walda—refugee camp in northern Marsabit District

Ethnic Groups Named in Text

Ariaal—cattle and camel pastoralists, a bridge culture between the Samburu and Rendille
Boran—cattle pastoralists of northern Kenya and southern Ethiopia, traditional enemies of the Ariaal and Samburu
Dorrobo—hunter and gathering group living in forests near Samburu communities
Gabra—camel pastoralists of northern Kenya
Giriama—KiSwahili speaking farmers and fisherman on Kenya's coast
Kamba—agricultural group of central Kenya
Kikuyu—agricultural and urbanized population of central Kenya
Laikipiak—Powerful Maasai group of the nineteenth century, vanquished by Purko-Kisongo Maasai
Maasai—cattle pastoralists of southern Kenya and northern Tanzania
Nandi—agro-pastoral group of western Kenya
Oromo—agro-pastoral people of southern Ethiopia; known as Borana in Kenya
Rendille—camel pastoralists of northern Kenya, allied to the Samburu
Samburu—cattle pastoralists of northern Kenya, related to the Maasai
Somali—camel and cattle pastoralists of northeast Kenya and Somalia
Swahili—coastal people of Kenya
Turkana—camel and cattle pastoralists of northwest Kenya, enemies of the Samburu and Ariaal

African Words Used in Text

ache-oling—thank you

akuya—grandfather (term of address)

apaiya—father (term of address)

awi—Turkana homestead

awulo—bush

l-barnoti—an male initiate before circumcision

bo'o—fenced livestock enclosure

busa'a—strong drink

changa'a—corn liquor (Swahili)

cho'oke l-kambau!—give me tobacco!

l-chota—water well, spring

duka—shop (Swa.)

emutai—disaster, hardship; refers to period of famine and disease in East Africa at end of nineteenth century

ero!—senior greeting to a youth

Ey—yes

fora—herding camps

n'go'o—here, have this

l-gume—nose, also Samburu nickname for Turkana

hodi—May we come in? (Swa.)

hoteli—hotel (Swa.)

a-ibon—power to predict

jambo—Swahili greeting (Swa.)

kaiyo paren—I have a favor to ask

kagol—strong, fierce

kai-yolo l-gomon poke—"I know all the parts of the face"

kedede—true, it is true (*mara kedede?* is this not true?)

l-keeok—ears

khat—plant and stimulant (*Catha edulis*), called *mira'a* by Samburu

kikoi—cloths (Swa.)

n-kong'u—eyes

kore?—where?

l-kukulai—root of *Rhamnus staddo* plant, used as "black" *ntasim*

kule na oto—sour milk, literally "milk that slept"

l-kuret—wedding ox

ku-tey—get away!

n-kutuk ol Loikop—Samburu language; literally "mouth" of Samburu

kwale—truly (Swa.)

laibon (*loiboni, loibonok*)—diviner, sorcerer, ritual specialist among Maa-speaking peoples

ol oiboni kitok—great laibon

lairuponi, lairupok—witches

lais, laisi—Rendille holy men

lameyu dorrup—"short hunger," the dry season

lameyu la'ado—"long hunger," drought

lapa ko twa—eclipse (lit. "the moon is dead")

lapa lonyokie—full or "red" moon

lauton—brother-in-law

lodua—rinderpest, cattle disease

lokochum—anthrax

loi-yei! loi-yei!—"boys! boys! Come quickly!"

lokore—a sacred tree

Longieli—Samburu and Ariaal clan

Lo'onkidong'i—Maasai clan of laibons

Lorukushu—Samburu and Ariaal clan

Lukumai—Samburu and Ariaal clan, also name of Dominic's nomadic village

Lukumai lol nkishu—Lukumai who keep cattle

Lukumai lol ntamesi—Lukumai with camels

maduup—a flightless bird

madai—crazy; also foolish

ma'alo—wooden container

ma'ape, ma'apeti (pl)—let's go!

maendeleo—progress (KiSwahili)

mei-yo—I don't want

meiyolo—I don't know

mandazi—fried dough (Swa.)

l-maneta—"the tying ones," objects used by the laibon for ritual protection

l-mangati—enemies

manyatta—a nomadic community, from Maasai *manyata, manyat*—a warriors' village

l-maoi—twin

mara—no, I don't want

mau mau—anti-colonial rebellion in Kenya in the 1950s

meti—there isn't any

miki-tajapa nkai—may God carry you

meti nbarabara—there is no road

milika—ghost (Swa.)

mira'a—stimulent and plant (*khat*)

mparingoi—type of warriors' dance

mparua—married women's neck ornament made of palm fibers

mpirrian—special age-mate friend

l-mugit—age-set ritual for Samburu warriors where ox is slaughtered

mugit lolai'ngoni—"*mugit* of the bull," final age-set ritual

l-murran, l-murrani—warrior, "those who are circumcised"

Mu tum! Tshombe iye!—You can't have any! Go away!

mwalimu—teacher (Swa.)

mzee—a respected elder, a "big man" (Swa.)

mzungu, wazungu—white person (Swa.)

na'abu (Rendille)—men's ritual center inside *nkang*

naikitok—wife of age-mate

naisho—honey, also honey wine

nanga—a cloth worn by men or women about their waists or over their shoulders

ndiyo—yes (Swa.)

ndotoi—African board game (also known as *mbau, mankala*)

ngolan—drought; hardship, also strength

nkai—God, the creator; *nkai neiyolo openy* "only God knows"

nkang—clan-based village

nkerai—girl, also girlfriend

nkerugwa—fever, malaria

nkidong, nkidongi—a container, specifically the laibon's divination gourd

nkurupore, nkuruporen—sorcery, sorcery poisons

nokore—woven rope from bark of *lokore* tree

ntasat—old women

ntasim, ntasimi—laibon's protective medicines

ntasim laisar—ritual fire

ntasim'l-ke'ene—"*ntasim* of the lion skin"

ol-Maa—language of Maasai and Samburu

oh-weh-nay—come with me

payian, payiani—elder(s)

l-paramunyo—root of *Toddalia asiatica* plant, used as "yellow" *ntasim*

paren—a favor; *paren kitok* a large favor

piki—motorcycle

pilipili—warrior's beaded ornament worn in back of head

pirantai—tree the desert rose

posho—maize meal

l-pus—a respiratory disease in livestock

l-reteti—fig tree

rungu—warrior's club, made of strong wood with thick knot or metal gear at end

sapa'ade—a special class of Rendille women formed every third generation

sara—leather aprons worn by Rendille womenon ritual occasions

sawa—"all right, enough" (Swa.)

serian—peace ("*Serian ake?* Is there peace?," "*Serian ntamesi?*" How are the camels?)

shamba—garden (Swa.)

shifta—bandits, also refers to Somalis who tried to secede from Kenya in the 1960s

shuka—a cloth worn around the body (Swa.)

sidai—ostrich; also beautiful

sikukuu—festival (Swa.)

soriu—ritual goat slaughter in Rendille and Ariaal

sotwa—special friends among men

taisho—stop it

l-tepes—acacia trees

l-tepes silipani, sucha, and *larasoro*—sacred trees

l-tipo—smallpox

tigerai—be still!

to-wana ene—sit here

tshomo iye!—Get away you!

l-Turia—clan community of Ariaal

Tu tum menye—"Your father will meet (and punish) you," term of derision

twiga—giraffe (Swa.)

ugali—maize meal cooked into moist cake (Swa.)

Ujamaa—Tanzania's socialist program under President Nyerere

ulukh—ritual fire

yeyo—mother (term of address)

Suggested Readings

Berntsen, John L. 1979. Maasai Age-Sets and Prophetic Leadership, 1850–1910. *Africa* 49 (2): 134–46.

Dombrowe, Christian. 2005. Review of *Divination and Healing: Potent Vision*, eds. Michael Winkelman and Philip Peek. *Shamans Drum Journal*, No. 70. Available at http://shamansdrum.org/Pages/ReviewsDivinationHealing.html.

Fratkin, Elliot. 1979. A Comparison of the Role of Prophets in Samburu and Maasai Warfare. In K. Fukui and D. Turton (eds.), *Warfare among East African Herders*, 54–65. Osaka: Senri Museum of Ethnology.

Fratkin, Elliot. 1991. The Loibon as Sorcerer: A Samburu Loibon among the Ariaal Rendille, 1973–1987. *Africa* 61 (3): 318–33.

Fratkin, Elliot. 1996. Traditional Medicine and Concepts of Healing among Samburu Pastoralists of Kenya. *Journal of Ethnobiology* 16 (1): 63–97.

Fratkin, Elliot. 2004. *Ariaal Pastoralists of Northern Kenya: Studying Pastoralism, Drought, and Development in Africa's Arid Lands*. Second edition. Needham Heights, MA: Allyn and Bacon.

Fratkin, Elliot. 2004. The Laibon Diviner and Healer among Samburu Pastoralists of Kenya. In Michael Winkelman and Philip Peek (eds.), *Divination and Healing: Potent Vision*, 207–26. Tucson: University of Arizona Press.

Fratkin, Elliot, and Eric A. Roth. 2005. *As Pastoralists Settle: Social, Health, and Economic Consequences of Pastoral Sedentarization in Marsabit District, Kenya*. New York: Kluwer Academic/Plenum.

Fratkin, Elliot, Eric A. Roth, and Martha A. Nathan. 2004. Pastoral Sedentarization and Its Effects on Children's Diet, Health, and Growth among Rendille of Northern Kenya. *Human Ecology* 32 (5): 531–59.

Greenberg, J. H. 1955. *Studies in African Linguistic Classification*. New Haven: Compass Press.

Harner, Michael. 1980. *The Way of the Shaman*. New York: Harper and Row.

Merker, Moritz. 1904. *Die Masai*. Second edition. Berlin: Dietrich Reimer.

Mol, Frans. 1978. *Maa: A Dictionary of the Maasai Language and Folklore English–Maasai*. Nairobi: Marketing and Publishing.

Mol, Frans. 1996. *Maasai Language and Culture Dictionary*. Limuru, Kenya: Diocese of Meru, Kolbe Press.

Payne, Doris L., and Leonard Ole-Kotikash. 2008. *Maa (Maasai) Dictionary*. Available at http://www.uoregon.edu/~maasai/Maa%20Lexicon/index-english/main.htm.

Schlee, Guenther. 1989. *Identities on the Move: Clanship and Pastoralism in Northern Kenya*. Manchester, UK: Manchester University Press.

Sobania, Neal. 1988. Pastoralist Migration and Colonial Policy: A Case Study from Northern Kenya. In Douglas Johnson and David Anderson (eds.), *The Ecology of Survival: Case Studies from Northeastern African History*, 219–39. London: Crook Greene.

Spear, Thomas, and Richard Waller (eds.). 1993. *Being Maasai: Ethnicity and Identity in East Africa*. London: James Currey.

Spencer, Paul. 1973. *Nomads in Alliance*. London: Oxford University Press.

Spencer, Paul. 2003. *Time, Space, and the Unkown: Maasai Configurations of Power and Providence*. New York: Routledge.

Straight, Bilinda. 2006. *Miracles and Extraordinary Experience in Northern Kenya*. Philadelphia: University of Pennsylvania Press.

Tucker, A. N., and J. Tompo Ole Mpaayei. 1955. *A Maasai Grammar with Vocabulary*. London: Longmans, Green.

Turner, Victor W. 1968. *The Drums of Affliction: A Study of Religious Processes among the Ndembu of Zambia*. Oxford, UK: Clarendon Press.

Waller, Richard. 1995. "Kidongoi's Kin: Prophesy and Power in Maasailand." In D. M. Anderson and D. H. Johnson (eds.), *Revealing Prophets: Prophecy in East African History*. London: James Currey Publishers.

Winkelman, Michael, and Philip Peek (eds.). 2004. *Divination and Healing: Potent Vision*. Tucson: University of Arizona Press.

Index

Mulugetta, 152
murder, 88, 92, 99
murratai (age-mates), 74, 78, 81, 139
Muslims, 26
mwalimu (teacher), 4, 110
mzungu (white person), 18, 61, 71, 98, 108

na'abu (ritual center), 12, 54, 124
Naiborr, 24, 26, 33–34; Dominic in, 34–35, 130, 134–36, 143–49, 151–52
naikitok (wife of one's husband's age-mate), 39
Nairobi, 3–4, 32, 33, 59, 113–16, 125, 128–29, 133
Naisaba, 37–39, 121
Naiseku, xii, 37–39, 45, 51–52, 56, 62, 105, 111; donkey of, 42, 76–77; "Lion and Ostrich's Children" told by, 121–23
naisho (honey wine), 19, 63–64
Naivasha, 82
Nandi people, 67
nanga cloth, 70, 74, 103, 123, 139
Nathan, Leah, 133, 135–37, 139–45
Nathan, Marty, xiii, 133, 135–37, 140–45, 147–48, 152
National Christian Council of Kenya, 24
National Geographic Society, xiii, 133
National Museum of Kenya, 4
ndotoi (board game), 43, 70, 81, 138
Ndoto Mountains, 6, 34–35, 81, 101, 141; sorcery in, 83–86
neocolonial policies, 115
Ngaldaiya, 99–100
n-golon (strength), 93
Ngong Hills, 128
Ngorongoro game park, 20
NGOs. *See* nongovernment organizations
Niger, 113

Nigeria, 3
nightjars, 84
Nilo-Hamites, 27
Nilotic languages, xiv, 8
Nixon, Richard, 3
Nkadume, 89–90
Nkai (God), 29, 50, 54, 96
nkang (village), 10
Nkarami, 108–9, 116, 131, 137–38
n-keju (leg), 93
nkerugwa (fever), 72–74
nkidong (divination gourd): of Lobata, 101; of Lokili, 100; of Lonyoki, 1, 15–16, 47, 78, 82–83, 92, 129–30
n-kiguana (meeting), 93
n-kiok (ear), 93
n-kiri (meat), 93
Nkitari, 41, 51–52, 77
nKong'ini, 43
n-kueni (peace, laughter), 93
Nkueny, 89
nkuruporen (sorcery poisons), 47, 83–85, 91, 100
nokore strings, 80
nomadism, 114
nongovernment organizations (NGOs), 6, 114
Northern Frontier District, 5
ntasat (old women), 45
ntasim (medicines), 1, 15–16, 18, 29; of Lembalen, 156–57; for Lengidi, 94–96; of Lonyoki, 47, 67, 80, 116
Ntenukwa, 39, 139
numerology, 93, 95–96, 124
Nyaparai clan, 40

objectivity, 65–66
Occupational Safety and Health Administration, U.S. (OSHA), 148
ochre, 9, 13, 31, 50, 74, 88
oil production, 115
ol-Maa language, xiv

About the Author

Elliot Fratkin is a professor of Anthropology at Smith College in Northampton Massachusetts where he teaches courses in Cultural Anthropology, African Studies, and the Anthropology of Development. He has studied nomadic pastoralists in East Africa for over thirty-five years, and has conducted research and worked in Kenya, Eritrea, Ethiopia, Chad, and Cameroon. Fratkin is author of forty academic articles and five books including the text *Cultural Anthropology* (with Daniel Bates, 2003), *Ariaal Pastoralists of Kenya* (2004), *As Pastoralists Settle: Social, Economic, and Health Consequences* (with Eric A. Roth, 2005), *African Pastoralists Systems: An Integrated Approach* (with Eric A. Roth and Kathleen Galvin, 1994) and *Surviving Drought and Development* (1991).

Elliot Fratkin has served with the World Bank Inspection Panel investigating complaints about indigenous peoples rights during the Chad-Cameroon Oil Pipeline Project (2002–2003), and has been a US Fulbright Scholar teaching anthropology at the University of Asmara in Eritrea in 2003 and Hawassa University in Ethiopia in 2011–2012. He is married to physician Marty Nathan and has three children, Leah, Mulugetta, and Masaye. When not thinking and writing about Africa, he enjoys playing folk music, working on his classic Triumph sports car, and demonstrating against injustice.